AGAINST THE NATIONS

WAR AND SURVIVAL
IN A LIBERAL SOCIETY

Stanley Hauerwas

A Seabury Book
WINSTON PRESS
Minneapolis • Chicago • New York

Cover design: Art Direction Inc.

Copyright © 1985 by Stanley Hauerwas.

Library of Congress Catalog Card Number: 85-50255

ISBN: 0-86683-957-7

Printed in the United States of America

5 4 3 2 1

Winston Press, Inc.
430 Oak Grove
Minneapolis, Minnesota 55403

To
Paul Ramsey
and
John Howard Yoder

CONTENTS

PREFACE

The more I write the less I feel able to claim what I do as mine. For writing is a constant reminder of how much one owes to others. Many of my debts are direct as I know how much I owe to people like David Burrell, Jim Burtchaell, Robert Wilken, John Howard Yoder, and David Solomon. After all they have been recent colleagues whom I forced to read much of this book and whose criticisms have never failed to make my work better. In the same way I am peculiarly aware of the debt I owe to the many graduate students who have worked with me over the last decade. Two of those students, Mark Sherwindt and Philip Foubert, were good enough to think through and write with me two of the chapters of this book. Charles Pinches was particularly helpful during the time I was writing the chapters on war. Greg Jones of Duke University made many useful suggestions. Good graduate students always remain skeptical about whether their professor is getting it right even if they think "he may generally be on the right track." I have been fortunate to have been blessed by students who were gracious enough to be "my" students but never followers.

Many debts are less direct but no less real. Over the past few years I have become peculiarly conscious of how much I owe to many people I hardly know who read my work and take it seriously. I do not mean they agree with every point, but rather they see what I am doing as making some contribution to their own projects. From time to time some ask me to address issues that force me to think about matters I might otherwise avoid. As a result they have forced me to think and rethink matters I would have thought settled or already sufficiently investigated by others. This book is the result of that kind of pressure.

In particular I owe a debt to Conrad Cherry for inviting me to deliver the Scholars Press Lecture at the 1982 meeting of the American Academy of Religion on the issue of nuclear disarmament. Jill Raitt and the Department of Religion at the University of Missouri were kind enough to ask me to address the same issue. On both occasions I learned more than I gave. I am also grateful to the

Department of Theology at Marquette University who honored me as the Marquette Lecturer in 1984. Marquette University Press, moreover, has been kind enough to permit me to reprint that lecture as the last chapter of this book.

I also need to thank the editors of *Center Journal* for asking me to respond to "Christianity and Democracy" as well as for permission to reprint it here. The chapter on imagination was the result of being asked to address that issue by *New Catholic World*, and the essay on the Kingdom of God was a response to a similar request by *Word and World*. Again I am in their debt not only for permission to republish those essays, but because they thought I might have something to say on such matters in the first place. "Remembering as a Moral Task" was originally written for a conference at Indiana University and published later in *Cross Currents*. I am indebted to both for giving me the opportunity to explore that most troubling issue.

Mike Bloy not only forced me to think about nuclear war by involving me in a conference at Cornell on the subject but he also made it possible for me to bring this book into final form through my participation in the Coolidge Colloquium. Tony Stoneburner and the other participants in that Colloquium provided the richest context for helping me understand what I wanted to say in this book. In that respect I am particularly indebted to Justus George Lawler as he made invaluable suggestions about the conception of this book. Without his continuing commitment to publishing serious work in theology we would all be the poorer.

A book on this subject reminds me how much I owe to my family. Those who love us and whom we love are constant reminders that none of us wish to survive for survival's sake, but rather we seek the space and time to develop those loves. Adam's interest in the subject of nuclear disarmament has been an inspiration for me; he made me realize that this is not just another "interesting" issue.

Finally, I am aware that many may find the approach of this book confusing if not confused. Such an impression may be confirmed by the fact I have dedicated this book to Paul Ramsey and John Howard Yoder. Surely an unlikely pair—the one the most prominent defender of just-war theory and the other a pacifist. I may be confused but I am not confused about how much I owe to each of them. Though convinced by Yoder's arguments for pacifism, I am not sure I would have been so if Ramsey had not argued so ably about war in the first place. Yet beyond what I owe to their particular reflections about war, I have dedicated this book to them because of their common commitment to maintaining the integrity of theological ethics. We are all in their debt.

1. INTRODUCTION:
THE SCOPE OF THIS BOOK

On Trying to Be a Performer

At the end of his *The Nature of Doctrine: Religion and Theology in a Postliberal Age*, George Lindbeck observes, "There is much talk at present about typological, figurative, and narrative theology, but little performance. Only in some younger theologians does one see the beginnings of a desire to renew in a posttraditional and postliberal mode the ancient practice of absorbing the universe into the biblical world" (135).[1] I do not know if I am a posttraditional or postliberal thinker, but I do know I want to be the kind of performer Lindbeck describes. Moreover I am aware I have done more talking about such performance than I have actually performed. Thus the reason for this book, for here I at least try to do what I have said should be done.[2]

Of course, I do not know if the kind of performance exemplified here is the kind Lindbeck had in mind. He may well be in fundamental disagreement with the position I work out and he may certainly dissent from some of my more particular judgments. Yet I find the position he develops extremely helpful as it allows me to make clear some of the primary presuppositions of my work. Therefore in the first part of this introduction I will try to position myself in terms of Lindbeck's analysis of modern theology in the hope of making explicit the basic perspective from which this book has been written.

By doing so I also hope at least to qualify some of the criticisms that have been directed at my work. For when my position is understood in terms of Lindbeck's analysis, my so-called "sectarianism" appears in a different light. I have no interest in legitimating and/or recommending a withdrawal of Christians or the church from social or political affairs. I simply want them to be there as Christians and as church. Nor do I harbor romantic assumptions about times past when community allegedly flourished as opposed to the individualism of liberal society. I assume our times and society are probably no better or worse than most times and most societies. The issue is not comparative judgments, but rather our ability to understand as

1

Christians the peculiar challenges facing the church in our times and in our society.

In this book I criticize as well as try to provide an alternative to the dominant mode of Christian ethics. Most contemporary Christian ethics corresponds rather closely to Lindbeck's characterization of the liberal theological enterprise. The liberal theologian, according to Lindbeck, assumes there is some universal experience that all people have that can be characterized as religious. The particular religions and their doctrines are but manifestations of that experience giving it expression in more or less adequate ways. The experience, however, always transcends particular religions so it can be called on as a basis for critique of their expression. In terms of ethics, liberalism provides the justification for the assumption that there is a strong continuity between Christian and non-Christian morality, especially in a liberal society.

In contrast the postliberal theologian, according to Lindbeck, argues that theology does not describe some universally available experience. Rather by our becoming members of a particular community, formed by Christian convictions, an experience not otherwise available is made possible. From this perspective Christian ethics does not simply confirm what all people of good will know, but requires a transformation both personally and socially if we are to be true to the nature of our convictions.

Postliberal theology is not just a theological program characteristic of Christianity; rather, Lindbeck suggests, it corresponds to a particular theory of religion he characterizes as cultural-linguistic. Such an account denies that there is an experiential core to religion because "the experiences that religions evoke and mold are as varied as the interpretative schemes they embody. Adherents of different religions do not diversely thematize the same experience; rather they have different experiences. Buddhist compassion, Christian love and —if I may cite a quasi-religious phenomenon—French revolutionary *fraternité* are not diverse modifications of a single fundamental human awareness, emotional attitude, or sentiment, but are radically (i.e., from the root) distinct ways of experiencing and being oriented toward self, neighbor, and cosmos" (40). In contrast the experiential-expressive theories of religion, assumed by liberal theology, tend to focus on one identifying mark of religion, such as a sense of the holy, which for many religions may have little or no importance. Such theories, thus, not only lack empirical grounding, but distort the fact that different religions may produce fundamentally different experiences of what it is to be human.

From this perspective postliberal theology is characterized by what Lindbeck describes as an intratextual method. Such a method does

> not make scriptural contents into metaphors for extrascriptural realities, but the other way around. It does not suggest, as is often said in our day, that believers find their stories in the Bible, but rather that they make the story of the Bible their story. The cross is not to be viewed as a figurative representation of suffering nor the messianic kingdom as a symbol for hope in the future; rather suffering should be cruciform, and hopes for the future messianic. More generally stated, it is the religion instantiated in Scripture which defines being, truth, goodness, and beauty, and the nonscriptural exemplifications of these realities need to be transformed into figures (or types or antitypes) of the scriptural ones. Intratextual theology redescribes reality within the scriptural framework rather than translating Scripture into extrascriptural categories. It is the text, so to speak, which absorbs the world, rather than the world the text" (118).

Lindbeck notes that liberal theology, which assumes an experiential-expressive view of religion more easily accommodates to present trends than does postliberal theology. "Liberals start with experience, with an account of the present, and then adjust their vision of the kingdom of God accordingly, while postliberals are in principle committed to doing the reverse" (125-6). Liberals often affirm what appear to be advances in the culture on the ground that they are advances toward the eschatological future, while the postliberal is committed neither to traditionalism nor progressivism. Yet postliberal resistance to making current experience revelatory means it may often resist current fashions, and thus give the impression of a conservative stance.

It is no wonder, therefore, that most who work in Christian or religious ethics are more naturally drawn to liberal theology—even those who are at least on record as favoring a more conservative theological outlook. Moreover, from a liberal perspective there is a sense that my position in ethics may appear "sectarian" as well as fideistic or irrational. Yet I think neither of these characterizations can be sustained, for in fact the perspective I develop in this book attempts to provide a Christian interpretation of our social situation, as well as suggest why it is so socially important to maintain the integrity of the church—both of which open up possibilities that otherwise would simply not exist.

However, a social ethic that emphasizes the distinctive nature of Christian ethics as well as the significance of the church is not only bucking the dominant trends of our time but may appear downright dangerous to many. For as Lindbeck notes, the present psychosocial situation is more favorable to liberalism than postliberalism. The rationalization, plurality, and mobility of modern life have dissolved traditional bonds. Created rootless, people now seek to discover meaning that must be created to be authentic.

> The churches have become purveyors of this commodity rather than communities that socialize their members into coherent and comprehensive religious outlooks and forms of life. Society paradoxically conditions human beings to experience selfhood as somehow prior to social influences. Selfhood is experienced as a given rather than as either a gift or an achievement, and fulfillment comes from exfoliating or penetrating into the inner depths rather than from communally responsible action in the public world. Thus the cultural climate is on the whole antithetical to postliberalism (126).

Moreover, it can be argued that we are fortunate that our situation is antithetical to the development of a postliberal perspective. If the world is to avoid nuclear annihilation we will have to become more unified. Rather than an emphasis on the distinctiveness of religious traditions the world will need some "kind of highly generalized outlook capable of providing a framework for infinitely diversified religious quests" (127). Therefore to criticize, as I do, current attempts to mount an effective anti-nuclear campaign for their false eschatologies, appears not only theologically doubtful but morally perverse.

It is important, however, that Lindbeck (or I) not be interpreted as emphasizing the distinctiveness of Christian convictions as an end in itself. There is no virtue in that. Rather it is our (or at least my) conviction that we must attend to the distinctiveness of our language, and to the corresponding distinctiveness of the community formed by that language, because it is true. I would say the same thing I am saying now even if I did not believe that such an emphasis more likely will help us meet "the needs of the future." Yet I think such is the case, because I believe that what Christians believe about what God has done for us through the life, death, and resurrection of Jesus of Nazareth is the truth and thus cannot but help us meet the future with hope and enthusiasm. But neither can I deny, as Lindbeck observes, that the position appears paradoxical since it seems "religious communities are likely to be practically relevant in the long run to the degree that they do not first ask what is either practical or relevant, but instead concentrate on their own intratextual outlooks and forms of life" (128).

Besides appearing "sectarian," the position I develop in this book will also appear to the liberal as dangerously fideistic. For as Lindbeck notes the great strength of the liberal is to try to make religion existentially intelligible to both the cultured and uncultured despisers and appreciators of religion. That is why the liberals are so committed to the foundational task in religion—namely, to show that particularistic convictions are the manifestation of universal principals or structures. Without such universals it is impossible to make faith credible to unbeliever or believer alike. In contrast the postliberal no more believes that religions can be translated into another medium than that one can learn French by reading translations. Religions, like languages, can only be understood in their own terms. From the liberal point of view such a claim can appear only as a counsel of despair since it seems to make impossible any rational account of religious convictions.

But if one takes the kind of antifoundationalist perspective that informs the following chapters, it seems that the choice between religions or between religion and no religion becomes irrational. The historicist perspective I develop seems from a liberal perspective to be trapped in the kind of confessionalism that cannot sustain rational discourse. As a result the strong stress on particularism offers no hope of lessening the violent conflicts of the world through the development of a rational ethic.

But as Lindbeck argues, antifoundationalism is not the same as irrationalism. "The issue is not whether there are universal norms of reasonableness, but whether these can be formulated in some neutral, framework-independent language" (130). All that is called into question is the idea of a foundational discipline that can determine the standards of rationality in every field, but the denial of such a discipline in no way commits us to standards of rationality within fields or even between fields. Reasonableness, as Aristotle maintained, is more like a skill than a universal principle. Rationality resides not in the mind but in intelligible practices which we must learn. Religious and theological claims are thus not immune to challenge, though they may be, like many other activities, not susceptible to definitive refutation or confirmation; they can nevertheless be tested and argued about. For finally "intelligibility comes from skill, not theory, and credibility comes from good performance, not adherence to independently formulated criteria" (131).

It is in this sense that this book is an attempt at performance. What I attempt in these chapters I suspect Lindbeck did not envision in his own critique of liberalism. For this is a book not in doctrine, but in Christian ethics. But I think the kind of performance here attempted is important for understanding how Christian convictions can more nearly be judged to be true or false. For the strong argument that gives this book coherence is simply that theological convictions have lost their intelligibility. They have lost their power to train us in skills of truthfulness, partly because accounts of the Christian moral life have too long been accommodated to the needs of the nation state, and in particular, to the nation state we call the United States of America. As a result the ever present power of God's kingdom to form our imagination has been subordinated to the interest of furthering liberal ideals through the mechanism of the state. To recover a sense of how Christian convictions may be true (or false) requires a recovery of the independence of the church from its subservience to liberal culture and its corresponding agencies of the state. For without the distinctive community we call the church, there is no place for the imagination of Christians to flourish if we are to sustain our ability to be a people of peace in a war-determined world.

It is in this manner that issues of rationality and the charge that my position entails a withdrawal-strategy by the church are interrelated. The charge seems substantiated by the pacifist position I take in this book, since it is alleged that by definition a pacifist must withdraw from political involvement. However I refuse to accept such a characterization not only because there is no intrinsic reason why pacifists must disavow all political involvement simply because they refuse to kill on behalf of the state, but also I refuse to accept such a characterization because it implies that all politics is finally but a cover for violence. That seems to me not only empirically unsupportable, but normatively a view that no Christian can accept. Rather than disavowing politics, the pacifist must be the most political of animals exactly because politics understood as the process of discovering the goods we have in common is the only alternative to violence. What the pacifist must deny, however, is the common assumption that genuine politics is determined by state coercion.

Therefore rather than being a "sectarian" position I understand the perspective developed in this book to be aggressively world affirming. Indeed, I find it odd that those who are so committed to the liberal values of the Enlightenment characterize the pacifist position as sectarian since they are usually the ones that develop justifications for Christians in one country killing Christians in another country on grounds of some value entailed by national loyalties. Surely if any position deserves the name "sectarian" it is this, since it qualifies the unity of the church in the name of a loyalty other than that to the Kingdom of God.

But what does all this have to do with rationality? If, as I have suggested, rationality is the kind of skill required by the Gospel, is it not decisively perverted when other authorities are allowed to determine how completely our lives are to be shaped by God's kingdom? Moreover, just to the extent that we allow our convictions as Christians to be so qualified, we lose the ability to see accurately the character of the world. For example we turn the Gospel into an ideal for peace that must wait on making the world just rather than the means to live and witness to God's peace among nations at war. The power of our imagination, and thus our reason, is blunted because we have let the Gospel be identified with utopian fantasies rather than face the Christian realism of the demand to live peaceably.

Yet even if the kind of nonfoundational position I defend in these chapters is neither relativistic or fideistic, the problem remains, as Lindbeck puts it, of how to exhibit the intelligibility and possible truth of the particularistic claims of the Gospel to those who no longer understand such traditional language (132). For Christianity is in that awkwardly intermediate stage in Western culture where having once been culturally established it is still not yet clearly disestablished. Such a situation still makes liberalism seem attractive both as a pastoral and social ethical strategy. For the biblical heritage is just present enough in our culture to make redescription a useful means to keep many people vaguely related to the church. Thus the Christian substance is translated into Marxism, into secularized forms of biblical eschatology, existentialism, and psychology; and it develops themes from Reformation anthropology divorced from Reformation theology. Moreover the identity of many people remains influenced by the religious past; such people often insist they are as genuinely Christian as those who go to church even though the former no longer believe in God as creator or in Jesus' cross and resurrection.

Lindbeck sees little possibility that any traditional catechesis, required by a postliberal perspective, is possible in our current situation. For such catechesis, rather than redescribing faith to confirm what is already known, requires us to learn a language and practices that transform the self and our relation to the world. As Lindbeck observes "pagan converts to the catholic mainstream did not for the most part, first understand the faith and then decide to become Christian; rather, the process was reversed: they were first attracted to the Christian community and form of life. They submitted themselves to prolonged catechetical instruction in which they practiced new modes of behavior and learned the stories of Israel and their fulfillment in Christ. Only after they had acquired proficiency in the alien Christian language and form of life were they deemed able intelligently and responsibly to profess the faith, to be baptized" (132).

However, the church no longer thinks of itself as living in missionary times. Instead we live in a time of progressive dechristianization in which the temptation of the church is to accommodate the prevailing culture rather than shape it. That such is the case cannot be the basis for prophetic denunciation, for if the church wishes "to embrace in one fashion or another the majority of the population" it must cater willy-nilly to majority trends. "This makes it difficult for them [Christian parents] to attract assiduous catechumens even from among their own children, and when they do, they generally prove wholly incapable of providing effective instruction in distinctively Christian language and practice. Those who are looking for alternatives to, for example, the American way of life turn instead to Eastern religions or to deviant offshoots of the Christian mainstream. This situation is not likely to change until dechristianization has proceeded much farther or, less plausibly, is fundamentally reversed." (133). Thus it is only when Christians have been reduced to a small minority that they again will be able to form communities that can without traditional rigidity cultivate their native tongue and learn to act accordingly.

Yet I refuse to wait for the process to occur. If such a refusal makes me a sectarian, so be it. I seek not, however, to make the church a minority, but simply to make it faithful not only in action but also in speech, for the two cannot be separated. That is why I have taken so much time and quoted so lengthily from Lindbeck. For it is my hope this book makes clear that questions of the integrity and truthfulness of our theology cannot be separated from questions that are normally classified as social ethics. Questions of dogmatics cannot be separated from how we think about war, the holocaust, suicide, and a host of other questions. That is the task I have tried to perform. How well I have done so I leave to the reader.

On the Structure of the Argument

Because of the complex nature of the themes running through this book, I think it is advisable to indicate how I understand their interrelationship. By doing so I do not mean to tell the reader what to find here, as it is my hope the discerning reader may well see things I have not about the relation between the chapters of this book. Yet I think it will be helpful for me to make clear the kind of cumulative case I try to build by arranging the chapters in the manner they appear.

The first chapter, "On Keeping Theological Ethics Theological," was written with the expressed purpose of challenging some of the dominant assumptions shared by most Christian ethicists. To explain why the subject of Christian ethics in America *is* America, I tell my version of the development of Christian ethics since the advent of the Social Gospel. I do so in order to understand why a tradition that began with a book titled, *Christianizing the Social Order*, could not many years later spawn a book called, *Can Ethics Be Christian?* The argument of this chapter constitutes the basic perspective for the book, since in the chapters that follow I try to show how Christian ethics' commitment to accommodating the liberal presuppositions of American society made it impossible to sustain the integrity of Christian ethics *as* Christian.[3] Particularly important in this respect is the failure to appreciate the role of the church in determining how we go about doing Christian ethics.

In some ways my argument is not unlike the one Paul Ramsey made in his famous attack on the World Council of Churches in *Who Speaks for the Church*.[4] Most reaction to Ramsey's attack has concentrated on his criticism of the "abstractness" of the concrete proposals made at the Council, particularly about Vietnam. As a result his primary concern with the church's ability to make a distinctive theological contribution has been overlooked. It was Ramsey's contention that when the church becomes identified with a number of specific partisan positions that may or may not be correct

> the church becomes a secular "sect" in its ecumenical ethics set over against the world as it is, instead of becoming truly a Christian sect concerned to nurture a distinctive ethos set over

against an acculturated Christianity or against a culture that is no longer Christendom. This is surely a form of culture-Christianity, even if it is not that of the great cultural churches of the past. This is, indeed, the most barefaced secular sectarianism and but a new form of culture-Christianity. It would identify Christianity with the cultural vitalities, with the movement of history, with where the action is, with the next and even now the real establishment, but not with the present hollow forms. By contrast, true prophecy to the most high God would be impelled in this or any other age to speak words of judgment to precisely the existing cultural vitalities—against both Baalism and Baalization of Yahwehism (55).

In contrast Ramsey suggests that "our quest should be to find out whether there is anything especially Christian and especially important that churchmen *as such* may have to say in the public forum concerning the direction of public policy—not directives for it" (16). That certainly sounds close to what I am saying yet there remains an important difference. For Ramsey still wants the church to create "the ethos out of which statesmanship may come" (41), leaving to the statesman the problem of working out concrete policies that will always involve some lesser goods and evils. While I do not think it is as easy to distinguish between "ethos" and "directives" as Ramsey suggests, my more primary concern with this way of putting things is that Ramsey is simply underwriting a different kind of cultural Christianity from what he found at the World Council.

For Ramsey the primary social contribution of the church is its ability to form an "ethos." In contrast I argue the church's social task is first of all its willingness to be a community formed by a language the world does not share. I do not deny the importance for the church from time to time to speak to the world in statements and policies, but that is not the church's primary task. The widespread attention given to the Catholic Bishops' recent Pastoral on nuclear war can be misleading in this respect since it looks as if they have had an impact on the public debate if not policy. Thus the churches are tempted to think they will serve the world well by drafting more and more radical statements. Yet the church's social ethic is not first of all to be found in the statements by which it tries to influence the ethos of those in power, but rather the church's social ethic is first and foremost found in its ability to sustain a people who are not at home in the liberal presumptions of our civilization and society.

That is why the next chapter deals with the imagination. Social reality no doubt, as is often claimed, involves institutions, coercion, and political considerations. But we too often forget that though the political often involves coercion, it is also an affair of the imagination. The imagination, however, does not simply fantasize about "what might be," but rather involves the concrete habits and language of a community. Imagination is the power, therefore, that makes it possible to avoid resorting to coercive violence. In particular for Christians the imagination is formed by learning to live the story of Christ in a world of violence and despair. As a result we should expect Christians to confront such a world by offering both intellectual and institutional alternatives to war. The truthfulness of our language will show itself by sustaining the hope necessary to face a world at war without despair and fear.

The next two chapters attempt to test this claim by offering interpretations of the Holocaust and Jonestown. In both I try to show how the church has failed to draw on its best imaginative resources precisely because it had far too readily accepted the liberal account of those events. Jews and Christians alike are tempted to misdescribe the significance of the Holocaust by making it intelligible in terms of universalistic presuppositions. I suggest that the very social policies Christians and Jews have pursued to try to insure that the Holocaust never happen again—that is, the social policies determined by liberalism—ironically undercut the particularity of the claims necessary to remember the Holocaust rightly. It is, of course, not my right to speak for Jews in this matter. Yet I am sure the Holocaust is one of the most significant challenges before the Christian community, for only if Christians are capable of remembering the Holocaust as part of *their* story will they have the resources to be a people of peace. If the church is able to do that, if it is able to grasp that as an imaginative possibility, then we may discover that we are more at odds with our culture than we had presumed. At the very least, this will require the church to recognize that we are no less particularistic than the Jews, no less particularistic because to be a community capable of remembering the Holocaust will force us to recognize that we are a people who are what we are because we live by forgiveness rather than coercion.[5]

The chapter on Jonestown is an attempt to contrast the liberal response to Jonestown—that is, who would ever think of taking religious belief *that* seriously?—to how I think Christians should have understood that terrifying event. What happened at Jonestown, and prior to that in California, is a judgment on the church's tolerance of "religion" as long as it seems to be helping someone. For in spite of the ambiguity surrounding the deaths of so many at Jonestown, I contend that we ought to respect the claim that their deaths were acts of revolutionary suicide. Only when we do so can we appreciate, first, why it is so important that Christians prohibit suicide and, second, what kind of community we must be to maintain such a prohibition. Moreover, such a prohibition again puts us at odds with the moral and imaginative capacities of liberalism. For it is anything but clear what grounds a consistent liberalism has to prohibit suicide or even to call the taking of one's own life unjustly, suicide. Suicide, from my perspective, therefore appears as part of the imaginative resources to sustain the Christian commitment to be a people for whom suicide is unthinkable.

It is my hope that this chapter will help prepare the reader for the way I approach questions of war and, in particular, nuclear war. For the criticism I develop of Jonathan Schell may make it appear I take a rather cavalier view of survival even when it is applied to the human species. As I hope the essay on Jonestown indicates, I certainly do not think that Christians are or should be in a hurry to die either as individuals, communities, or species. Our first task is in living. But we do not live because we are afraid to die, but because we believe our living is a gift that offers us opportunity for service. Such a perspective, that is, a vision of life fueled by the eschatological hopes of our faith, cannot help but make a difference in how we understand and in how we respond to the threat of nuclear war.

That is why the next chapter deals with the nature of the Christian hope for the Kingdom of God. There I argue against attempts to interpret the Kingdom in terms of liberal presumptions about what constitutes human progress. Instead, I argue that the Kingdom is a present reality, just as the Kingdom was made fully present through the life, death, and resurrection of Jesus of Nazareth. Thus, while the church certainly does not contain the Kingdom, it at least is that community that creates the space and time in this world that makes it possible for us to live peaceably. Moreover the peace the church embodies is not that derived from our fear of death, but rather the peace that is possible because Christians are a people who have had their attention captured by the only subject worthy of complete love.

The next chapter marks a transition in the book. It is a response to Richard Neuhaus' statement, "Christianity and Democracy." It is transitional because it continues to develop the theme of the centrality of the church for Christian ethics, but it also raises the issue of war that the rest of the book involves. Neuhaus' argument in "Christianity and Democracy" I regard as an extremely fine statement of the claim that Christians have a peculiar stake in democracy and, in particular, American democracy. My criticism of his position is meant to be taken very seriously since it means I am rejecting one of the key presuppositions of a great deal of contemporary Christian ethics. Yet it is just that presupposition I think that has prevented the church from understanding as well as responding faithfully to the reality of war.

The primary theme that unites the essays on war is the importance of an eschatological perspective for understanding the nuclear predicament. On the surface such a perspective appears innocent enough, but I argue it makes a very significant difference to the attitude with which Christians should approach the challenge of nuclear war. For the eschatological presuppositions of Christians are radically different from those of many who currently sustain the campaign for nuclear disarmament. I fear a "peace without eschatology" can too easily become a stance that justifies the next war.

I make no attempt to hide my own pacifist convictions in these chapters. Yet I make no attempt to develop or defend such a position; I do not because I have done so elsewhere,[7] but more importantly because I want to claim that my attempt to put war, and in particular, nuclear war, in an eschatological perspective does not stand or fall with the validity of my pacifism. I do hope, however, that the approach I take in the present book may invite others to reconsider the validity of pacifism as a stance for Christians (and non-Christians). For I think this discussion makes clear that the pacifist position which I hold by no means entails the naive and idealistic assumptions its critics often attribute to it. Christian pacifism is not just another form of the liberal assumption that war is some kind of ghastly mistake. Rather, as I hope this book exhibits, it would be hard to find a tougher "realism" than that demanded by pacifism. Of course the issue is not which position is the more "realistic"; the issue is how Christians should witness to their profound conviction that God has created us to be people at peace.

The relation of these chapters on war to the first part of the book is complex. At the most obvious level the way I approach issues of war involves an attempt to free Christians from the assumption that we have a "side." That is particularly difficult when the very structure of the way we have been taught to think presupposes that Christian ethics has a stake in furthering democratic liberalism as integral to the growth of God's kingdom. The very ideals most Christian ethicists underwrite in the name of developing a more nearly just society also legitimate Christian participation in war in the interest of preserving such putative moral gains. It is not my purpose to call into question attempts to secure more just institutions, though I do not always share liberal assumptions about what such institutions should be; rather it is my purpose to remind us that the church is the institution that claims the first loyalty of Christians.

The Catholic Bishops' Pastoral, *The Challenge of Peace: God's Promise and Our Response*, is extremely instructive from this perspective. For the Bishops sought to speak at once to the Christian people and also to address issues of nuclear strategy. Insofar as they attempted the latter task, they almost unavoidably began to write as if the Catholic people of America had a particular nuclear policy. To address issues of policy they had to assume what would or would not be in the United States' best interest. As a result the thrust of their challenge to the Catholic people was blunted.

I suspect if they had spoken more *to* the church than *for* the church their message would have been even more challenging. For it is the responsibility of the Bishops to challenge us with the knowledge that we, the Christian people, have not been a people of peace. We have been neither pacifist or just warriors but rather a people who have been ready to kill if our leaders asked us to do so. The Pastoral, written from such a perspective, would have called us to be a people ready to create and support actions that would take risks to make us less liable to be part of a nation planning murder as part of its policy. If the Bishops had written from such a perspective they might well have found their message even more controversial than *The Challenge of Peace*. For such a stance would first ask Christians to change their lives rather than ask statesmen to change their policies.

In a less obvious way the very manner and style of these chapters on war depend on the perspective developed in the first section. For I do not begin by talking about "the ethics of war" as if that is what Christians are concerned about in relation to war.[8] Nor do I witness the kind of urgency many think so important to the question of nuclear war—namely, how do we go about creating conditions that make sure it does not happen? While I am certainly concerned with the latter question and think it important to know how to make discriminating ethical judgments about war, my methodological perspective forces me first to ask how we are to understand theologically the situation in which we find ourselves. In that respect I try to show that many of the assumptions about human destiny present in the antinuclear movement are quite similar to those that have justified our building nuclear weapons in the first place.

Put starkly, the chapters on war presume that the church does not have something to say about war so much as the church *is* what God has said about war. The church does not have an alternative to war. The church is our alternative to war. That is why questions of the unity of the church should be our most urgent agenda. Questions of Christian unity, and I am not talking about simply the reunification of denominational organizations, and the Church's ability to respond to a world at war cannot be separated. More important, therefore, than what the church says about war is what kind of people Christians are that our very being provides an alternative to war for ourselves and the world.

There is one last connection between the first set of chapters and the chapters on war that is important to make explicit. What Lindbeck calls the antifoundationalist position, which I represent, clearly has implications for how one approaches the question of war. Once one assumes that there is no place outside the various histories we inherit to "ground" an ethic, then it seems we are caught in a web of warring communities with no possibility of an ordered peace. In other words we lack the means to secure rational agreement because we share nothing in common. From such a perspective the modern nation state is an extraordinary invention for peace since at least it limits the number of warring factions on this limited globe.

I could wish the situation might be different, but I do not believe any universal ethic exists sufficient to ground a vision of world peace. I do, however, believe that it is often possible to achieve greater peace between differing people than the "realist" assumes. What is necessary for such an achievement, however, is not the assumption of universal principles of reason but actual contact as peoples. Peace simply depends on people being in touch with one another.[9] As Christians we believe the church is one of the means God has given us to be in touch with one another so that peace may be not just an ideal but a reality in this world. Therefore questions of rationality and the existence of a people constituted into a fellowship throughout the nations are inextricably interrelated.

On Liberalism and Catholicism

One of the obvious criticisms some may feel inclined to make on reaching the end of this book is that I have unfairly characterized liberalism; or worse, that I do not clearly indicate what I take liberalism to be. Such criticism is fair, but I am not sure how I could have done otherwise without having written an entirely different book. For part of the difficulty is that liberalism itself is such a protean phenomenon.[10]

In the most general terms I understand liberalism to be that impulse deriving from the Enlightenment project to free all people from the chains of their historical particularity in the name of freedom. As an epistomological position liberalism is the attempt to defend a foundationalism in order to free reason from being determined by any particularistic tradition. Politically liberalism makes the individual the supreme unit of society, thus making the political task the securing of cooperation between arbitrary units of desire. While there is no strict logical entailment between these forms of liberalism I think it can be said they often are inter-related.

Yet even if I were able to give a more accurate account of liberalism, the problem still remains if in fact America is correctly characterized as a liberal society. The continuing enthusiasm for religion in America, especially the rise of the new religious right, might be taken as an indication that America is not a liberal society. Certainly there are many aspects of our culture that are not liberal. I am extremely sympathetic with those who remind us of America's republican and biblical heritage.[11] Yet I think, whether or not America has been a liberal society, liberalism has become a self-fulfilling prophecy for we have no other imaginable public philosophy.

I hope I have avoided the temptation to attribute to liberalism everything that is wrong with our society. It has not been my purpose or desire to underwrite the current miasma gripping American society; or at least the miasma that grips many in American society. I certainly believe there is much right about our social order. Moreover, I think that liberalism has, sometimes almost in spite of itself, had some beneficial results. It is still unclear if some of those results, such as freedom of religion, can be sustained in a consistently worked out liberal society. For liberalism has been successful partly because it could depend on social structures and habits it did not create and in fact over time undermines. It is my view that the concern of the religious right and of neoconservatives to reclaim "traditional moral values" is ironic since the very values they want to recover have been undermined by the very liberalism they support in other spheres of life. What must be recognized is that liberalism is not simply a theory of government but a theory of society that is imperial in its demands.

Yet it would be a mistake to make the church look good by making American society look bad. The issues before church and society are far too serious for that kind of strategy. Rather the issue is how to help the church recover a sense of its own integrity that it might better be able to make discriminating judgments about the society which we happen to call America.

One last issue needs mentioning for fear of misunderstanding. In this book I deal rather critically with the American Bishops' Pastoral, *The Challenge of Peace*. Some might well think that I have a peculiar animus against Roman Catholics when the exact opposite is the case. The reason I so often criticize Roman Catholic sources is very simple—they are the ones I know the best. For fourteen years I worked and lived among Roman Catholics, and the very title of this book, with its intentional echo of St. Thomas' smaller *Summa*, reflects my concern with Catholic thought. The Roman Catholic agenda often became my agenda, not in a conscious manner but simply because that was the way the issues came before me. Therefore if it appears I am "picking on" Roman Catholics it is only because they have had a tradition where serious use of moral language has been maintained to an extent they are able to say something interesting even if I sometimes think it wrong.

But in fact, I think we no longer live at a time when we can or should think of ourselves as exclusively Protestant or Roman Catholic theologians. This may appear to some a liberal sentiment I have yet to purge from my soul. However I should like to think it is instead a profound affirmation of the unity of the church which God is making possible, a unity that hopefully can sustain the attempt to live peaceably in a world at war.

Notes

1. George Lindbeck, *The Nature of Doctrine: Religion and Theology in a Postliberal Age.* (Philadelphia: Westminster, 1984).

2. This claim may appear odd since there are few explicit or extended discussions about narrative or virtue in this book. That is partly because the subjects treated simply do not require such a discussion. Moreover I have consciously tried to avoid saying the same thing over and over again, as I think there is nothing more tiresome than for an author to "push a line" in a manner that breaks no new ground. So what I have tried to do in the following chapters is not say again what I have already said, but test out the implications of what I have said over a different set of problems. Obviously the stress on eschatology I develop, especially in the chapters on war, is of a piece with my more general methodological presupposition that ethics (and theology) cannot avoid a historicist starting point. From such a perspective war becomes a peculiar challenge since war cannot be judged as an aberration or failure of a universal ethic. Rather war is what one should expect if we live in a world that lacks a common history. How, therefore, I can at once hold the methodological assumption I do and yet remain a pacifist is the crucial problem that sets the agenda for this book.

3. I am not suggesting that James Gustafson's *Can Ethics Be Christian?* is the result of such an accommodation, as his position derives much more directly from his theological perspective. My point, rather, is more like Gustafson's own complaint in *Protestant and Roman Catholic Ethics* (Chicago: University of Chicago Press, 1978) that the current attention by Christian ethicists to moral philosophy, while in many ways useful, has exhibited a corresponding loss of interest in the theological aspects of Christian ethics (45–46).

4. Paul Ramsey, *Who Speaks For The Church* (Nashville: Abingdon Press, 1967).

5. For reflections on forgiveness and the Holocaust see my "The Holocaust and the Duty to Forgive," *Sh'ma*, 10, 198 (October 3, 1980), 137–139. See subsequent issues for responses.

6. Richard Neuhaus, "Christianity and Democracy," *Antor Journal*, 1,3 (Summer, 1982), 9–25.

7. In particular see my *The Peaceable Kingdom: A Primer in Christian Ethics* (Notre Dame: University of Notre Dame, 1983) and "Pacifism: Some Philosophical Reflections," *Faith and Philosophy*

(Forthcoming). More convincing cases have been developed by John Howard Yoder and many others.

8. There is a peculiar historical method in the Bishops' pastoral that makes them open to the charge of ignoring the international situation in which we find ourselves. Thus James Finn contrasts the Bishops' methodology with that of John Courtney Murray who argued that one cannot begin with the just war criteria, but rather with the exact nature of the international conflict. Such an analysis Murray argued, "will be [able] to furnish an answer to a complex of questions that must be answered before it is possible to consider the more narrow problem of war. What precisely are the values, in what hierarchical scale, that today are at stake in the international conflict? What is the degree of danger in which they stand? What is the mode of the menace itself—in particular, to what extent is it military, and to what extent is it posed by forms of force that are more subtle? If these questions are not carefully answered, one will have no standard against which to match the evils of war." Quoted by Finn in "Pacifism, Just War, and the Bishops' Muddle," *This World*, 7 (Winter, 1984). According to Finn from this perspective the Bishops have failed to adequately assess the nature of the Soviet foreign policy and thus they have failed to suggest a realistic policy alternative. Of course one can ask Finn in response what has happened to the just war logic. I suppose he would answer by suggesting that such an analysis shows why the principle of proportionality must finally control that of discrimination.

9. It is important this not be read in a sentimental fashion for, as I argue in "Should War Be Eliminated?", cooperation between people does not insure peace, but to the contrary may be the occasion for violence.

10. For an excellent attempt to provide a more positive account of political liberalism and its significance for Christian ethics, see William Werpehowski, "Political Liberalism and Christian Ethics: A Review Discussion," *The Thomist* 48, 1 (January, 1984), 81–115. Werpehowski's defense of Rawls against critics such as Michael Sandel is certainly sophisticated, but I doubt that he is ultimately successful. For if, as he alleges, Rawls has a richer account of the necessity of social cooperation than the original position suggests, then Rawls' account no longer can claim the same kind of rational compellingness. I also doubt, even if Werpehowski is right in theory about liberalism, whether liberalism in fact sustains the kind of self-worth and respect for persons he thinks necessary for political community. Of course he can respond that the resources are there if we will only exploit them. Moreover as

Christians, given our sense of what society should be like, we should do so. I have no objection to such an attempt as long as it does not underwrite a nationalism that legitimates an uncontrollable self-righteousness.

11. See, for example, John Coleman's *An American Strategic Theology* (New York: Paulist Press, 1982) for such an attempt.

2. ON KEEPING THEOLOGICAL ETHICS THEOLOGICAL

The Ethical Significance of Saying Something Theological

"Say something theological," is a request, as Gustafson notes, theologians frequently hear.[1] Such a request, often made in a more oblique manner, may be entirely friendly, as the inquirer—possessed by an archaeological curiosity in still living antiquities—simply wants an example of a religious relic. More likely, however, the request is really a challenge: "Say something theological in a way that convinces me that you are not talking nonsense." Such a challenge thus assumes that anyone using theological language seriously —that is, as though that language is essential for telling us about how things are or how we ought to be—bears the burden of proof.

This is particularly the case in matters having to do with ethics. For even though at a popular level many continue to assume there must be a close connection between religion and morality, this has not been compellingly evidenced on the philosophical level. Indeed the persistence of such an assumption only testifies how hard it is to kill certain habits of thought. For the assumption that there is a strong interdependence between religion and morality is but the remains of the now lost hegemony of Christianity over Western culture. That many still persist in assuming religion is essential to motivate us to do the good is an indication, however, that no satisfactory alternative has been found to replace Christianity, as world view and cult, in sustaining the *ethos* of our civilization. We, therefore, find ourselves in the odd situation where many of our society's moral attitudes and practices are based on Jewish and Christian beliefs that are thought to be irrelevant or false in themselves. This situation does not provide an argument for the continued viability of religious practices, but only an indication that as a culture we still have not fully faced the implications of generating a genuine secular morality.

Our culture's lingering failure to find an adequate substitute for Christianity has presented theologians with a temptation almost impossible to resist. Even if they cannot demonstrate the truth of

23

theological claims, they can at least show the continued necessity of religious attitudes for the maintenance of our culture. Of course it would be unwise to continue to use the explicit beliefs derived from the particular historic claims associated with Christianity (and Judaism) as the basis of a secular morality. Such beliefs bear the marks of being historically relative and contingent. If religion is to deserve our allegiance, so the thinking goes, it must be based on the universal. Thus, theologians have sought, at least since the Enlightenment, to demonstrate that theological language can be translated into terms that are meaningful and compelling for those who do not share Christianity's more particularistic beliefs about Jesus of Nazareth. In short, theologians have tried to show that we do not need to speak theologically in order to "say something theological," as other forms of speech are really implicitly religious. After all, hasn't talk of God always really been but a way to talk about being human?[2]

Even though this understanding of the theological task is relatively recent, there is ample precedent for this endeavor in Christian tradition. As early as the second century, Christians felt their faith contained enough in common with the nonbeliever to legitimate an apologetic strategy. Moreover, such a strategy seems required by a faith that claims a strong continuity between the God who redeems and the God who creates. Thus Christians should not be surprised to find their specific religious beliefs confirmed by the best humanistic alternatives.

Without denying some continuity between recent theological strategies and some modes of past Christian theology, it is equally important that we see the fundamental differences. The apologist of the past stood in the church and its tradition and sought relationship with those outside. Apologetic theology was a secondary endeavor because the apologist never assumed that one could let the questions of unbelief order the theological agenda. But now the theologian stands outside the tradition and seeks to show that selected aspects of that tradition can no longer pass muster from the perspective of the outsider. The theologian thus tries to locate the "essence," or at least what is essential to religion, in a manner that frees religion from its most embarrassing particularistic aspects.

Ironically, just to the extent this strategy has been successful, the more theologians have underwritten the assumption that anything said in a theological framework cannot be of much interest. For if what is said theologically is but a confirmation of what we can know on other grounds or can be said more clearly in nontheological language, then why bother saying it theologically at all? Of course there may still be reason to keep theologians around to remind us of what people used to believe, or to act as a check against the inevitable perversities of those in our culture who persist in the more traditional forms of religious practices and belief, but theology as such cannot be considered a serious intellectual endeavor. Nor is this meant to deny that theologians may have important insights concerning general human and moral issues, but that situation testifies to their individual intelligence and insight rather than their particular theological convictions or training.

For example, much of the recent work in "medical ethics" has been done by theologians, but their prominence in that area has been purchased largely by demonstrating that they can do "medical ethics" just as well as anyone who is not burdened by a theological agenda. As a result it is very hard to distinguish between articles in medical ethics written by theologians and those written by nontheologians except that often the latter are better argued.[3]

The fact it has become hard to distinguish work done by theologians in ethics from that of philosophers has only reinforced the impression that theologians have nothing interesting to say as theologians. Theologians and religious ethicists avidly read philosophers; the compliment is seldom returned. There are signs, however, that philosophers are beginning to turn their attention to matters that were discussed in the past by theologians. We may, therefore, have the odd situation where philosophers began thinking about religious issues while theologians continue to plumb issues no longer at the center of philosophical discussions.

For example, many philosophers writing about ethics are beginning to challenge the assumption that ethics is best understood on analogy with law, or at least, how many assume lawlike morality should function. For centuries Christian theologians have discussed that question and at no time more intensely than the Reformation.

That discussion has had rich results, for Christian thinkers have
consistently maintained that the law is not sufficient to depict the
Christian moral life.[4] In a related manner many challenge overly
optimistic assumptions about humanity and moral rationality.
Nowhere in modern literature have such assumptions been more
decisively challenged than by Reinhold Niebuhr.[5] And still further,
some suggest that ethicists must free themselves from their fascina-
tion with quandaries and rules, and pay more attention to the virtues
and character. Again religious traditions provide rich resources for
such an analysis and some theologians, for example, James Gustafson, have developed well-argued accounts of ethics so understood.[6]
Yet each of these significant developments in theology has largely
been ignored outside the theological community. Why is that the
case?

At least part of the fault can be attributed to the sheer prejudice
of many secular thinkers. They are simply ignorant of the disciplined nature of theological reflection and assume any reflection
informed by religious claims cannot possibly be intelligible. But I
suspect that there is a further reason, not so easily addressed, that is
internal to how theological reflection about ethics has been done in
our time: the lack of attention to the inability of Christian theologians to find a sufficient medium to articulate their own best
insights for those who do not share their convictions. In order to
understand why that is the case, it will be necessary to describe the
development of Christian ethics during this century. For it is only
against this historical background that we can understand the failure of Christian ethics to command attention, and furthermore, why
that failure should not be perpetuated, since those convictions still
offer a powerful resource for ethical reflection, even for those who
find they are unable to envision and construe the world through
them.

The Difficulty of Keeping Christian Ethics Christian

The very idea of Christian ethics as a distinct discipline is a relatively recent development.[7] Of course, Christians have always had
a lot to say about moral matters, but neither in their practical

discourse nor their more systematic reflection did they try to make ethics a subject separable from their beliefs and convictions. The Church fathers did not write ethics *per se*; rather their understanding of theology shaped their view of the moral life. Prior to the Enlightenment, the notion that there might be an independent realm called "morality" to which one must try to determine one's relation religiously and theologically simply did not exist.

The story of the development of "Christian ethics" as a distinct field, at least in the Protestant context, has two different strands—one philosophical and the other more pastoral. The first begins in Europe, especially in Germany, where Protestant liberalism tried to save the soul of theology by rescuing its essence—the fatherhood of God and the brotherhood of man. The great exponent of this solution, of course, was Kant who, with his characteristically admirable clarity, maintained that

> since the sacred narrative, which is employed solely on behalf of ecclesiastical faith, can have and, taken by itself, ought to have absolutely no influence upon the adoption of moral maxims, and since it is given to ecclesiastical faith only for the vivid presentation of its true object (virtue striving toward holiness), it follows that this narrative must at all times be taught and expounded in the interests of morality; and yet (because the common man especially has an enduring propensity within him to sink into passive belief) it must be inculcated painstakingly and repeatedly that true religion is to consist not in the knowing or considering of what God does or has done for our salvation, but in what we must do to become worthy of it.[8]

Thus morality becomes the "essence" of religion, but ironically it is understood in a manner that makes positive religious convictions secondary.

The other part of our story does not begin with such an explicit intellectual agenda, but involves a group of Protestant pastors in the late nineteenth and early twentieth centuries and their attempt to respond to the economic crisis of their people.[9] These men challenged the widespread assumption that poverty was the fault of the poor. Taking their bearings from the prophetic traditions of the

Hebrew Scripture, they preached against political and economic structures which they believed were the roots of poverty. In the process they thought they discovered an old truth that had been lost through centuries of Christian accommodation with the status quo —namely that the essential characteristic of the Christian religion is its insistence on organic unity between religion and morality, theology and ethics.[10] For Christian salvation consists in nothing less than

> an attitude of love in which we would freely coordinate our life with the life of our fellows in obedience to the loving impulses of the spirit of God, thus taking our part in a divine organism of mutual service. God is the all-embracing source and exponent of the common life and good of mankind. When we submit to God, we submit to the supremacy of the common good. Salvation is the voluntary socializing of the soul.[11]

The "social gospel," as we learned to call this movement, cared little for the development of Christian ethics as a reflective mode of discourse. Rather Christian ethics meant for them the mobilization of the energy and power of the church for social renewal. That does not mean they were unsophisticated, for they were deeply influenced by Protestant liberalism, particularly the Kantianism of Albrecht Ritschl. Thus they were adamant in their opposition to all eschatologies that might justify passive Christian response to societal injustice. The social gospel sought "to develop the vision of the Church toward the future and to cooperate with the will of God which is shaping the destinies of humanity."[13]

Yet with the social gospel, for the first time, serious courses began to be taught in American Protestant seminaries in Christian ethics —though they were often called Christian sociology. Taking their inspiration from the social gospel, these courses tended to be primarily concerned with why Christians should be committed to social justice and what economic and social strategy best accomplished that end. As a result, one of the central agendas of Christian ethics, still very much present, was a concern to make use of the social sciences for social analysis and action.[14] A Christian ethicist often became but a social scientist with a religious interest. More importantly, however, this emphasis meant that the primary conversation partners for most Christian ethicists were not philosophers but social scientists.

It was not long, however, before some of the more naive theological and social assumptions of the social gospel began to be questioned in the light of experience and historical criticism. For example, the social gospel's conviction that "the first step in the salvation of mankind was the achievement of the personality of Jesus"[15] was rendered problematic by the increasing knowledge that the Gospels do not pretend to portray Jesus "the way he really was." Thus the attempt of liberal Protestantism to free Jesus from past "schemes of redemption," to base his divine quality not in metaphysical questions but on the free and ethical acts of his personality, ironically failed to meet the challenges of a critical approach to Scripture.

Moreover the social strategy of the social gospel was soon called into question by the change of attitude occasioned by World War I and the intractability of many social problems with regard to unambiguous solutions. In spite of their trenchant criticism of American capitalism, the social gospelers were after all completely committed to American progressive ideology and policies. They never doubted the uniqueness of the American experience or entertained any critical doubt about the achievement of the American ideal, which they saw as nothing less than the realization of the Kingdom of God. The only question was how to bring the economic institutions of American life under the same spirit of cooperation that our political institutions had already achieved. The primary difference between "saved and unsaved organizations" for the social gospel is that the former are democratic and the latter are autocratic and competitive. Their attempt to turn American business into worker cooperatives was but the continuing attempt to create the secure "saved institutions."[16]

Though often more realistic and theologically profound than these aims suggest, it was clear that the movement started by the social gospel required a new theological rationale as well as social strategy.[17] "Christian ethics" became the discipline pledged to find just such a rationale and strategy. The great figure representing this project was Reinhold Niebuhr, who began his long career as a social gospel advocate, became its most powerful critic, and was quite possibly the last publicly accessible and influential theologian in America. Niebuhr seemed to be saying something theological that was compelling to a wide range of people, including people in government, but, as we shall see, his accomplishment was fraught with ambiguity.

Niebuhr's criticism of the social gospel originally centered on his increasing dissatisfaction with its optimistic view of social institutions and change. His own experience as a pastor in Detroit during the great labor struggles taught him to distrust any idea that institutions *qua* institutions are capable of moral transformation, much less salvation.[18] Rather, under the influence of Marx, he began to appreciate the necessity of power and coercion as essential for achieving, not a saved society, but at least one that might be more relatively just.

Niebuhr's theological transformation was at least partly the result of his having to wrestle with the implications of this changed perspective on social action. Theologically, how can we come to terms with living in a world which might well require us to kill for a relative political good, and with the full knowledge that any achievement of some justice that may require violence necessarily results in some injustice. Thus Niebuhr came to conclude that "the tragedy of human history consists precisely in the fact that human life cannot be creative without being destructive, that biological urges are enhanced and sublimated by demonic spirit and that this spirit cannot express itself without committing the sin of pride."[19]

Though by education a theological liberal, Niebuhr found the liberal optimistic understanding of mankind insufficient to sustain his social vision. He turned to that line of Christian theology represented by Augustine, Luther, and Kierkegaard, who emphasized humanity's fallenness and the need for a redemption not of human making. What we need to sustain us in the struggle for social justice is not, as the social gospel presumed, a grand idealistic vision, but a forgiveness which is necessarily a "moral achievement which is possible only when morality is transcended in religion."[20] Thus, for Niebuhr, Jesus' cross represents the ultimate sacrificial love that will always call into question every social and political order. Such a cross is necessary to sustain moral action in an inherently unjust world, for only as it stands on the edge of history do we have the basis for a hope that does not result in either despair or utopianism.[21]

Under Niebuhr's influence, the agenda of Christian ethics became, for many, the attempt to develop those theological, moral, and social insights necessary to sustain the ambiguous task of achieving more relatively just societies. Although this would seem to indicate a decisive break with his social gospel forebears, in fact Niebuhr continued their most important theological and social presuppositions. Like them he assumed that the task of Christian ethics was to formulate the means for Christians to serve their societies, particularly American society. His understanding and justification of democracy was more sophisticated, but like the social gospelers he never questioned that Christianity has a peculiar relationship to democracy. For Niebuhr and the social gospelers the subject of Christian ethics was America.[22] They differed only on how nearly just such a society could be and the theological presupposition necessary to understand and sustain social involvement.

Niebuhr, far more than was seen at the time, continued to be essentially a liberal theologian. His emphasis on the sinfulness of man in his magisterial *Nature and Destiny of Man* led many to associate him with the "neo-orthodox" movement of Bultmann, Brunner, and Barth. Yet Niebuhr never shared Barth's theological rejection of liberalism as a basic theological strategy; he, like Bultmann, continued liberal theology's presumption that theology must be grounded in anthropology. Thus, his compelling portrayal of our sinfulness, which appeared *contra* liberal optimism, only continued the liberal attempt to demonstrate the intelligibility of theological language through its power to illuminate the human condition. In spite of Niebuhr's personally profound theological convictions, many secular thinkers accepted his anthropology and social theory without accepting his theological presuppositions.[23] And it is not clear that in doing so they were making a mistake, as the relationships between Niebuhr's theological and ethical positions were never clearly demonstrated.

It was becoming increasingly apparent that Christian ethics must be written in a manner that allowed, and perhaps even encouraged, the separation of ethics from its religious roots. Perhaps this seems an odd result for a movement that began by asserting the "organic unity" between religion and ethics, but it was a development that was a necessary outgrowth of the social gospel commitments. The social gospelers were able to make direct appeals to their religious convictions to justify their social involvement, because in the late nineteenth century they could continue to presuppose that America was a "religious" or even a "Christian civilization and country." Niebuhr, more aware of our religious pluralism as well as the secular presuppositions underlying the American experience, attempted to provide a theological rationale for why Christians should not seek to make their theological commitments directly relevant for social policy and strategy. Even though he appeared extremely critical of the Lutheran law-Gospel distinction, in fact, he drew on the resources of that tradition, now reinterpreted in existential categories, to justify an understanding of justice and its attainment that did not require any direct theological rationale.

Niebuhr's views prevailed for no other reason than that they were more in accord with the changing social and religious situation in America. American society was increasingly becoming a pluralist and secular society.[24] As a result Christian theologians, particularly as they dealt with social issues, felt it necessary to find ways in which their ethical conclusions could be separated from their theological framework. In the hope of securing societal good, the task of Christian ethics thus became the attempt to develop social strategies which people of goodwill could adopt even though they differed religiously and morally.

Therefore, even though Niebuhr criticized the Catholic natural law tradition for "absolutizing the relative," he nonetheless was a natural law thinker. Only the natural law, through which justice was defined, involves "not so much fixed standards of reason as they are rational efforts to apply the moral obligation, implied in the love commandment, to the complexities of life and the fact of sin, that is, to the situation created by the inclination of men to take advantage of each other."[25] In fact, Niebuhr's understanding of the "law of love" as an unavoidable aspect of the human condition was in many ways a powerful attempt to provide a natural theology that could make the cross intelligible as a symbol of human existence.[26]

If Reinhold Niebuhr's work resulted in an ambiguous account of Christian ethics, in many ways his brother's work proved to be a more decisive challenge for that task. H. Richard Niebuhr was less concerned with the difficulties of sustaining the social imperatives of the social gospel; instead, he tended to pursue the theological difficulties that the social gospel had occasioned. Deeply influenced by Troeltsch, he was acutely aware that the social gospelers' attempt to move directly from their theological convictions to social strategies was fraught not only with social ambiguities but with theological difficulties. Moreover, he was increasingly doubtful of any position which assumed that God could be used to underwrite mankind's interests, even if those interests were most impressive.

Under H. Richard Niebuhr's influence it became the business of Christian ethics to find the most adequate conceptual means to explicate what kind of moral implications might follow from Christian convictions.[27] Thus, Christian theologians began to give more serious attention to what philosophers were doing, hoping they would supply just such conceptual tools. But the kind of philosophical ethics to which Niebuhr's students looked had exactly the opposite effect. They learned from those philosophical sources that there was an inherent problem in trying to move from theological claims to normative recommendations, for in doing so one commits the "supernaturalistic fallacy."[28] As a result, theological ethicists began to pay even less attention to positive theological claims and instead attempted to show that, formally, a theological basis for ethics was not inherently incoherent and, in particular, that theological claims could underwrite anti-relativist and objectivist concerns.[29] In the hands of some, Christian ethics became but another form of metaethics. In the process, it became just as ahistorical as its philosophical counterpart.

That was certainly not a result which would have made H. Richard Niebuhr happy. Even though in his work Christian ethics was less an aid to action than an aid to understanding, he did not want Christian ethics to lose its theological agenda. On the contrary, his attempt to focus attention on the question "What is going on?" rather than "What should we do?" was an attempt to

keep theological questions primary for ethical reflection. It was
H. R. Niebuhr's task to show that the former question could only be
answered adequately in theological terms. Thus, in the *Responsible
Self*, he maintained the central Christian claim is "God is acting in
all actions upon you. So respond to all actions upon you as to respond
to his action."[30]

For H. R. Niebuhr the problem was not how to secure justice in
an unjust world, but rather how to account for moral activity amid
the relativities of history. His theological project was to provide a
theological interpretation of the relativity of our existence so that
the knowledge of our finitude was relativized by our relation to a
God who alone deserves our complete loyalty. For H. R. Niebuhr
the task of Christian ethics was a theological task, but, ironically, his own theology made it difficult to keep Christian ethics
Christian. For the very idea of "Christian ethics" suggested a far too
narrow conception of God to do justice to the relativities of our
existence.[31]

In spite of the undeniable influence of Barth on H. R. Niebuhr,
the influence of Schleiermacher was stronger. He strongly reacted
against the christocentrism of Barth, but just as importantly, like his
brother he continued the liberal project to secure the intelligibility of
theological discourse by demonstrating how it reflects as well as
describes the human condition. Therefore, while differing deeply
with his brother on particular theological issues, he remained essentially in the tradition of Calvinism, as opposed to Reinhold's Luther-
anism, but in many ways the structure of their theologies was
similar. H. Richard Niebuhr's *The Responsible Self* was an attempt
to analyze the inherent relatedness of human to human, human to
nature, human and nature to God who enters a covenant with his
creation.[32]

The recent history of Christian ethics has largely been the story of
the attempt to work out the set of problems bequeathed to us by the
social gospel and the Niebuhrs. The other figure in the drama of late
has been Roman Catholic moral theology. Under the impetus of
Vatican II, Roman Catholic moral theologians have increasingly
made contact with their Protestant counterparts in hopes they could
learn from them how to put their natural law commitments in a

more compelling theological framework. Protestant thinkers, struggling with the failure of their own tradition to develop discriminating forms of argument, looked to the Catholic casuistical tradition for help in thinking about such issues as marriage, abortion, and war. No thinker better represents this tendency of Protestant thinkers than Paul Ramsey. For Ramsey continues to assume that the task of Christian ethics is to address the American body politic. Yet now the issue is not the transformation of that polity but how the ethos that underwrites that polity can be sustained under the increasing onslaught of relativistic and consequential moral theories. The heir of both Niebuhrs, Ramsey found that neither the Niebuhrs nor Protestant thought in general provided the framework appropriate for disciplined ethical argument. Thus Ramsey looked to the Catholic tradition for principles to structure arguments that, at least in principle, would be publicly acceptable. Still, the influence of the Niebuhrs meant that Ramsey could not accept Roman Catholic assumptions about the relative autonomy of natural law and morality. As a result, his work clearly manifests the tension inherent in the development of Christian ethics—namely, a concern to provide a theological account of the moral life while at the same time underplaying the significance of theology for purposes of public discussion.[33]

Much of Ramsey's perspective on this wider set of issues was set by the situation ethics debate of the 1950s and '60s. Against Joseph Fletcher's acceptance of act-utilitarianism as the most appropriate expression of Christian love, Ramsey insisted that Christian love must be in-principled. Moreover, the principles he thought best expressed or embodied their love were very much like the traditional Roman Catholic prohibitions against unjust life-taking, lying, sexual misconduct, and so on. Thus Ramsey maintained that Christian ethics, as well as Christian responsibility to maintain the best moral insights of Western civilization, was clearly aligned with deontological normative theories and against all consequentialism.[34]

Perhaps it is hard to see how this agenda has anything in common with the social gospel, but in many interesting ways Ramsey stands in continuity with that project. Even though he does not seek to underwrite a social activism that the social gospelers thought was required by the "organic unity between religion and ethics," Ramsey nonetheless shares their assumption that the first subject of Christian ethics is how to sustain the moral resources of American society. Moreover, like Reinhold Niebuhr he assumes that this project requires an account sufficient to underwrite a politics of realism in which we see that we may well have to kill in the name of a lesser evil; but unlike Niebuhr, Ramsey sought to provide, through a theological reinterpretation of the just war tradition, a control on realism's tendency to consequentialism.[35]

Ramsey claims that what makes ethics Christian is that theological convictions are necessary to sustain the deontological commitments of our culture. Therefore, in Ramsey's work in such areas as medical ethics, most of the theology can be done in the "Preface" of his books. As a result, even many of those who are sympathetic with Ramsey's construal of the ethos of medicine in deontological terms see no reason why those deontological commitments require Ramsey's peculiar theological views about the significance of covenant love to sustain that ethos. Or again, many may well side with Ramsey against the act-utilitarianism of Fletcher, but see no reason why that debate involves theological questions, since it is simply a straightforward philosophical matter involving whether a coherent deontological or teleological normative theory can be defended. All the talk about love by both Fletcher and Ramsey is but a confusion of the issue.

Therefore, contemporary theologians find themselves in a peculiar situation. Increasingly they turned to philosophical sources to help them illumine the logic of their ethical commitments, but just to the extent they did so it became harder to say what, if anything, Christian ethics had to contribute to discussions in ethics. What they failed to see was that the very philosophical sources from which they drew to clarify the nature of their normative claims made it difficult to suggest how religious convictions might challenge just those philosophical frameworks. Thus theologians assumed, along with their philosophical colleagues, that ethics must basically be about dealing with quandaries, the only question being whether Christian convictions are more basically deontological or teleological or some as yet unspecified combination of the two.

The distinctive nature of theological ethics continued to be shown not in its philosophical expression, but rather in the range of interests each theologian addressed. By continuing to draw on the inspiration of the social gospel, the theologian continued to be concerned about questions of social and economic justice, marriage and the family, the status of the nation state, that hitherto had tended to be ignored by the philosopher. Yet, with the work of Rawls and the rise of journals such as *Philosophy and Public Affairs*, the theologian could no longer even claim that mark of distinction. The only alternatives left seemed to be to retreat to working in a confessional stance or analyzing the methodological issues and alternatives for understanding how theological ethics has been or should be done.

Much of the later work has been done by James Gustafson—a student of H. R. Niebuhr—who has sought through careful analysis of historical and current options within theological ethics to keep the discourse alive.[36] Though much of Gustafson's work is descriptive, his concerns are primarily constructive. It is, therefore, not accidental that Gustafson began to direct attention to the importance for ethics of the "sort of persons we are," of character and virtue, as the appropriate context for assessing the significance of theological language for ethical behavior.[37]

Above all, Gustafson's work is centered on the question "Can ethics be Christian?" For him the Christian theologian's ethical task is done for the sake of a community which shares a set of common experiences and beliefs about God and his particular revelation in Jesus Christ.

The Christian community is not, however, the exclusive audience. Since the intention of the divine power for human well-being is universal in its scope, the historically particular medium through which that power is clarified for Christians also has universal significance. The theologian engaged in the task of "prescriptive" ethics formulates principles and values that can guide the actions of persons who do not belong to the Christian community. They will be persuasive to others, however, on the basis of supporting reasons different from those that Christians might respond to. In effect, the theologian moves from the particular Christian belief to a statement of their moral import in a more universal language. These statements will be persuasive to nonreligious persons only by the cogency of the argument that is made to show that the "historical particularity" sheds light on principles and values that other serious moral persons also perceive and also ought to adhere to. Indeed, since the Christian theologian shares in the general moral experience of secular people, and since one facet of this work that is theologically warranted is the inferring of principles and values from common experience, he or she need not in every practical circumstance make a particular theological case for what is formulated. The theologian ought, however, to be able to make a Christian theological case if challenged to do so.[38]

Gustafson's reasoning is based on his theological belief that God's purposes are for "the well-being of man and creation," and thus on most occasions the reasons that justify any moral act would justify the moral acts of Christians. The only case he can give that might be an exception to this is some Christians' commitment to nonviolent resistance to evil, since the justification of such a response clearly must rely on appeal to certain "religious" reasons that go beyond what we mean by morality.[39]

If this is all that is to be gained by speaking theologically about morality, then one may well question if it is worth the effort. As I have tried to show through this brief history of the development of the "discipline" of Christian ethics, the primary subject theologically became how to keep Christian ethics Christian. This situation is no doubt partly the result of the changing historical and sociological stance of the churches vis-a-vis American society. For as that society increasingly becomes secular, Christians, insofar as they endeavor to remain political actors, must attempt to translate their convictions into a nontheological idiom. But once such a translation is accomplished, it becomes very unclear why the theological idiom is needed at all.

The difficulty of making and keeping Christian ethics Christian, however, derives not only from social strategies, but, as we have seen, also from theological difficulties. For the recovery of the ethical significance of theological discourse was part of a theological movement within Protestantism that in large measure sought to avoid the more traditional particularistic claims of Christianity. Ironically, just to the extent that the development of Christian ethics as a field was a success, it reinforced the assumption that more positive theological convictions had little purchase on the way things are or should be. It is no wonder, therefore, that the dominant modes of philosophical ethics received little challenge from the theological community. Indeed, exactly to the contrary, theologians and religious thinkers have largely sought to show that the modes of argument and conclusions reached by philosophical ethicists are no different from those reached by ethicists with more explicit religious presuppositions. The task of Christian ethics, both socially and philosophically, was not revision but accommodation.

A Revision of Theological Ethics

I have tried to suggest why the development of Christian ethics during this century provided no significant alternative to the dominant modes of ethical reflection done by philosophers. To be sure there are aspects in the work of Rauschenbusch, the Niebuhrs, Ramsey, and Gustafson that stand in sharp contrast with the accepted mode of doing philosophical ethics. But it is simply the case that their work has failed to influence or even to be taken very seriously by others working in ethics in a nontheological context.

Of course part of the reason for that is more sociological than intellectual. Religion has increasingly become marginal in our culture, both politically and intellectually. Those types of religion that attempt to assert their relevancy in the social and political realm do so with a crudeness that only underwrites the general assumption that our society will do better to continue to relegate religious concerns to the private and subjective realm. This same kind of relegation has occurred in the intellectual realm, often with much less good reason. Few modern intellectuals feel the obligation to read the better work done in theology, because they prejudicially assume that theology must inherently be a form of special pleading.

As I suggested at the beginning, attempts to address this prejudice on its own terms are doomed to failure. The more theologians seek to find the means to translate theological convictions into terms acceptable to the nonbeliever, the more they substantiate the view that theology has little of importance to say in the area of ethics. It seems that the theologian is in a classical "no win" situation.

Yet I think in many ways this is not the case. It may be that theology can make a virtue of necessity. In many ways the social and intellectual marginality of the church in our culture is an intellectual resource that can provide the opportunity to recover some of the more important aspects of Christian reflection, particularly concerning morality. As I have tried to suggest, the very development of "Christian ethics" as a branch of theology was inspired by an attempt to reawaken Christian social responsibility. But the very terms of that reawakening and its underlying theology had already accommodated itself far too much to the secular ethos. Therefore, in spite of the significant advances in Christian reflection represented by the development of Christian ethics, in many ways it failed to represent adequately the resources for ethical reflection within the Christian tradition. Thus one of the ironies is that many of the challenges made by philosophers against the reigning paradigm could have been made, and perhaps made even more forcefully, from a theological perspective. But they were not, and they were not because Christians in general and theologians in particular continued to assume that they had built a home within Western civilization that they had a stake in continuing. As a result, Christian ethicists accepted an account of the social good that fails to manifest the struggle, the transformation of the self necessary for any adequate account of the moral life.

It is odd that Christians, of all people, could have made that mistake, since who could know better than they that the moral good is not an achievement easily accomplished by the many, but a demanding task that only a few master. Christians have not been called to do just the right, to observe the law, though doing the right and observing the law are not irrelevant to being good. Rather, for Christians the moral life, at least scripturally, is seen as a journey through life sustained by fidelity to the cross of Christ, which brings a fulfillment no law can ever embody. Thus Aquinas says

> there is a twofold element in the Law of the Gospel. There is the chief element, namely, the grace of the Holy Ghost bestowed inwardly. And as to this the New Law justifies. Hence Augustine says: "There (that is, in the Old Testament) it is given in an inward manner, that they might be justified." The other element of the Evangelical Law is secondary; namely the teachings of faith, and those commandments which direct human affections and human actions. And as to this, the New Law does not justify. Hence the Apostle says: "The letter killeth, but the spirit quickeneth" (II Cor. 3:6), and Augustine explains this by saying that the letter denotes any writing that is external to man, even that of the moral precepts such as are contained in the Gospel. Therefore the letter, even of the Gospel would kill, unless there were the inward presence of the healing grace of faith.[40]

From such a perspective Christian thinkers, above all, should have been among the first to criticize the attempt to model the moral life primarily on the analogy of the law. Instead, fearing moral anarchy, like our philosophical colleagues, Christian thinkers assumed that questions of "right" were more primary than questions of good, that principles were more fundamental than virtues, that for morality to be coherent required some one principle from which all others could be derived or tested, that the central task of moral reflection was to help us think straight about quandaries, and that we had to see the world as neatly divided into facts and values, rather than an existence filled with many valuational possibilities, some of which may well be in conflict. Perhaps most ironical, Christian theology attempted to deny the inherent historical and community-dependent nature of our moral convictions in the hopes that our "ethics" might be universally persuasive.

But as Schneewind reminds us, the justification of our moral principles and assertions cannot be done from the point of view of anyone, but rather requires a tradition of moral wisdom.[41] Such a tradition is not a "deposit" of unchanging moral "truth," but is

made up of the lives of men and women who are constantly testing
and changing that tradition through their own struggle to live it. The
maintenance of such a tradition requires a community across time
sufficient to sustain the journey from one generation to the next. The
Christian word for the community is church.[42]

It is my suspicion that if theologians are going to contribute to
reflection on the moral life in our particular situation, they will do so
exactly to the extent they can capture the significance of the church
for determining the nature and content of Christian ethical reflection. This may seem an odd suggestion, for it seems such a move
would only make the theologian that much further removed from
being a serious conversation partner. It is assumed, by theologian
and philosopher alike, that any distinctive contribution of theological ethics must begin with beliefs about God, Jesus, sin, and the like,
and the moral implications of those beliefs. And of course there is
much truth to that. Yet the problem with putting the matter in that
way is that such "beliefs" look like descriptions of existence, some
kind of primitive metaphysics, that one must then try to analyze for
their moral implications. To force Christian moral reflection into
such a pattern is to make it appear but another philosophical
account of the moral life.

But that is exactly what it is not. For Christian beliefs about God,
Jesus, sin, the nature of human existence, and salvation are intelligible only if they are seen against the background of the church—that
is, a body of people who stand apart from the "world" because of
the peculiar task of worshipping a God whom the world knows not.
This is a point as much forgotten by Christian theologians as by
secular philosophers, since the temptation is to make Christianity
another "system of belief." Yet what was original about the first
Christians was not the peculiarity of their beliefs, even beliefs about
Jesus, but their social inventiveness in creating a community whose
like had not been seen before. To say they believed in God is true but
uninteresting. What is interesting is that they thought that their
belief in God as they had encountered him in Jesus required the
formation of a community distinct from the world exactly because of
the kind of God he was. You cannot know what kind of God you
disbelieve in, from a Christian perspective, unless you see what kind

of community is necessary to worship him across time. The flabbiness of contemporary atheism is, thus, a judgment on the church's unwillingness to be a distinctive people.

Therefore, when asked to say something theological, especially when the questioner is seeking to understand the ethical significance of religious convictions, we should perhaps not say with Gustafson "God," but "Church." For the criticism of the emphasis in contemporary ethics on law, on rights, on principles, on quandaries, on facts distinguished from values, is the result of trying to write ethics for anyone, as if ethics can be abstracted from any community. It is not surprising that the law becomes the primary analogue for such an ethic as law is often seen as the minimal principles needed to secure order between people who share little in common. Ethics, like law, thus becomes the procedural means to settle disputes and resolve problems while leaving our individual "preferences" and desires to our own choice. To say more about morality requires not simply a conception of the good, but a tradition that carries the virtues necessary for training in movement toward the good.

Many philosophers and theologians are calling for a fuller account of the moral life. They rightly criticize the thinness of much of contemporary ethical theory; yet they offer no persuasive alternative. They point to the need for revision, but the social and political practices necessary for that revision to be institutionalized are missing. Moreover, any attempts to create them appear utopian or totalitarian. Of course, appeals can be made to particular individuals as paradigms of the kind of moral life desired, but moral geniuses are never sufficient to sustain our best moral convictions. For sustenance we need a community to direct attention toward, and sustain the insights of, those who have become more nearly good.

As Christians we believe we not only need a community, but a community of a particular kind to live well morally. We need a people who are capable of being faithful to a way of life, even when that way of life may be in conflict with what passes as "morality" in the larger society. Christians are a people who have learned that belief in God requires that we learn to look upon ourselves as creatures rather than as creators. This necessarily creates a division between ourselves and others who persist in the pretentious assumption that we can and should be morally autonomous. Of course Christians are as prone to such pretensions as non-Christians. What distinguishes them is their willingness to belong to a community which embodies the stories, the rituals, and others committed to worshipping God. Such a community, we believe, must challenge our prideful pretensions as well as provide the skills for the humility necessary for becoming not just good, but holy.

Theologians, therefore, have something significant to say about ethics, but they will not say it significantly if they try to disguise the fact that they think, write, and speak out of and to a distinctive community. Their first task is not, as has been assumed by many working in Christian ethics and still under the spell of Christendom, to write as though Christian commitments make no difference in the sense that they only underwrite what everyone already in principle can know, but rather to show the difference those commitments make. At least by doing that, philosophers may have some idea how the attempt to avoid presuming any tradition or community may distort their account of the moral life as well as moral rationality. Our task as theologians remains what it has always been—namely, to exploit the considerable resources embodied in particular Christian convictions which sustain our ability to be a community faithful to our belief that we are creatures of a graceful God. If we do that we may well discover that we are speaking to more than just our fellow Christians, for others as a result may well find we have something interesting to say.

Notes

1. James Gustafson, "Say Something Theological," 1981 *Nora and Edward Ryerson Lecture* (Chicago: University of Chicago, 1981), 3. Gustafson notes that he has the presence of mind to say "God."

2. This development is as true of Roman Catholic as well as Protestant theology. See, for example, Thomas Sheehan's review of Karl Rahner's *Foundations of Christian Faith*, in which he applauds Rahner's attempt to carry out Feuerbach's program of transforming theology into anthropology. Of course, the odd thing about Sheehan's enthusiasm for this move is that Feuerbach assumed that to do so was the agenda of atheism, not theism. "The Drama of Karl Rahner," *New York Review of Books*, February 4, 1981, 13-14.

3. That is not to say that much of the work done by philosophers in medical ethics is free from difficulty. By "better argued" I mean it is more adept at working within the set paradigms of philosophical analysis. However I am by no means happy with those paradigms. For example, see my *Suffering Presence: Essays on Medical Ethics, the Mentally Handicapped, and the Church* (Notre Dame: University of Notre Dame Press, 1985).

4. See, for example, Edward Long's fine article "Soteriological Implications of Norm and Context," in *Norm and Context in Christian Ethics*, edited by Eugene Outka and Paul Ramsey (New York: Scribner's, 1968) 265-296.

5. In particular, see Reinhold Niebuhr, *The Self and the Dramas of History* (New York: Scribner's, 1955).

6. James Gustafson, *Can Ethics Be Christian?* (Chicago: University of Chicago Press, 1975).

7. I am keenly aware of the inadequacy of the brief overview of the development of Christian ethics over the last century. Not only do I leave out of the account many of the main actors, even those I treat are not analyzed with the nuance they deserve. I hope soon to write a more adequate book-length account that will do justice to this complex story. However, for present purposes I thought it worthwhile to tell the history in a somewhat contentious manner, since my interests are more systematic than historical. Moreover, I am certainly ready to defend the interpretive features of my account, even though I have not taken the time here to document them adequately.

8. Immanuel Kant, *Religion Within the Limits of Reason Alone*, translated with an introduction by Theodore Greene and Hoyt Hudson (New York: Harper, 1960), 123.

9. C. H. Hopkins, *The Rise of the Social Gospel in American Protestantism, 1865-1915* (New Haven: Yale University Press, 1940).

10. Walter Rauschenbusch, *A Theology for the Social Gospel* (Nashville: Abingdon Press, 1945), 140.

11. Ibid., 98–99.

12. Ibid., 210.

13. Ibid., 224.

14. For example, in his fine article on one of the early social gospelers, Francis Greenwood Peabody, David Little observes that "like many of his contemporaries, Peabody recommended wide exposure to the methods of social science as the basis for sound moral action. Since the ethical aims of true religion and manifest patterns of social development were believed to be rooted in one and the same phenomenon, inductive empirical investigation of social life could only complement and enrich the moral task. He is very clear about this: 'Ethics is finally social science and social science is ethics. *Ethics* is the end of sociology.'" "Francis Greenwood Peabody," *Harvard Library Bulletin* 15, 3 (July 1967), 287–300.

15. Rauschenbusch, 151.

16. Rauschenbusch, 112–113.

17. For a particularly able defense of Rauschenbusch see Max Stackhouse's, "The Continuing Importance of Walter Rauschenbusch," which introduces Rauschenbusch's *The Righteousness of the Kingdom* (Nashville: Abingdon Press, 1968), 13–59.

18. Niebuhr's reflections on his change of mind can be found in his *Leaves from the Notebook of a Tamed Cynic* (New York: Living Age Books, 1957). See also Niebuhr's "Intellectual Autobiography," in *Reinhold Niebuhr: His Religious, Social, and Political Thought*, ed. Charles Kegley and Robert Bretall (New York: Macmillan, 1956), 1–24.

19. Reinhold Niebuhr, *The Nature and Destiny of Man* (New York: Scribner's, 1941), 1:10–11.

20. Reinhold Niebuhr, *An Interpretation of Christian Ethics* (New York: Living Age Books, 1956), 201. It is interesting that Niebuhr's stress on forgiveness as the hallmark of Christian ethics is not carried forward in his later work. Rather his emphasis is almost entirely on self-sacrificial love. It is my hunch that Niebuhr was much closer to being right by

focusing on forgiveness than love as more important for the systematic display of Christian ethics.

21. In his *Christian Realism and Liberation Theology* (Maryknoll: Orbis Books, 1981) Dennis McCann suggests that rather than providing a strategy for social action Niebuhr is best interpreted as trying to form a "spirituality" necessary to sustain political activity. That seems to me to be a particularly fruitful way to read Niebuhr, as it helps account for the lack of any conceptually clear connections between Niebuhr's theological views and his strategic judgments.

22. See, for example, Niebuhr's *The Children of Light and the Children of Darkness* (New York: Scribner's, 1944) and *The Irony of American History* (New York: Scribner's, 1962). This perhaps helps explain the oft made observation that Niebuhr paid almost no attention to the social significance of the church—for finally, in spite of all the trenchant criticism he directed at America, America was his church. Thus the criticism that failed to sustain his trenchant perspective in the last years of his life in some ways is misplaced, since it fails to note that Niebuhr from beginning to end was involved in a stormy love affair with America. In some ways the social gospelers were less accommodationist than Niebuhr in this respect; Rauschenbusch, in particular, assumed the necessity of the church to stand as a critic against American society.

The importance of America as the subject of Christian ethics can also be seen in the tendency of many Christian ethicists to think of ethics as a form of "American studies." H. R. Niebuhr's *The Kingdom of God in America* (New York: Harper, 1937) remains the classical text for this genre.

23. Niebuhr profoundly influenced such people as Hans Morgenthau, George Kennan, Arthur Schlesinger, Jr., and many others. It is, perhaps, a mark of the instability of Niebuhr's position that often both sides of a political issue, particularly in foreign affairs, can claim with some justice to be Niebuhrians.

24. Arthur Schlesinger documents this well in his "The Political Philosophy of Reinhold Niebuhr," in *Reinhold Niebuhr: His Religious, Social, and Political Thought*, 125–150. Schlesinger rightly notes that Niebuhr, the penetrating critic of the social gospel and of pragmatism, ended up "the powerful reinterpreter and champion of both. It was the triumph of his own remarkable analysis that it took what was valuable in each, rescued each by defining for each the limits of validity, and, in

the end, gave the essential purposes of both new power and vitality. No
man has had as much influence as a preacher in this generation; no
preacher has had as much influence in the secular world" (149).

25. Reinhold Niebuhr, *Faith and History* (New York: Scribner's, 1951),
188–189.

26. Niebuhr's stress on the sinfulness of man leads some to forget that for
Niebuhr theology is still primarily anthropology. As a result Niebuhr
never answered satisfactorily how the cross of Jesus is necessary for
our adequately understanding why the cross is the necessary symbol of
"the perfection of *agape* which transcends all particular norms of
justice and mutuality in history." (*Nature and Destiny of Man*) 2:74.

27. For the best short introduction to H. R. Niebuhr's work see James
Gustafson, "Introduction," in H. R. Niebuhr, *The Responsible Self:
An Essay in Christian Moral Philosophy* (New York: Harper and
Row, 1963), 6–41.

28. H. R. Niebuhr was not himself very taken with ethics done out of the
analytical tradition, but instead was influenced more by the pragmatist
tradition of Royce and Perry. However, a latter generation of students,
trained by Gustafson, turned increasingly to Moore, Ross, Hare, in
attempts to think through the problems they had inherited from
Niebuhr.

29. Art Dyck's enthusiasm for and theological justification of the "ideal-
observer" theory is a good example of this tendency. See his *On
Human Care: An Introduction to Ethics* (Nashville: Abingdon, 1977).

30. H. R. Niebuhr. *The Responsible Self*, 126.

31. For H. R. Niebuhr, Jesus is normative only as he "represents the
incarnation of radical faith," which is faith that "Being is God, or
better, that the principle of being, the source of all things and the
power by which they exist, is good, as good for them and good to them"
Radical Monotheism and Western Culture (New York: Harper and
Row, 1960), 38.

32. Thus he says, "Man responsive and responsible before nature, fitting
his actions into those of nature; man responsive in political or economic
or cultural society as responsible citizen; responsible businessman,
responsible educator, responsible scientist, responsible parent, responsible churchman—such men we know and understand. But what ties
all these responsivities and responsibilities together and where is the
responsible *self* among all these roles played by the individual being?
Can it be located within the self, as though by some mighty act of self-

making it brought itself into being as one 'I' among these many systems of interpretation and response? The self as one self among all the systematized reactions in which it engages seems to be the counterpart of a unity that lies beyond, yet expresses itself in, all the manifold systems of actions upon it. In religious language, the soul and God belong together; or otherwise stated, I am one within myself as I encounter the One in all that acts upon me" *The Responsible Self*, 122.

33. The theological side of Ramsey's work was more apparent in his early work where he was emphatic that "natural law" must be transformed by love. See in particular his *War and the Christian Conscience* (Durham, N.C.; Duke University Press, 1961). Ramsey's shift to the motif of covenant fidelity as the central metaphor for Christian reflection also seems to have been accompanied with a greater appreciation for the continuity between the "natural" covenants we find in our lives and that which God has made with us. As a result he is able to proceed with much less direct appeal to theological warrants. See, for example, his *The Patient as Person* (New Haven: Yale University Press, 1970).

34. Thus Ramsey argues that "Protestant Christian ethics is often too profoundly personal to be ethically relevant, if in this is included even a minimum of concern for the social habits and customs of a people. Ordinarily, we do not take Christian ethics with enough seriousness to illumine the path that men, women, and *society* should follow today. This suggests that only some form of rule-agapism, and not act-agapism, can be consistent with the elaboration of a Christian's social responsibilities. No social morality ever was founded, or ever will be founded, upon a situational ethic." *Deeds and Rules in Christian Ethics* (New York: Scribner's, 1967), 20.

35. Ramsey's profound debt to Niebuhr can be most clearly seen in his *The Just War: Force and Political Responsibility* (New York: Scribner's, 1968). There Ramsey, like Niebuhr argues that the failure of all peace movements is they presume the illusion that force can be avoided in politics and as a result only increase the likelihood of war. In contrast the just war tradition influenced by the theological insights of Augustine rightly sees that war can never be fought for peace, but only for more relative just ends. Thus Ramsey argues the ethos necessary to control violence through just war principles must ultimately draw on religious presuppositions. For only if you think death is not ultimate power over life can you be willing to expose yourself to death and to kill others for the limited moral goods of political community.

36. See, for example, Gustafson's *Christian Ethics and the Community* (Philadephia: Pilgrim Press, 1971) and *Theology and Christian Ethics*. (Philadelphia: Pilgrim Press, 1974), both of which are collections of his essays that attempt to bring some intellectual clarity to the activity of other Christian ethicists.

37. This emphasis, of course, is but an indication of Gustafson's indebtedness to H. R. Niebuhr's attempt to identify the central issue of Christian ethics as that of the "self." Unfortunately many of the interpreters of H. R. Niebuhr tend to stress more his account of "responsibility" and, as a result, fail to see that Niebuhr's primary concern was the "self."

38. Gustafson, *Can Ethics Be Christian?*, 163.

39. It is telling, I think, that in his recent constructive work, *Ethics from a Theocentric Perspective* (Chicago: University of Chicago Press, 1981), Gustafson thinks John Howard Yoder's "sectarian" stance to be the most intelligible alternative to his own position.

40. Thomas Aquinas, *Summa Theologia*, I-II.106.2 translated by Fathers of the English Dominican Province (Chicago: William Benton Publisher, 1952). Many others besides Aquinas could be quoted to substantiate this point. I purposely chose Aquinas, since many who defend a natural law approach to Christian ethics appeal to him as their primary authority. Yet as the quotation makes clear, Aquinas assumed that an adequate theological ethics could not be limited to or based on an analogy with law.

41. J. B. Schneewind, "Moral Knowledge and Moral Principles," in *Revisions: Changing Perspectives in Moral Philosophy*, edited by Stanley Hauerwas and Alasdair MacIntyre (Notre Dame: University of Notre Dame Press, 1983), 113–126.

42. For a fuller account of this prespective see my *A Community of Character: Toward a Constructive Christian Social Ethic* (Notre Dame: University of Notre Dame Press, 1981).

3. ON KEEPING THEOLOGICAL ETHICS IMAGINATIVE

with Philip Foubert

Imagination and Morality

Imagination and morality are concepts we do not often link. We customarily associate imagination with spontaneity, creativity, the unique genesis. Artists are imaginative. Painters, poets, and novelists are subject to the unpredictable and fertile powers of imagination, for it is their task to create fabulous worlds unconstrained by our normal habits. So imagination invents a world not subject to discipline and necessity. As a result, the imaginative is often the province of disillusioned individuals isolated from society. For just to the extent that imagination creates the unexpected or disrupts our normal way of seeing, so also does it threaten. Indeed, it frequently challenges the cherished social conventions we consider our basic morality.

In contrast, we usually think that to be moral is to do what is required. Persons of good character are those who have learned to make their own the common good of society. They seek not to challenge society but to foster practices which promote the ends of the social order. The moral life flourishes not on the unexpected but on the trust built by observance of obligation. Morally we try to live in the actual world rather than an imaginary one, for the real world houses the everyday interactions which are the very substance of morality.

Though this understanding of imagination and morality pervades our culture, we contend that it is a misconception which profoundly distorts the Christian moral life. For we intend to suggest that Christians, as a people of hope, are obligated to be morally imaginative in the formation of our lives together. Christians' very ability to live morally as a community of the new age makes it imperative that we live by trusting our imagination. Yet our imagination is not simply the unique talent of a gifted few—though certainly some are so gifted—but the imagination of people searchingly faithful to the

51

God who never ceases to challenge us through Jesus' cross and
resurrection.

Imagination Disciplined by Hope and Courage

Many of our most important notions prove elusive when analyzed.
Hence we must begin by trying to discover what we mean by imagination. We ordinarily associate imagination with mental facility
since we suppose it involves the power of the mind to produce and
organize previously unrelated images or ideas. Thus the imagination
entertains "entities" located not "out there" but "in the mind." That
does not mean they are nonexistent; but the subjects of the imagination seem to have only a hypothetical status when compared to the
factual objects of our experience. Typically, we say, "I must have
imagined it" when admitting a mistake. This suggestion of unreality
underwrites our connecting imagination with creativity and its allied
lack of constraint, discipline, or necessity.

But such a contrast between "fact and fancy" appears wide of the
mark when the testimony of creative people is considered. For they
commonly report that their new invention, discovery, or vision
springs principally from discipline and training, providing them with
the skills to notice and make use of the unexpected. Often the
"unexpected" dwells in our midst but is overlooked or taken for
granted since we lack the skills to see its significance. Great art is
not, as so often portrayed by the enduring Romantic response to the
Enlightenment, unprecedented achievement, but the culmination of
extensive discipline which has learned to make a virtue of necessity.[1]

Such training, of course, entails acquiring the skills of the
craft. Musicians must repeatedly practice playing their chosen
instruments. Painters must learn to imply form and apply color with
brush strokes. Poets and novelists must master nuances of language.
These skills are disciplines necessary to perform and project the
creations of artists. Spontaneity, often a felt accompaniment to
artistic production, is but the outcome of years of training and
practice and thousands of experiments.

Yet the training required for artistic achievement must be culti-
vated further by learning to accept the limits of a given medium.
Imagination cannot sail in unlimited possibility but must navigate a

world of limitations. Musicians cannot produce just any sounds, but must respect the tonal range of their instruments. Painters cannot design just any piece, but must use this canvas and that palette of colors with brushes. Novelists are not free to invent entirely new languages, but must compose with words we share and use in common. Of course, artists constantly press against the limits and necessities of their media, but they are able to do so only because they have first come to understand the limits of what they leave behind. Thus musicians modify accepted assumptions about musical theory or even alter their instruments. Painters try materials other than chalk, water, and oil to apply color. Novelists transform conventions of language and narrative display. By doing so they teach us all to listen, receive, and read differently. They school our imagination in the exercise of new skills. We may learn a more appreciative quality of attention to reality because we have been disciplined by others' achievements.

The relationships between imagination, creativity, and discipline have often been observed and discussed, but such discussions often overlook the moral dimension at the heart of the imaginative adventure. For the virtues of hope and courage are at least as important as disciplined skills in the creative process. Often those who have acquired the skills of their specific craft fail to bring new insight to their work not because they lack talent, but because they lack hope and courage. Artists must have a profound confidence that their efforts to stretch their craft will broaden the vision and enlarge the lives of others. Such confidence and hope, precisely because it ventures to risk, frequently appears in the distorted form of arrogance and highhandedness. But arrogance is still a form of hope without which we would all be poorer.

Courage is as important as hope. Indeed, arrogance may well be but a form of hope unschooled by the courage that produces humility appropriate to the task. For imagination is not merely a process "in the mind" taking place apart from a person's character. We do not "imagine" with our "minds" but with our passions, our hands and feet; in short, with everything we are. For we can only act in the world we can see. To imagine, to envision life anew as having possibilities which we almost fear, apprehensive of

disappointment, requires that we be people of courage.[2] For there is
much to dread in our lives; to seek enrichment through the creation
of new possibilities in many ways only makes the world more threat-
ening. Most of us prefer convention, though we find ultimately no
safety there. The task of imagining, of skillful revisioning, must be
thoroughly disciplined by the virtues of hope and courage if it is to
be sustained.

The Necessity of the Virtues

"Imagination" and "the moral life," therefore, are not two separate
subjects which must be brought into relation; rather, they are but
two aspects of the same reality. For "imaginative" persons cannot be
such without some virtues, and "moral" persons cannot be so without those virtues which compel us to be imaginative.[3] This does not
mean that "creative" people or artists will always manifest the
requisite virtues of hope and courage in aspects of their lives apart
from their work, though they certainly may. But it does mean that
artists, in relation to their art, often will have begun to acquire skills
crucial to the moral life more generally understood.

How or why, then, is imagination indispensable to the moral
person? Even more, why have we asserted that the moral community
as such should live only through imagination? Precisely the opposite
seems true, as morality is usually thought to deal with decisions in
the normal round. Indeed, ethical theories emphasizing the unique
and the exceptional, on the order of situation ethics, fail to account
for the significance of moral constants, such as trust and obligation,
which depend on maintaining "the normal."

While we do not dispute the recognition that the moral life has a
heavy stake in upholding normality, we wish to emphasize how
profoundly "the normal" requires and depends upon imagination.
For the "necessities" of our "normal" obligations generate the need
for imagination in moral life. Our character as a Christian community, after all, is but the normal result of our extraordinary conviction that in Jesus the Christ we witness God's kingdom. That
conviction, making us who we are, is the source and basis of our
ability to remain imaginative people. To be sure, our convictions

have a brand of necessity to them, but exactly one which demands that we exert our imagination if we are to be faithful. For our moral existence is not a given; rather, we insist, as moral convictions structure our vision of reality, that the world be a certain kind of place, by refusing to betray our convictions because they make our lives more difficult.

Creativity in the moral life, far from implying an escape from the constraints of habit, transforms what is into what ought to be by displaying through the virtues the implications of our obligation to witness to God's rule. Thus Christian moral casuistry should become our manner of imaginatively and courageously reckoning with the unanticipated costs of discipleship. Imagination is morally required because we refuse to allow the "necessities" of the world, which are often but stale habits, to go unchanged or unchallenged when they are in fact susceptible to the power of imagination.[4]

The Kingdom of God: The Challenge to Imagination

Put starkly, moral obligations create the necessities that empower imagination. We can illustrate this by citing the consummate artistry of the Gospel of Mark. That narrative, crafted to train us to see and to follow Jesus as God's ruling presence, was first proclaimed for a community whose courage was tested by "wars and rumors of wars" and whose hope remained in a crucified and risen messiah. Their mission to preach "Christ crucified, a stumbling block to Jews and folly to Gentiles," despite the disappointment of normal messianic expectations, makes the very form of the Gospel an imaginative accomplishment. For there we discover the kingdom of God as an imaginative possibility just to the extent that we have been seasoned by discipleship to see Jesus' cross as bringing the new order of God's rule.

Like the prophets who challenged the public imagination of Israel, Jesus arrives suddenly on the scene in Galilee preaching the nearness of the kingdom of God and calling disciples. Though we learn the secret of Jesus' identity as the Son of God in the opening moments, we are schooled by Mark's dramatic irony to see the blindness of the disciples and opposing officials to the way of God.

Fascinated by Jesus' power, the disciples must struggle to follow him because they cannot imagine delivering up their lives or becoming servants. They resist the necessity of Jesus' passion despite his warning of that destiny on the journey to Jerusalem. They disregard Jesus' teachings about renouncing the self, taking up the cross, welcoming children, and serving others. As suffering and death threaten, the disciples do not envisage the possibilities available through faith; in fearful self-concern they maneuver all the more for advantage. Their reluctance to risk repentant following on the way of God evidence their failure of imagination.

So too the authorities are blind to God's reconciling presence in Jesus' ministry. They prevent the "traditions of God" from charging their imaginations into recognizing Jesus as the very integrity of his Father. The office holders misuse their power by "lording over" people and separating themselves from those in need of compassion. They seek to save their lives by "looking to the reactions" of people and "doing the satisfactory thing for the crowd." So completely do the powers that be repudiate the one who sent Jesus that they resort to violence to secure the illusion of their own importance.

Neither disciples nor authorities, then, rightly see God's way in Jesus. But Jesus himself faced the necessity of death with courageous trust in the possibilities open to his Father. For he faithfully employed the authority he received from God only to serve and to heal. Indeed his preaching did not promote the nature or status of his own person, but steadily proclaimed the already partly present kingdom of God. Because he never imagined his hope to reside in anything other than dependence on God, he lost his life, abandoned and murdered by uncomprehending strangers, rather than turning to power to save himself.

Mark's narrative artistry surfaces when we see that only by following Jesus' way to the cross can his disciples come to recognize his true character as the Son of God. For trusting God enough to lose one's self in graciously serving the many "little ones" is the very discipline of the kingdom. Mark skillfully trains us to see the rule of God in Jesus' death and resurrection, and we are thereby invited into the exacting journey of discipleship.

It is an imaginative commitment to be a community capable of living with such demands and finding the resources to remain faithful. It is an imaginative exercise to be a servant people when the gift of others' existence may seem to threaten our desires, our possessions, our very lives. For our obligation to the helpless and nameless who come into our world is as "normal" for us as that to the next child born into our own family. That the weak should call forth our unconditional care grows out of Jesus' command that following him necessitates nothing less. Our convictions, then, are much like the skills of artists, forming us to be the kind of people capable of corresponding to the way the world ought to be but is not. Our imagination prompts us to do what is necessary to share in God's way with his world.

This analysis of imagination helps us to appreciate what an extraordinarily imaginative feat it is to describe the destruction of children as abortion. For "abortion" is a moral notion created to remind us that we ought to be a people welcoming children into the world.[5] At times such hospitality may impose hardship, yet such hardship turns out to be the very source of our creativity as a moral community. For it is from all children that we learn to acknowledge that our lives are not our own, but belong to God. Without them we would literally be impoverished, for we would lack the capacity to see beyond the limits of our own selfish history.

Christians are a people whose imagination has been challenged by a God who has invited us into an otherwise unimaginable kingdom. For only God could have created a world in which forgiveness rather than force could be both a possibility and a duty. Our own limited imagination often occasions our sin, as we imprison ourselves in attachments for which we are normally willing to kill. Only as we fulfill our obligation to let our vision be governed by the kingdom inaugurated in Jesus can we become free to face death as faithful servants. For it is a kingdom which challenges our conventional assumptions that security can be achieved only through violence, that our relations with others should be determined by fear, and that our history is finally a tale of despair.

Rather, we have been schooled to see that our security comes only by trusting in God's care, that we must serve others as God's good creation, and that our lives have a place in God's kingdom. Because we have been called to discipleship in a community of the new age proclaimed by Jesus of Nazareth, we have become capable of the unimaginable: forgiveness of enemies even unto death, loving service knowing no boundaries or limits, trust in the surpassing power of God's peace.[6] In short, God has invited us to learn the skills, disciplines, and necessities of his kingdom through which we may display to the world the unceasing innovations made possible by being his people.

For what could be more challenging to our imagination than that in Israel, Jesus, and the Church God has gathered to himself a historic people? That is why God's rule in Jesus is not merely an "image," however arresting or vivid. We can risk our lives in hope and courage only because God has entered our history to make possible our going beyond the seeming "necessities" of our available options. Indeed the central task in the conversation between Israel and Christianity must be to imagine and explore how it can be true that the one God of Israel has come with unprecedented authority as a crucified messiah. We must be able to renounce our "normal" expectation that the world in which we live will continue to exist indefinitely. That God is the lord of history means we must be able joyfully to imagine that things need not and will not go on just as they are but as God will have them. The Christian skill of seeing our present and future in the hands of God frees us from the necessity of wielding violence to control history.[7]

Accordingly, Christians should never profess a contrast between imagination and moral life, however ingrained in culture such a distinction may be. For the traditional literature of the Hebrew Bible and New Testament alerts our imagination to the need for radically changing our hearts. As we learn from the prophetic vision of Isaiah, the God whom we worship has destined us for a kingdom in which he would have "the wolf dwell with the lamb" and in which "no more shall there be an infant that lives but a few days." We may, of course, avoid such moral direction by neglecting to take seriously its implications. For example, it is a sign of our lackadaisical imagination as well as our infidelity that the Christian community has failed to generate the enlivening discussion about the eating of animals that is appropriate to our imagination. At least we have remained faithful in the measure that we have not suppressed those very scriptural images of God's kingdom which may well challenge our lives. For there is perhaps no more serious Christian offense than to fail in imagination, that is, to abandon or forget the resources God has given as the means of calling us to his kingdom.

The Christian community lives through a hope fastened on the imaginative world created by God. His kingdom, we believe, is not some fabulous ideal yet to be realized, but a present possibility made real in the life, death, and resurrection of Jesus who is an "image" only because he is so real. His reality as the Christ is the resource empowering Christians with the courage to create the necessity of being a peaceable people in a violent world. That we will not abandon the weak when serving them may demand that we deliver up our lives, without resorting to violence though it may well challenge us to be more imaginative than we had anticipated. Christians live on hope and learn to trust in an imagination disciplined by God's peaceable kingdom into accepting the cross as the alternative to violence. Our imagination is the very means by which we live morally, and our moral life is in truth the source of our imagination.

Notes

1. The discipline moreover is carried by a tradition into which the artist must be initiated even if later they break from it. For example, see E. H. Gombrich's account in *Art and Illusion* (New York: Pantheon Books, 1960).
2. For a fuller account of the relation between seeing and virtue see my *Vision and Virtue* (Notre Dame: University of Notre Dame Press, 1974).
3. In many ways Aristotle's account of the relation between the "intellectual" and "moral" virtues remains unsurpassed. See *Nichomachean Ethics*, translated by Martin Ostwold (Indianapolis: Bobbs-Merrill, 1962), Book Six.
4. Thus most of us assume that there is no alternative but to use violence to resolve social conflicts. Our very inability to imagine an alternative makes our lack of imagination a self fulfilling prophecy.
5. By "created" we do not mean that it is an arbitrary invention that has no basis in reality. Rather created denotes that "abortion" is the result of a community's prior assumption about the significance of children. Such notions, moreover, are not "created" at once but rather reflect a community's long experience learning the implication of their convictions.
6. For a defense of this account of the Gospel see my *The Peaceable Kingdom* (Notre Dame: University of Notre Dame Press, 1983).
7. Pacifists, have no corner on knowing how to live peaceably. Indeed I suspect that most of us who call ourselves "pacifist" have little idea what is entailed by such a description. To say that I am a pacifist in fact is an attempt to make a commitment public in the hopes that others will force me to explore what such a commitment entails—i.e. it is a challenge to the imagination.

4. REMEMBERING AS A MORAL TASK: THE CHALLENGE OF THE HOLOCAUST

Emancipation (of the Jews) did not depend on who won the arguments, but on the process of secularization that shaped the modern state and which could not tolerate self-governing groups apart from the monolithic organizations of the nation-state. It was on these grounds that the Jews had to either be drawn into a secular definition of citizenship, based on nationalism or else be regarded as incapable of assimilating into this national identity and eliminated by expulsion (or extermination). It was here that liberal philosophy and theology played an ambivalent role. Their definition of religion, either as universal, national religion of reason, or else as profound inwardness, made Judaism the antithesis of the concept of "religion." Since Judaism was not a religion, according to either Christian rationalist or Christian romantic theories, Judaism came to be defined in this tradition of thought in nationalist, quasi-racial terms. Judaism was said to be, not a religion, but the laws of a nation. Jews were not a religious group, but a foreign nation. The antithesis of Judaism and Christianity was translated into an antithesis between Jews and Europeans, or Jews and Germans.[1]

We can deal only with the history of that church which contained within itself, from its first beginning, the seed and the principles of the objective unity of the true and *universal* religious faith, to which it is gradually brought nearer. And first of all it is evident that the Jewish faith stands in no essential connection whatever, i.e., in no unity of concepts, with the ecclesiastical faith whose history we wish to consider, though the Jewish immediately preceded this (the Christian) church and provided the physical occasion for its establishment. The *Jewish faith* was, in its original form, a collection of mere statutory laws upon which was established a political organization; for whatever moral additions were then or later appended

61

to it in no way whatever belong to Judaism as such. Judaism is really not a religion at all but merely a union of a number of people who, since they belonged to a particular stock, formed themselves not into a church; nay, it was *intended* to be merely an earthly state so that, were it possible to be dismembered through adverse circumstances, there would still remain to it the political faith in its eventual reestablishment.[2]

The Holocaust: The Methodological Challenge

"In what ways has the Holocaust had an impact on the way Jewish and Christian thinkers make judgments and decisions about modern moral and political problems? What implications does the Holocaust have for the interaction between Jewish thinkers and Christian theologians as they confront contemporary moral and political problems? What are the implications of the Holocaust for the Jewish and Christian assessment of Liberalism and the ideals of liberal democracies?"[3]

These questions presuppose that one already has an understanding of the reality, causes, and the meaning of the Holocaust—issues that most agree continue to require further critical investigation. Therefore, it seems those who address the ethical significance of the Holocaust must shed our "scholarly detachment" and say what we think should be said about its relevance. In particular, it seems I should address the relevance of the Holocaust for religious ethics and the social strategy of Jews and Christians in a liberal society. And even though I feel a bit burdened by this demand, I must admit there seems something right about it. For in spite of the various issues surrounding the causes and meaning of the Holocaust, few would deny its significance for how we understand ourselves and act today. If it fails to have such significance, then the deaths that occurred there are even more meaningless and Hitler will seem to have his victory.

Yet as important as the task is, I feel completely unequal to it. I have read and thought about the Holocaust since I was a seminarian and I still feel I have almost nothing to say about it. I am still not sure how the Holocaust should be assessed from a secular or theological point of view. For me it simply continues to stand there starkly as sheer horror. The horror lies not just in the massive numbers of those murdered, but in the systematic and effective attempt of the Nazis to rob those deaths of all meaning. As Emil Fackenheim suggests, "Auschwitz was the supreme, most diabolical attempt ever made to murder martyrdom itself and, failing that, to deprive all death, martyrdom included, of its dignity."[4]

Moreover, I remain unsure how, if at all, the Holocaust was unique in Jewish or world history. I am not even sure if the question of uniqueness is the right question, though I will suggest why it seems so unavoidable for us. Nor am I even sure which theological issues are raised by Auschwitz or how to answer those that are asked. It may even be that the fundamental rethinking about Christianity in the face of the continuing existence of the Jews is misdirected when the Holocaust is made the central issue. I certainly do not know what should be said about God and his relationship to us in the light of the Holocaust. One part of me tends to favor those who counsel silence as the only appropriate theological response simply because they know of no alternative.[5]

Yet we rightly feel that we cannot or should not, especially when it involves questions of ethics and social policy, let silence be our only response. Therefore, it seems we must say something about what the implications of the Holocaust are or should be. But what? I have no answer that I can unhesitatingly put forward for anyone. Therefore I will try to suggest how the Holocaust has influenced the way I attempt to do Christian ethics as well as how the Church should be related to liberal society. For even though I have not been able to develop any position or "theory" about the Holocaust, I have always assumed that the Holocaust, and Christian complicity in the Holocaust, is a decisive test case for anyone attempting to think ethically as a Christian.

That may seem an odd claim since I have seldom directly discussed the Holocaust. But it seems odder still, since I have been one of the few persons working in contemporary religious ethics who has called for Christian ethics to be unapologetically Christian. I have emphasized those aspects of the moral life—character, narrative, the separateness of the church—that make Christian convictions about Jesus morally intelligible and significant.[6] Therefore, in contrast to those who would attempt to interpret religious ethics as but a qualification or addition to a more universal ethic I have been characterized as a "voice crying in the wilderness" because I argue that "accounts of the moral life are not conceptually or existentially separable from one's religious narrative, one's story."[7] Even more shocking, I am said to assert that "the notion of a common morality is an illusion; believers and non-believers simply have their stories through which their characters are shaped."[8]

This characterization is essentially correct, although given more space I would put the matter in a more nuanced fashion. Christian ethics for me is governed by frankly theological commitments. Thus I have not called attention to the narrative form of ethical convictions simply to make a philosophical point, but because I think Christians have a story that they rightly claim to be true. Therefore I do not pretend, in the name of nature, natural law, or some general anthropological claims, to be doing ethics for anyone, but rather I claim that Christian ethics must begin and end with the God we find revealed in the life, death, and resurrection of Jesus Christ.

But from the perspective of many, and especially those concerned with Auschwitz, this reassertion of the particularity of Christian ethics cannot but appear as a dangerous new tribalism. It may even be an indication that Christians, realizing that their theological claims cannot pass modern evidential muster, are retreating into self-protective enclaves. As a result they lack moral resources to prevent another Holocaust just as they were devoid of a universal ethic to challenge the narrow loyalties that led to the Holocaust.[9]

Therefore, it would seem that if Christians, as I am encouraging them to do, took seriously the particularity of their convictions as primary for forming their morality, they would lack the means to challenge the subtle and implicit anti-semitism that constantly threatens to reawaken in our society and the church. What then of my claim that the challenge of the Holocaust should be a decisive test case for Christian ethics? The claim still stands, for it is my conviction that Christian anti-Semitism, without which the Holocaust would not have been possible, is rooted in an account of Christian existence that ignores the particularity of our convictions.

Moreover, it is my contention that the failure to appreciate the particular nature of our convictions was fueled by a social policy and ethic that, often with the best intentions and idealism, perversely attempted to make the "ethic of Jesus" an ethos sufficient to sustain a civilization. In the process, Christians lost exactly those convictions concerning God's judgment on all nations that should have prevented them from identifying with as well as cooperating with those powers that perpetrated Auschwitz.

I first became aware of the Holocaust in the context of studying modern German theology. I approached that study assuming that those theologians who represented Protestant liberalism would have been the first to stand against the Nazis and their anti-semitic program. Much to my surprise, I discovered that it was not the liberals but Barth who had the resources to recognize and challenge the Nazis at their deadly game.[10] Just as Barth's own mind was changed in the face of his theological mentor's capitulation to earlier German war aims, so I began to understand that the relationship between theological convictions and their social expression was not as simple as I assumed. For it seemed to me that the liberal attempt to make Christianity a "reasonable" set of beliefs turned out to be an ideology for theological and social imperialism.[11] Of course, I am not accusing the liberals of being anti-semites, though some were; nor am I suggesting that Barth's own challenge to the rise of the German Christians was as sharp as it should have been, especially on the question of the persecution of the Jews. I am simply indicating that the strategy of Christian theology to accommodate the challenge of the Enlightenment, in both its intellectual and social forms, may have social implications that should be questioned.

Liberal theologians were right to force the issue of the truthfulness of Christian convictions. But too often they failed to see that the question of the truthfulness of those convictions did not lie in their "universality," but in their practical force that was dependent on their particularity.[12] And it is in this context that the Holocaust stands as a challenge to Christian convictions. For certainly one of the basic tests of the truthfulness of any significant set of convictions lies in the kind of lives in which they are embodied. If it can be shown that the Holocaust lies at the heart of Christian claims about the kind of life required to be a disciple of Jesus, it would surely provide strong evidence that Christianity is a false and perverse faith.

Only by recovering the particularity of Christian convictions and their correlative ethical implications can we gain a perspective by which the Holocaust can be seen as perversion of the Gospel and gain a better sense of how Christians should relate to the world. This does not mean to deny or excuse the centuries of Christian anti-semitism that prepared the way for countless injustices against the Jews culminating in the Holocaust. Christians have much for which to be guilty, but we cannot let our guilt guide what we must now say.[13] I am not suggesting that the particularity of our claims about Jesus must be recovered in order to prevent another Auschwitz, but rather how a renewed appreciation of the particularity of Jesus helps us to understand more truthfully Christian failure in the Holocaust. For it is my contention that the church lost the means to challenge the Nazis exactly to the extent it tried to base its "ethics" on grounds other than those made possible by the faithful life of Jesus of Naza-reth. In doing so it necessarily attributed to culture and the state a hegemony they cannot and should not have.

From a Jewish point of view, my position may entail some deep losses. For if the political significance of the Gospel lies exactly in its power of forming a people who are able to maintain a separated existence among the nations, that means we cannot promise "never again." Put more strongly, those who continue to do Christian social ethics from the perspective of forming a culture which will insure "never again" are but continuing to be caught in the same logic that resulted in Christian complicity with the Holocaust. Moreover, I think this is particularly true of those who would have us support and underwrite the ethos and procedures of liberal culture in the hopes of preventing another Auschwitz.

Jew and Christian in a Secular Society

Many will find this an odd claim, since the dominant assumption is that liberal and secular cultures—social systems that seek to free politics from religious presuppositions and involvement—are the best strategy to prevent another Auschwitz. Liberalism, in the many different forms it has assumed since the Enlightenment, stands as the uncompromising challenge to those who would seek to control any society and state by religious presuppositions.[14]

Yet the presumption of the moral advantage of liberalism for Jewish and Christian existence must be challenged. By issuing such a challenge, I do not mean to suggest that liberalism, especially in its social form, is worse than other social systems, but only to remind Christians and Jews that it involves peculiar challenges for each of us. To be sure, liberalism offers moral opportunities that should be exploited, but it also involves subtle temptations that can rob Jewish and Christian communities of their substance.

As a way to explore this contention I want to call our attention to Eliezer Berkovits' account of the implications of the Holocaust.[15] Berkovits is attractive in that he has little use for ecumenical etiquette. He deeply distrusts, and I suspect dislikes, Christianity, and thus is not impressed by the recent attempts of Christians to take a more positive attitude toward Judaism. Moreover, he also sees with great clarity that relations between Jews and Christians have entered a new period, not because of the Holocaust, but because Christianity can no longer dominate Western culture or states. The crucial question for Berkovits, therefore, is what the proper social strategy for Jews should be in a post-Christian era.

Berkovits argues that the Christian era did not begin with the birth of Jesus, but dates from the first half of the fourth century when Constantine made Christianity the state religion. "The characteristic mark of that era was militancy. This was inherent in its beginnings: Christianity did not capture the Roman Empire by the power of a religious idea but by the sword of the emperor. As soon as Christianity was established, Judaism was declared an odious heretic sect whose propagation was forbidden under the penalty of death. Even the vast missionary activities in Asia and Africa were possible only because the Western colonizing powers which opened up these new lands were Christian. The preachers of the gospel marched in the wake of the swift and terrible sword of Constantine" (p. 38).

But according to Berkovits this era has come to an end. The sword of Constantine has been passed to numerous other hands, the Soviets, the Chinese, Moslems, and many developing nations, where Christianity has no decisive role. Berkovits suggests that this is what accounts for the new Christian ecumenism and tolerance. After centuries of resisting the principle of tolerance and freedom of religion, Christians now have seized those slogans as their own simply because "Christianity is no longer supreme in the world. When the Church leaders speak of freedom of religion, they mean first of all freedom for Christians to adhere to their faith in Communist lands. Christianity is now on the side of tolerance because this is the post-Christian age of world history, because in this post-Christian era the old policies of intolerance are no longer viable" (pp. 39–40).

This change in our social situation means that for the first time since the fourth century the confrontation between Jews and Christians can take place in freedom. In such a time it is the responsibility of the Jew to confront Christianity with the meaning of the Christian—which is nothing less than the accusation of the moral and spiritual bankruptcy of Christian civilization and religion. "After nineteen centuries of Christianity, the extermination of six million Jews, among them one and a half million children, carried out in cold blood in the very heart of Christian Europe, encouraged by the criminal silence of virtually all Christendom including that of an infallible Holy Father in Rome, was the natural culmination of this bankruptcy. A straight line leads from the first act of oppression against the Jews and Judaism in the fourth century to the holocaust in the twentieth"(p. 41).

Berkovits is therefore little interested in entering a "fraternal dialogue" with Christians. Indeed, there is no reason why Jews should be interested in it. Unlike Christianity, "it is not Judaism's ambition to save mankind, because it never maintained that mankind was lost without it. Judaism is the only possible way of life for Jews. Judaism is free from missionary zeal"(p. 46). Jews, therefore, are not interested in whether Christians are now willing to acknowledge the "fragmentary truths of Judaism." Rather, all they desire from Christians is to "keep their hands off us and our children! Human beings ought to treat each other with respect and hold each other dear, independently of theological dialogues, Biblical studies, and independently of what they believe about each other's religion. I am free to reject any religion as humbug if that is what I think of it; but I am in duty bound to respect the dignity of every human being no matter what I may think of his religion. It is not interreligious understanding that mankind needs but interhuman understanding —and understanding based on our common humanity and wholly independent of any need for common religious beliefs and theological principles."

Berkovits does not deny the possibility of Jewish and Christian cooperation in some areas of endeavor. "A common front is useful and necessary in the struggle for freedom of conscience and worship, for peace and social justice; our interests are identical in these fields of human striving. In the post-Christian era, however, these goals of freedom, peace, and social justice have universal validity. It would be extremely foolish to seek their realization by means of a narrowly Jewish-Christian front"(p. 48). Indeed Berkovits suggests even in the field of ethics the Jew should be very cautious about Jewish-Christian endeavors. Because Christianity has been so compromised by its involvement in Western imperialism, it is not easy to determine what is humanitarian-ethical idea and what is Christian propaganda. As an example he offers Pope Paul VI's speech before the United Nations on behalf of world peace. Berkovits thinks it was a fine speech but one that came too late in history since in earlier periods a pope's stand on universal peace could have stopped wars. "Unfortunately, when it could have been most effective—in the Christian era—the papacy was unaware of its universal mission for peace"(p. 49). On the whole, therefore, Berkovits thinks it better for Judaism simply to go its own way.

This kind of attack tends to invite from Christians a defensive posture. And certainly Berkovits' case is weakened by a lack of nuanced historical and theological judgment.[16] In many ways Rosemary Ruether has presented a more compelling case against Christian anti-Semitism by tracing Christian persecution of the Jews to the Gospel itself. Ruether, however, confirms the main lines of Berkovits' attack. For even though she points out that Judaism remained the only legal dissenting and non-Christian faith after the fourth century, after Constantine "what had previously been the hostile tradition of an illegal sect toward its parental faith now became the official creed of the civil religion of the Christian Roman Empire.[17]

I have no interest, however, in trying to qualify or answer the Berkovits argument. For I think the main lines of his case are correct —Christians and Jews do now live in a different world where the sword of Constantine has passed to new hands. But I question whether Berkovits has rightly read the implications of this transition to the "post-Christian age" and whether his acceptance of the values of "universal validity" constitute the most appropriate framework to think about the relation of Christianity and Judaism with each other in the kind of world in which we both must now live. In particular I question whether his claim of Judaism's lack of "missionary zeal" is not due more to his adherence to those values than to an accurate reading of Judaism's task to be a "light to the nations." But even more I doubt whether Berkovits has provided an analysis of what it means to live in a "post-Christian" world that alerts us adequately to the challenge such a world presents for Judaism as well as Christianity. For Berkovits fails to understand that societies putatively founded on values of "universal validity" cannot help but interpret the particularistic commitments of the Jewish people at best as a moral curiosity, and more likely as morally retrogressive.

In this respect I think it is interesting to compare Berkovits' commitment to those values—freedom, justice, and peace—to that of liberal Christianity. From Berkovits' perspective such values and their institutionalization represent an advance because they now provide the means to keep the Christian foot off the Jewish neck. Indeed elsewhere in his book Berkovits suggests he has little sympathy with the idealism of secular societies with their illusions of our "common humanity."[18] Therefore Berkovits' adherence to and support of liberal societies is but a continuation of the classical Jewish defense strategy. Insofar as these values help Jews survive they will use them, but not place their trust in them.

But from certain Christian perspectives these values are not just strategy for survival—they are the continuation of the divine mission of the church to make the world more nearly God's kingdom.

Christian advocates of these values can and do share Berkovits' condemnation of the shameful history of Christian coercion through the state, but they have not given up the assumption that Christians have a stake in forming the ethos of societies that embody the "universal" values of the Gospel. Thus "Constantinianism" is shifted to a new key. No longer able or willing to try to control the governmental apparatus itself, Christians seek to form societies that embody their values on the assumption that those values are universal.

This presumption has dominated the strategy of Christian social ethics for the last century and could easily be documented from the writing of Christian social ethicists. It is equally true of the liberal and conservative, Catholic or Protestant, social ethic. It is reflected in the social group as well as in Reinhold Niebuhr.[19] It continues to be found in recent debates about whether America has a civil religion as well as in discussions regarding the theological meaning of secularity. Such debates are but an indication that, contrary to Berkovits' assumption, Christians are anything but ready to let go of our civilization. Thus Berkovits may well find that those values he accepts as "universally valid" continue to have peculiar Christian colorings he might not have anticipated.

Moreover, if Rosemary Ruether is right, Berkovits has failed to read correctly the implications of the transference of power from the Christian era to more secular governments. For the universal values appealed to in order to justify emancipation of the Jews exacted a price as it revivified anti-Judaism in new forms, "translating the basis for contempt from theological to nationalist and then racial grounds. Where the Middle Ages was intolerant of the religious alien, the modern state was intolerant of the person of alien national identity. It had no place for Jewish self-government, such as was possible in the medieval corporate state. The Jew in the modern state became the representative of the 'outsider' to nationalist identity. But the same stereotypes, the same set of psychological attitudes were preserved in this change of theoretical grounds. Philosophical liberalism provided the theoretical basis for emancipation, but at the same time suggested the basis for this transition from religious to nationalist anti-Semitism. Protestant theology and biblical studies absorbed and deepened this cultural anti-Semitism."[20]

Of course, it may be objected that this "nationalistic anti-Semitism" was a perversion of the liberal values that provided for emancipation. The test case should not be Europe, and in particular Germany, with its centuries of religious anti-Semitism, but America. It is here, in America, that the Jew has benefited from the liberal faith in the common brotherhood of man. It is in America that Judaism rightly supports the development of a secular society not only as the means of the survival of Judaism but also as a more nearly just society for all people.

None of us is in a position to assess whether such a claim is true or not.[21] Indeed, I think the fairest thing to say is that the evidence is still out. For in effect the Jew in America has until recently been affected by the disadvantages and advantages of diverse forms of an anti-Semitism which is still far from absent. Rather than trying to judge the success of the American experiment for Judaism (which is surely a task best left to the Jews), I simply want to call attention to the problem such a society as America presents for a proper assessment of the Holocaust.

I think it fair to say that for American Jewry the Holocaust has become nothing less than an obsession in the past ten years. There has been much of value that has resulted from this heightened awareness, but at the same time religiously much remains ambiguous. For many secular Jews in America the Holocaust has become the means to reassert Jewish identity—an identity often downplayed in the interest of being just another good American.[22] But when the Holocaust becomes the basis for being Jewish, then the very reason why the Holocaust is such a serious challenge for Jews and Christians is lost.

As Michael Wyschogrod has pointed out, "it is necessary to admit that we are fixated on the Holocaust to an extent quite unacceptable in a universalistic framework. The moral force of those who cannot share this fixation must be recognized. It is, I believe, necessary to abandon the attempt to find 'objective' criteria in accordance with which such a fixation on the Holocaust will be made plausible, simply because any and all such criteria bestow uniqueness on the

Holocaust at the expense of diminishing the other occasions of human suffering. To argue that one is asserting only the uniqueness of the Holocaust and not that it is a greater or more tragic crime than all others, simply won't do because the uniqueness which is asserted ('groundless, infinite hate indiscriminately directed against adults and children, saints and sinners, and so relentlessly expressed in action') turns out to be morally decisive and not just an attribution of abstract uniqueness. It is necessary to recognize that, from any universally humanistic framework, the destruction of European Jewry is one notable chapter in the long record of man's inhumanity against man, a record which compels the Holocaust to resign itself to being, at most, a first among equals."[23]

Wyschogrod goes on, however, to argue that he and Fackenheim are right to have a fixation on the Holocaust, but such a fixation is only justified theologically. The uniqueness of the Holocaust lies in the claim of Israel to being God's chosen people. "The fate of Israel is of central concern because Israel is the elect people of God through whom God's redemptive work is done in the world. However tragic human suffering is on the human plane, what happens to Israel is directly tied to its role as that nation to which God attaches His name and through which He will redeem man. He who strikes Israel, therefore, engages himself in battle with God and it is for this reason that the history of Israel is the fulcrum of human history. The suffering of others must, therefore, be seen in the light of Israel's suffering. The travail of man is not abandoned, precisely because Israel suffers and, thereby, God's presence is drawn into human history and redemption enters the horizon of human existence."[24]

Wyschogrod admits this must appear as a scandal in the eyes of the non-believer. For how can the non-believer be expected to concede that the fate of Israel is more central than the fate of any other people? Wyschogrod thinks the Jew cannot and must not expect this, and therefore the Jew must neither be surprised nor outraged when the Holocaust, as it inevitably will, fades from general consciousness. But Jews must remember the Holocaust because only a believing "community can transcend time, can fixate on events of very limited 'historic' significance (how 'significant' was the Exodus to the ancient world whose records never mention it?) and find in them the significance of a redemption history apparent only to the eyes of faith. For believing Israel, the Holocaust is not just another mass murder but, perhaps, the final circumcision of the people of God. But how else, except by the power of God, can anyone believe that?"[25]

A people who are determined to remember in this way will never rest easy in a culture which pretentiously believes that it represents universal values. Such a people are especially offensive when those values are thought to represent mankind's control of our own lives.[26] For the faith that God, not man, rules and determines the value of our lives is antithetical to the very presumption of modernity. Berkovits is surely right to underwrite those values that freed the Jew from feeling the direct power of Christian anti-Semitism at the hands of the power of the state, but it is not clear that those values do not result in a more subtle but no less destructive form of anti-Semitism. It is more subtle because now the Jew is tempted to remember the Holocaust for the wrong reasons.

It is not my place to try to work out the social strategy for the Jew vis-a-vis liberalism. Rather, my concern must be with what the implications of this may be for how Christian ethics is conceived and executed. Earlier I suggested that the reality of the Holocaust made me more convinced that Christian ethics must begin not with the assumption that our liberal society is grounded on universal values, but on the basis of the particular convictions of the Church. I think I can now explain more clearly why I think this, and what implications this has for Christian social ethics done in a liberal social order.

A Community of Remembrance: The Social Implications

Like the Jews, Christians are called to be a community and a people capable of remembering: indeed this is their first social task. The social significance of being such a community is often ignored today since "social ethics" is primarily identified with issues set by our wider social order. But the "social ethics" of the church is not first of all what the church can or should do to make the societies in which it exists more just. The church does not *have* a social ethic in that sense, but rather the church *is* a social ethic as it serves this or any society by first being the kind of community capable of nourishing its life by the memory of God's presence in Jesus Christ.[27]

But if that is the case, the great social challenge for Christians is learning how to remember the history of the Jews, as part of and as essential to our history.[28] Such remembering cannot be based on feeling guilty about the Holocaust, since guilt soon fades or becomes a substitute for honest appraisal. Rather we must learn to remember with the Jews a history which certainly includes the Holocaust because we are learning that the Jews are our partners in discerning God's way in the world.[29] To learn to remember in this manner is a radical political act in that it must of necessity change our understanding of the Christian community and its relationship to our world.[30]

As Rosemary Ruether points out, "Learning history is never really an act of 'detached' scholarship, as academicians like to think. Learning history is, first of all, a rite of collective identity. Christians learn who they are by learning the story of Jesus, and through Jesus, carrying down a history created by the Christian Church and society. The history of the Jews disappears at the time of Jesus. This testifies to the Christian claim that it is the true Israel which alone carries on the biblical legacy. This Christian way of learning history negates ongoing Jewish existence. If we learned not only New Testament, but rabbinic Midrash; if we viewed the period of the Second Temple, not merely through the eyes of early Christianity, but through the eyes of the disciples of Rabban Yohanan ben Zakkai; if we read Talmud side by side with the Church Fathers; if we read the Jewish experience of Christendom side by side with Christian self-interpretation, this Christian view of history would fall into jeopardy. For this reason, Jewish history 'after Christ' is not merely unknown but repressed. Its repression is essential for the maintenance of Christian identity. For Christians to incorporate the Jewish tradition after Jesus into their theological and historical education would involve ultimately the dismantling of the Christian concept of history and the demythologizing of the myth of the Christian era."[31]

And it would, I am suggesting, mean a radical change in the political form of the church. For to be a people of remembering is nothing less than a prophetic call for the church to respond to the

God who has called them to be a new people amid the nations. It would mean that the church would have to give up the security of having its ethos enforced or at least reinforced by wider social structures, trusting rather in the power of the Holy Spirit to be its sustainer and guide.

Some may think this would require Christians to qualify our commitment to Jesus as the source of our life and the object of our worship. I think that is not the case. Certainly it would require a challenge to some christological formulations, but christology after all is not the object of our faith. [32] God is the object of our faith, and as Christians we must affirm that it is in the presence of this Jesus that we have been most decisively drawn into fellowship with God.[33] Nor can we qualify our obligation to witness to others the joy of the fellowship and our wish for them to share it. However, the obligation to witness does not mean that we are in possession of a universal truth that can compel assent or serve as the basis for an ethic of wider society.

Christianity may be a "universalistic" religion in a way that Judaism is not, though I doubt it.[34] However, what is certainly the case is that the nature of our universalism has been deeply misunderstood and subject to ideological perversion. Again, as Ruether points out, "Catholic Christianity regarded itself as the universal messianic fulfillment of the election of the Jews. Some of the verisimilitude for this perspective on the Church, as the fulfilled messianic in-gathering of the nations of Zion, rested on its later fusion with the ecumenical empire. After Christianity became the established religion of this empire, Christian theologians came to imagine that the religion of the biblical God had literally captured all peoples and all lands. Christianity took the universalism of the messianic hope and fused it with the ideological universalism of the ecumenical empire. The result was a doctrine of the Church as the one Catholic faith for all people which could no longer tolerate the concessions to particularism possible for a polytheistic empire. One God, one faith, and one Church, founded on this revelation, the cultural and political vehicle for which became the Roman Empire."[35]

What often goes unnoticed about such "universalism" is that it not only results in cultural and social imperialism, but it also distorts the nature of faith itself. For too often in order to sustain the presumed universality of our convictions, the convictions are transformed into general truths about "being human" for which "Christ" becomes a handy symbol.[36] Our universalism is not based on assumed commonalities about mankind; rather it is based on the belief that the God who has made us his own through Jesus Christ is the God of all people. Christian universality is too often based on a high view of the human, rather than a high view of Jesus.[37]

When the universality of humanity is substituted for our faith in the God of Abraham, Isaac, and Jacob, the eschatalogical dimension of our faith is lost.[38] Christian social ethics then becomes the attempt to do ethics for all people rather than being first of all an ethic for God's eschatological people who must learn to wait between the times. Our conviction that the God whom we worship is in fact the God of all creation does not give us the warrant to assume that others *must* already share our faith and/or moral presumption, but only to hope that if we manifest in our own social life some of the marks of what it means to be a new people, others will be converted to the reality of his kingdom. Otherwise, what does it mean for the church to be an eschatological community whose primary task is not to make the world the kingdom, but rather to witness to the power of God to transform our lives more nearly appropriate to service in that kingdom?[39] To be sure, as Christians we do believe that the unity of all peoples has been established in principle, but this unity is not an accomplished fact nor can it be presumed to be the basis of a universal ethic. Rather it can only be manifested in the kind of community made possible by a people who have learned to remember and thus tell rightly the story of God's choosing and caring for his people—both Jews and Christians.

Rosemary Ruether has suggested that the end of Christendom means Christianity now must think of itself as a Diaspora religion.[40] I am trying to suggest that Christianity, whether it is forced to or not by the end of Christendom, must always be a Diaspora religion. But we have hardly begun to think through the social implications of that claim. Certainly the mainstream of Christian social ethics continues to be written as if Christians share the primary values of their culture and/or that Christians should seek to be the primary political and social actors in that culture.

As long as that strategy is simply assumed I think there is little chance that Christians can make the Holocaust part of their own existence, integral to their own identity. And as a result I further suspect, under the spell of liberal assumptions, we lack the means to recognize the significance that indeed the sword of Constantine has passed to many other hands. For we will continue the illusion that Christians, unlike the Jews, are not simply a people who must find the means to survive among the nations. We will thus continue to lack the means to help the world see how deeply divided it is and why in fact it needs redemption.

From the world's perspective, being a community capable of remembering the Holocaust cannot appear politically significant. But from the perspective of the Gospel, there can be no more potent political task.

Notes

1. Rosemary Ruether. *Faith and Fratricide: The Theological Roots of Anti-Semitism* (New York: Seabury Press, 1979), 220.
2. Immanuel Kant, *Religion Within the Limits of Reason Alone*, Tr. by Theodore Green and Hoyt Hudson (New York: Harper and Brothers, 1960), 116.
3. These are the questions I was asked to address at the International Scholars Conference, "Thinking About the Holocaust," at Indiana University, November 3–5, 1980. Previous sessions had dealt with historical and theological issues. Because my interests are primarily constructive I have dealt very little with the first question. However it ought to be noted that the Holocaust has not commanded the attention of most Christian ethicists or affected the way they work.
4. Emil Fackenheim, *God's Presence in History: Jewish Affirmations and Philosophical Reflections* (New York: Harper and Row, 1970), 74.
5. For an excellent account of various theological options for interpreting the Holocaust see Pinchas Peli, "In Search of Religious Language for the Holocaust," *Conservative Judaism*, 32, 2 (Winter, 1979), 3–24. Peli ends by suggesting that silence is required as a response, but it must be the silence that is "part of conversation, silence that incorporates a relationship to a 'thou' ('for Thee')—but not silence that ends all communication and removes all possibility of discovering meaning." For what I take to be a similar point see Alvin Rosenfeld's insightful analysis of Wiesel's use of silence, "The Problematics of Holocaust Literature," in *Confronting the Holocaust: The Impact of Elie Wiesel* (Bloomington: Indiana University Press, 1978), 1–30. Rosenfeld rightly suggests that it is no accident that Wiesel has increasingly turned toward Midrashic literature as a model of how silence can be made to speak without being domesticated by conventionalities.
6. See, for example, my *Vision and Virtue* (Chicago: Fides Claretian, 1974) and *Truthfulness and Tragedy* (Notre Dame: University of Notre Dame Press, 1977). Perhaps more relevant is my *A Community of Character: Toward a Constructive Christian Social Ethic* (Notre Dame: University of Notre Dame Press, 1981). One of the dangers of ethicists', and in particular Christian ethicists', discussion of the Holocaust is the temptation to have it confirm views they have arrived at on other grounds. I hope I am not guilty of this, though it is true that the Holocaust is a more decisive challenge for those, like me, who are

intent to do Christian ethics rather than simply some form of "religious ethics."

7. John P. Reeder, "Recovering the Connections," paper given at American Academy of Religion, 1979.

8. Ibid.

9. In this respect it is interesting to note Richard Rubenstein's comment that he was able to encounter the Christian world "without anger or resentment," because "we could only be angry or resentful if we expected some standard of conduct from the Christian world which it failed to observe. But, if Auschwitz has taught us anything, it is that in times of stress rights and dignity are operative only within one's primary or kinship group, if indeed they are operative at all." Quoted by Robert E. Willis in his "Christian Theology after Auschwitz," *Journal of Ecumenical Studies*, 12, 4 (Fall, 1975), 494. Rubenstein's own fuller view is worked out in his *After Auschwitz: Radical Theology and Contemporary Judaism* (Indianapolis: Bobbs-Merrill Co., 1966). Rubenstein's point is a bit different than mine but he seems to assume that the only check against tribalism is some form of universalistic ethic and community standard. That is exactly what I am suggesting we do not have, but that does not mean that the kind of behavior he notes is any less morally reprehensible. It was reprehensible for Christians, not because they violated "rights and dignity" but because they betrayed the very God they claim to worship.

10. For an account of Barth's role, see Arthur Cochrane, *The Church's Confession Under Hitler* (Philadelphia: Westminster Press, 1962). I am aware that there were, of course, many kinds of "liberalism" that resulted in diverse forms of political expression. It is certainly, therefore, not my intention to "blame" the Holocaust on "theological liberalism," but I am suggesting that liberalism in its many modes lacked the resources that might have rightly acted as a check against the nationalism that underwrote Auschwitz.

11. As Ruether points out, "even the liberalism with which Jews allied themselves in their struggle for emancipation harbored fundamental ambivalences toward Jews. The price of emancipation was also seen as one of cultural assimilation. Most liberals actually thought of this as paving the way for Jewish conversion to Christianity. All liberals took it for granted that ghetto Judaism represented a bad moral, spiritual, and intellectual condition. The price of emancipation was the destruction of Jewish self-government and autonomous corporate identity, possible in the medieval corporate state, which had allowed the Jews to

keep a sense of peoplehood within Christian society. It was this sense of autonomous corporate identity and peoplehood which the modern nationalist state could not tolerate and which became the basis of modern anti-Semitism. Now Jewish identity in an ethnic sense was seen as intrinsically evil. It must be dissolved as the Jew could become a 'German' or else it was seen as indissolvable, and so the Jew must be expelled. In any case, the Jew must pay for emancipation by ceasing to be a Jew in a corporate sense." *Faith and Fratricide*, 217–18. This process appears more benign in America as here the Enlightenment was qualified for a period by the Puritan and Republican political traditions. However it has become increasingly the case that America has become the best example of Enlightenment political thought and as a result Judaism has been interpreted, by Jew and non-Jew alike, to be a matter of "personal conviction." Ironically, in spite of claims about the pragmatic nature of American society and government, no society and state has ever been more the product of a theory than America.

12. Indeed, even to have the question of truthfulness posed as an alternative between particularistic claims already presupposes an Enlightenment understanding of conditions necessary for truth. From the Enlightenment's perspective the idea that a particular community could make (and even represent) universalistic claims simply appears anomalous. To force a choice between being "universalistic" or "particularistic" creates a false alternative for Jews (and Christians), whose particular sense of their own history is the basis for their claim to worship the God of all people.

13. See, for example, my "The Holocaust and the Duty to Forgive," *Sh'ma*, 10/198 (October 3, 1980), 137–39; and my "Forgiveness & Forgetting," *Sh'ma*, 11/202 (November 28, 1980), 15–16. Interestingly enough, forgiveness turns out to be essential for historical objectivity, since only by forgiveness can we avoid denying our past wrongs or perpetrating an ideology that only continues to underwrite our assumed righteousness.

14. The relationship between liberalism (both political and theological) and the Enlightenment is obviously complex and needs a more careful rendering than I provide here. Moreover, English liberalism is in many ways quite different than that of Germany and France, and liberalism in America is quite different from each. However, by liberalism I simply mean those societies that take as their primary aim the freeing of the individual from arbitrary "accidents" of birth and community. I

assume that such an ideal was given birth in the Enlightenment's concern with the autonomy of the individual as the necessary condition (or ideal?) for moral action.

15. Eliezer Berkovits, *Faith after the Holocaust* (New York: KTAV Publishing House, 1973). All references to Berkovits are in the text.

16. For example, Robert Wilken has argued persuasively that the spread and influence of Christianity was great prior to Constantine. See his *John Chrysostom and the Jews* (Berkeley: University of California Press, 1983). Yet even if that is the case Berkovits is no doubt right to suggest that state acceptance of Christianity helped secure its position to the detriment of the Jews. For, as Wilken also documents, Judaism was seen by many non-Christians as a viable alternative if not decisive challenge to Christianity. For if Jesus was a Jewish messiah, then why did the Jews continue to reject him?

17. Ruether, *Faith and Fratricide*, 184–5.

18. But Berkovits believes that Judaism does underwrite the ideal of "common humanity." For "mankind is not a group; it is not a historical entity. Mankind is an idea, an ideal. The comprehensive group to be created to suit the comprehensive deed as a historical reality is a people in sovereign control of the major areas of its life. The faith of Judaism requires such a comprehensive deed. Realization through and within the all-comprehensive collective, mankind, is the ideal; the instrument of its realization in history is the people. Since our concern is with the comprehensive need of Judaism, the people of Israel, of necessity, the covenant had to create the people with which the covenant was concluded" (149).

19. Of course Niebuhr never talked about "Christianizing the Social Order" in as direct a way as the social gospel, but he continued the assumption that the primary subject of Christian social analysis is wider society. Thus in the *Nature and Destiny of Man*, II (New York: Scribner's Sons, 1941) he simply assumed the task of Christian ethics was in "reorienting the culture of our day" (205). Niebuhr's realism obviously placed a check on how much such a "reorienting" could accomplish, but in spite of his devastating critique of liberalism he continued to assume liberal values as primary for guiding and forming social policy.

   One of the ironies (to continue a Niebuhrian theme) of the current situation is the use of the Holocaust by Christians as the reason why they should continue to try to pursue some form of Constantinian social ethic.

20. Ruether, *Faith and Fratricide*, 215. For documentation of Ruether's last point see Charlotte Klein, *Anti-Judaism in Christian Theology*, Tr. by Edward Quinn (Philadelphia: Fortress Press, 1978).

21. I suspect that in many ways America does present both a different kind of opportunity and challenge for Judaism than Europe. For example, Lucy Dawidowicz suggests that "The 'Christian' state had once been meant to serve 'Christian' purposes, that is, the expansion of Christianity. The Volkist state appropriated that purpose. The Jew, by definition an outsider in the 'Christian' state, remained an outsider in the Volkist conception of the state." *The War Against the Jews, 1933-1945* (New York: Bantam Books, 1979), 36. America's lack of "history" and the necessity to deal with pluralism seems to avoid some of the most explicit forms of anti-semitism that still plague Europe. However, I think it would be extremely unwise to underestimate the depth of anti-semitism that is often embodied in American commitments to "tolerance." Too often tolerance becomes a formula for condemning anyone who demands that their differences be taken morally and politically seriously. Moreover, the justification of American "secularism" as a non-ideological solution to the problem of religious pluralism and totalitarianism has beguiled too many Christians to overlook the fact that we live not in a "Christian society" but in the time of a new paganism—a paganism made all the more destructive and potent because it uses the symbols of Christian civilization.

22. See for example Eugene Borowitz's criticism of this tendency in his "Liberal Jews in Search of an 'Absolute'," *Cross Currents* 29 (Spring, 1979), 9–14. An article in the *New York Times Magazine* documents how many are concerned that the popularization of the Holocaust may lead to trivialization. Paula E. Hyman, "New Debate on the Holocaust," *New York Times Magazine* (September 14, 1980), pp. 65–67, 78–82, 86, 109.

23. Michael Wyschogrod, "Faith and the Holocaust," *Judaism*, 29, 3 (Summer, 1971), 299.

24. Wyschogrod, p. 293. I do not mean to suggest that Wyschogrod and Fackenheim are thus in agreement on the Holocaust. Indeed, Wyschogrod's position stands as a challenge to Fackenheim's view that the Holocaust must be the starting point for Jewish theological reflection. While it is perhaps wrong for a Christian theologian to take sides on this issue, it should be clear that my sympathies are with Wyschogrod. From this perspective Richard Rubenstein's position seems to me to involve a deep pathos. For he argues that Auschwitz means nothing

less than for the Jew to reject the "myth" of their special destiny, yet he provides little or no alternative other than vague appeals to the necessity of "true dialogue." *After Auschwitz,* 74–75. Yet at the same time Rubenstein has no faith in the attempt to build a completely secular society, for such a society lacks a sense of the tragic (79). Thus we seem left with two people ready to talk but who have nothing to say to one another since they have been denied any appeal to any sense of their own history.

25. Wyschogrod, 293. It would be interesting to contrast Wyschogrod's sense of the Holocaust to that of the Eckardts in terms of the theological presumptions of both. I suspect that Eckardt's claims of "transcending uniqueness" betrays a commitment to liberal Protestant theology for which Wyschogrod would have little sympathy. See, for example, Alice Eckardt and A. Roy Eckardt, "The Holocaust and the Enigma of Uniqueness: A Philosophical Effort at Practical Clarification," *The Annals,* 450 (July, 1980), 165–178.

26. One of the curious aspects about the current enthusiasm among Christian ethicists for more universalistic and humanistic accounts of the moral life is how quickly Reinhold Niebuhr's critique of those modes of thought has been forgotten. For it was Niebuhr's contention that "rationalism" always failed to "subject human righteousness to a transcendent righteousness, the righteousness of God. Thus it tempts men to 'go about establishing their own righteousness' and finally degenerates into a fanaticism more grievous than that of dogmatic religion. The logic of the decay of modern culture from universalistic humanism to nationalistic anarchy may be expressed as follows: Men seek a universal standard of human good. After painful effort they define it. The painfulness of their effort convinces them that they have discovered a genuinely universal value. To their sorrow, some of their fellow men refuse to accept the standard. Since they know the standard to be universal the recalcitrance of their fellows is a proof, in their minds, of some defect in humanity of the non-conformists. Thus a rationalistic age creates a new fanaticism. The non-conformists are figuratively expelled from the human community." *Beyond Tragedy* (New York: Scribners, 1965), 237. Interestingly enough, Niebuhr understood the implication of this for the question of the Jews. To his credit, as early as 1942, he was defending Zionism. In doing so he did not deny the right of the Jews to be assimilated if they desire, but he saw that there is an aspect of the Jewish problem not solved by this strategy. "That is the simple right of the Jews to survive as a people. There are both Jews and

Gentiles who deny that the Jews have such a survival impulse as an ethnic group, but the evidence of contemporary history refutes them, as does the evidence of all history in regard to the collective impulses of survival in life generally. Modern liberalism has been blind to this aspect of human existence because its individualistic and universalistic presuppositions and illusions have prevented it from seeing some rather obvious facts in man's collective life. The Jews have survived in spite of the fact that they have been a nationality scattered among the nations, without a homeland of their own, since the dawn of Western European history. They are a people of the Diaspora." *Love and Justice,* edited by D. B. Robinson (New York: Meridian Books, 1967), 135–6.

27. For a fuller elaboration of these themes see my *A Community of Character.*

28. The remembering of such a history depends on a story as much as it does historical "fact," though of course the story cannot be without fact. For an account of the complex interrelation of "story" and "history" see Julian Hart's chapter "Story as the Art of Historical Truth," in his *Theological Method and the Imagination* (New York: Seabury, 1977), 219–54.

29. Paul Van Buren is surely on the right path in this respect as he has formed his recent attempt at "systematic theology" around the metaphor of being on a journey—that Jews and Christians must necessarily walk together. See his *Discerning the Way* (New York: Seabury, 1980).

30. See, for example, Robert E. Willis, "Auschwitz and the Nurturing of Conscience," *Religion in Life* (Winter, 1975), 432–48.

31. Ruether, *Faith and Fratricide,* 257.

32. See, for example, Van Buren's extremely interesting suggestions about how such a Christology might be done in his *Discerning the Way,* 78–86. However I do not want my remarks to imply I think it is possible for there to be an easy resolution to the differences between the Jewish and Christian communities. The differences remain no matter how much we may wish the pain they cause to go away. We must each continue to say what we think we have found to be true as otherwise we will be unfaithful not only to ourselves but to the other.

33. In his unfortunately ignored book, *Jesus and the Nonviolent Revolution* (Scottdale, Pennsylvania: Herald Press, 1973) André Trocmé contends, "If the New Testament should be demythologized, it should not be done with the help of our modern myths but with the assistance of the Old Testament. The more the strict monotheistic faith in the God of Israel is exalted, the more visible becomes the thought of Jesus

Christ. Let us never forget that the God of Jesus Christ was the God of Israel. The Christian faith dissolves into mythology as soon as it no longer leans upon Judaism. Nothing can be lost by rejudaizing Christianity. Judaism is the point of departure for all research destined to rediscover the Jesus of history. We need not hesitate to examine those ideas which the authors of the New Testament borrowed from sources other than the Old Testament in order to explain Jesus to their Jewish and Greek contemporaries. But let us not sacrifice the Old Testament" (2). Fortunately, Trocmé's views have found expression in John Howard Yoder's widely read *The Politics of Jesus* (Grand Rapids: Eerdmans, 1972).

34. Fackenheim maintains, for example, "Jewish Messianism always requires the particularity of Jewish existence. Its God is universal; but, because His presence is in history and does not (or not yet) transfigure history, it can only be a particularized presence, and for this if for no other reason, it is a fragmentary presence. The saving divine Presence at the Red Sea had revealed its fragmentariness, if only because the Egyptians were drowning; the divine commanding Presence at Mount Sinai had been fragmentary, if only because it could be rejected as well as accepted; the law has not yet put in the inward parts (Jer. 31:33). For the Jew to experience or reenact such a fragmentary divine presence is, on the one hand, to be singled out by it and, on the other, to be made to hope for wholeness; that is, to be made witness to the Messianic future and to remain stubbornly at this post until all has been accomplished. This Jewish particularity, however, has been a scandal, first, to ancient pagans (who denied that history stood in need of redemption) and, subsequently, to Christians (to the degree to which they hold that the redemption affirmed by the Jewish testimony has already arrived)" *God's Presence in History,* 52–53. Like the Jew, however, Christian universalistic claims must always be eschatalogical.

Interestingly, Jews and Christians are communities of memory exactly because their existence is necessarily historical. If they were founded as a "truth" that could be known without remembering then they would be no more than philosophical alternatives. That they are fundamentally communities of memory, that is they depend on scripture, ritual, and holy people, denotes that the character of their understanding of the truth is particular and historical.

35. Ruether, 233–4.

36. "Logos Christologies" in particular tend to reduce all theology to anthropology. Though such christologies at first appear more tolerant and open to other religions than those that emphasize the particularity of Jesus' person and work, in fact they are in principle more imperialistic. For example, Michael McGarry suggests "Confronted by the fact of pluralism some form of logos-Christology may prove most fruitful as a way for Christians to recognize the validity of other religions (and, a fortiori, of Judaism). Karl Rahner employs logos-Christology as a way of working out a Christology in the fact of the plurality of religions, and the success of this effort with regard to leaving theological room for Judaism has been noted by Eugene Borowitz. It can at least be said that logos-Christology, properly understood, does not see Judaism as only preparatory to Christology, as destined to disappear from the earth. Rather it sees Judaism as one of God's ways of speaking to his world through his continued election of the Jewish people in terms which Christians can understand. Logos-Christology does not dictate a Christian understanding to the Jews." *Christology After Auschwitz* (New York: Paulist Press, 1977), 101-102. McGarry's emphasis that this is only the way that Christians should understand the matter cannot avoid the uncomfortable fact that the assumption remains that Christianity provides a perspective from which the other religion's "validity" is to be evaluated. Only now that perspective is not the humble man on the cross, but the assumption that Christians, unlike other folk, understand the "logos" of God's creation more completely than others. More troubling to my mind, however, is the assumption that Christology should be done primarily with the issue of religious pluralism in mind. Christology is first of all reflection about what kind of truth about God Christians find or should find in Jesus Christ. Christology is not apologetics, but rather a task seeking understanding and truth.

37. Philip Hallie provides an interesting example of this in his *Lest Innocent Blood Be Shed: The Story of the Village of Le Chambon and How Goodness Happened There* (New York: Harper and Row, 1979). In this highly praised book, Hallie tells the story of André Trocmé, the pastor of the village of Le Chambon in France, who led his people to provide shelter for Jewish children during the war. Hallie tells well how they did this and indicates that the Huguenot background of the village no doubt helped prepare the people to assume a position of resistance. But what Hallie is completely unable to do is explain

Trocmé's own commitments that led him to take such a courageous stand. Hallie suggests several times that Trocmé's commitment was based in his belief about Jesus (34, 161), but he is never able to tell us what in fact those beliefs were. Instead he constantly reiterates throughout the book that Trocmé's action was based on his belief in the preciousness of all human life (42, 48, 53, 54, 274). That Trocmé believed in the preciousness of all human life is certainly true and that such a conviction was related to his belief in Jesus was also true. For example, see his *Jesus and the Nonviolent Revolution*, 145–6. But what is not true is that Trocmé's belief in nonviolence was grounded in a general humanistic concern about each individual's life. Rather his nonviolence was based on his deep belief that Jesus had inaugurated a social revolution based on the jubilee year that necessarily entailed the church to be a counter culture to all social orders with their humanistic pretensions. As Trocmé says, "Christian nonviolence is not a part of the fabric of the universe, as in Hindi nonviolence. Rather, it has a temporary character. It is tied to the delay God grants men because of the voluntary sacrifice of the messianic King. By deriving nonviolence not from a philosophy of the universe (which may be utopian) but from His sacrifice on the cross, Jesus gives it historical precision and a much greater impact. Through redemption, nonviolence thrusts itself upon all Jesus' disciples. It becomes an article of faith, a mark of obedience, a sign of the kingdom to come as it was for Jesus Himself." *Jesus and the Nonviolent Revolution,* 66. That Hallie was only able to explain this kind of conviction in the pieties of general humanistic rhetoric is understandable, but such an account misses entirely the force of Trocmé's position. I should note in passing that the kind of social ethic I am attempting to develop is closer to Trocmé's views than that of mainstream Christianity.

38. For a defense of the necessity of Christianity to "spiritualize" eschatology see John Pawlikowski's "The Historizing of the Eschatological: The Spiritualizing of the Eschatological: Some Reflections," in *Antisemitism and the Foundations of Christianity,* edited by Alan Davies (New York: Paulist Press, 1979), 151–66. Pawlikowski writes in criticism of Ruether's "historizing of the eschatological" and defends the view that Jesus' primary importance is that in him people came to see clearly for the first time that humanity is an integral part of God. This means that each person is divine, that he or she somehow shares in the constitutive nature of God. As we learn from the latter strata of the New Testament materials, this humanity has existed in

the Godhead from the beginning. So in a very real sense God did not explain why, if this is the case, it is only in Jesus that it was first seen. In this respect I think Ruether is exactly right to suggest that Pawlikowski is not "spiritualizing eschatology," but "spiritualizing the messianic." Moreover she is correct to argue that such a spiritualization is basically a denial of the messianic as it robs the category of messianism of the Jewish hope in a historical fulfillment. She does not deny that one may well "solve" the problem of Christ that way, "but do not call it christology; just call it by its right name, Platonic soteriology." Rosemary Ruether, "The *Faith and Fratricide* Discussion: Old Problems and New Dimensions," in *Antisemitism and the Foundation of Christianity,* 224–45.

In substantiation of Ruether's point, Pawlikowski goes on to suggest that in one sense the final version of the Church's christology is the culmination of the Jewish tradition not in terms of "the fulfillment of the messianic prophecies, but the fulfillment of the growing sense of the dignity and uniqueness of the human person" (162). Judaism retains a "unique and distinctive role" in the sense it has maintained a sense of peoplehood and the belief that no individual person can achieve salvation without the whole human family having attained salvation." But that surely is a "truth" separable from the "existence" of the Jews and hardly makes intelligible the persistence and suffering the Jews have experienced over the centuries. Moreover, Pawlikowski thinks Christians' contact with Judaism is necessary if the Church is to correct its longstanding tendency to overcome a false "privatization of religion," but that is exactly the social implication written into his christology. Even more troubling is his suggestion that his christology recaptures the sense of the "human person as Co-creator, as responsible for history and for the world God has created" (163). It is hard for me to understand how anyone can use such language in the light of the Holocaust. If any event has taught us that we are not co-creators, it is that. What we require is not a god that underwrites our pretensions, but one who is capable of calling us from our false notions of power and control.

39. The criticisms above of Pawlikowski may appear too harsh especially in the light of his work on the relation of Jews and Christians. His intention has been to "liberalize" Roman Catholic attitudes by emphasizing those "universalizing" tendencies in Catholicism. Thus, for example, he points out that Pius XII was primarily concerned to keep the Church alive, no matter what the cost in non-Catholic lives,

because he thought the Church was the institution through which "the principal components for human salvation—the Eucharist and the other sacraments—were made available to the Human community." "Method in Catholic Social Ethics: Some Observations in Light of the Jewish Tradition," in *Formation of Social Policy in the Catholic and Jewish Tradition,* edited by Eugene Fisher and Daniel Polish (Notre Dame: University of Notre Dame Press, 1980), 172–73. Pawlikowski points out that this ecclesiology was not intentionally indifferent or hostile to the rights and very existence of non-Catholics. "Rather it so envisioned the Church and its purpose for existence that in moments of crises, when hard decisions were required concerning the institution's survival, non-Catholics occupied no central role in the definition" (173). I have no doubt that Pawlikowski sees his emphasis on a more universalistic Christology as a corrective for this, but as a result he fails to challenge the most decisive failure of Catholic ecclesiology—the idea that the primary task of the Church is to survive. The task of the church is not to survive, but to be failthful to its eschatological mission. The "success" of that mission is not measured by whether the Church survives or not, but whether her survival or non-survival serves the ends of that kingdom. Any time Christians presume that the "success" of God's kingdom depends on the "success" of the Church they have already betrayed our belief in God's lordship of history.

40. Ruether, *Faith and Fratricide,* 226–7.

5. ON TAKING RELIGION SERIOUSLY: THE CHALLENGE OF JONESTOWN

The Moral and Religious Challenge

When confronted by such horrors as happened in Jonestown we naturally seek to provide explanations that leave our everyday world intact. For Jonestown is a challenge to some of our most cherished assumptions. We like to think that we live in a modern age where people are beyond this kind of behavior. Therefore the fact that more than nine hundred relatively normal people could commit mass suicide simply lies quite beyond our comprehension. It seems to raise questions like "How could the most advanced society the world has ever produced develop a political system that resulted in the murder of six million Jews and others?"

We assume that being modern involves at least agreement that no one ought to take religion too seriously, especially if it is going to ask any real sacrifices from us. Thus advocates of religion, from the more sophisticated to the craziest, tend to hawk their wares by promising that religion will provide us with meaning or at least reinforce our profoundest desires about what a fulfilling life should be. Any idea that religious convictions might challenge our deepest beliefs about ourselves or ask us to make extraordinary sacrifices is simply unthinkable.

Therefore we can look at the pathetic deaths at Jonestown only as some kind of pathological mistake. How did these people miss the important lesson that the lowest possible priority for anyone should be willingness to die in the name of a religious cause? What must be remembered is that religion is a dangerous thing and that being dangerous it must be properly domesticated before being given any allegiance. Religion, like certain kinds of drugs, should be taken only in moderate amounts and under carefully controlled conditions.

We thus think ourselves protected from terrible events such as Jonestown by our assumption that religious convictions do not really involve matters of truth or falsity. Rather, religious beliefs are matters best left to the conscience of each person since religious convictions are largely a matter of opinion. And after all, who would be willing to die for an opinion? Like Pilate, we look on the deaths at Jonestown, wash our hands, and ask "What is truth?"

Yet it will be my argument that our attempts to dismiss or explain what happened at Jonestown as a mistake or as pathology—though certainly much that happened there was pathological—are dangerous trivialization. In contrast, I will suggest, we should take seriously what happened there as an act of revolutionary suicide that should initially be morally honored and respected. Not to honor the people's willingness to take their own lives in a cause they believed true and good is to avoid far too easily the challenge of Jonestown for our secular society as well as for our established religions. Yet it is my contention that what happened at Jonestown was not just a mistake but a form of the demonic that must be recognized and condemned. What went wrong at Jonestown is not that people died for what they believed but that they died for false beliefs and a false god. Their willingness to take their own lives demonstrates the demonic character of their beliefs. I contend that the traditional condemnation of suicide, both personal and revolutionary, by Jews and Christians turns out to be an essential test for considering whether religious convictions might stand the test of being truth.

We often forget that Jews and Christians, no less than Jim Jones, have held and continue to hold beliefs for which they think it is worth dying. The question was not whether they should die for their convictions, but how they should die. Jews and Christians believe that their lives are not theirs to do with as they wish. Rather they belong to an Other who alone has the right to determine when they will live and when they will die, their existence has value only if such a God exists. Therefore they are prohibited from taking their lives but are equally required to be ready to give their lives if their continued existence depends on their renouncing loyalty to the very Being that made their lives worthy in the first place.[1]

Only in the context of such a tension can the moral significance for the category of martyrdom be appreciated. To be a martyr means that one's death can be clearly distinguished from the immorality of suicide and thus honored as a necessary consequence of one's faith.[2] But it is obviously difficult to distinguish clearly between an act of suicide and an act of martyrdom since isolated acts of either may appear similar. There is no final empirical test to be able to separate the one from the other; rather, final determination must rest on the good judgment and wisdom of the witnesses.

However, Christians and Jews have developed some strong checks through which we may be able clearly to distinguish suicide from martyrdom. An essential one is the refusal of Christians and Jews to lay hands on themselves to end their lives.[3] To lay claim to being a martyr requires that the person be put to death. Christians and Jews believe their task is to live, not to die. We do not seek our death and we refuse to be agents of our death. The agent, if any, must be someone else.

It is tempting in our age to think such distinctions at best irrelevant, even positive distortions of reality. Thus we think irrational those who would be willing to stop life-maintaining measures on an irreversibly ill and dying patient but refuse to administer a drug or inject an air bubble that would precipitate the patient's death. It is our view that if the patient is going to die anyhow it matters little how, that if some people are stupid enough to hold beliefs that might put them in danger it matters little whether they take their own lives or have others do the deed for them.

Yet such objections fail to understand the profound values that such symbolic scruples are seeking to preserve. By making those who seek to destroy us do the actual killing, Jews and Christians make clear their conviction of the goodness of God's creation. It is not their business or their prerogative to determine when they should die —that they leave to God. Their task is learning how to live faithful and true to the God they deem the source of all that is true and good about our existence. Only when we can make this kind of distinction can we simultaneously honor those who died at Jonestown and condemn what they did. However, before developing this point it is necessary to suggest why those who would explain what happened at Jonestown as pathological fail to deal with its moral and religious reality.

The People's Temple Experience: Can There Be An Explanation?

The first thing anyone feels about Jonestown is naturally the sheer horror of what happened there. It is important not to lose too quickly our sense of horror. For horror is a particularly important moral response as it indicates an appropriate reaction to what we simply feel is incomprehensible. What is truly horrible cannot and should not be explicable in terms of our conventional categories. Rather we must be willing to let the horrible remain foreign and frightening if we are to avoid self-deceptive accounts that may only reinforce more deeply our false perceptions.

To let the matter rest there, however, is almost an impossibility for those of us with intellectual pretensions. Our task is to explain and an event such as Jonestown is simply too rich not to have an explanation attempted. Indeed, Jonestown in many ways is a boon because it invites the kind of intellectual speculation that can make a career. At the very least it offers the opportunity to demonstrate whatever theory we may have about what is the nature of our society or what is causing our particular problems. It is of particular interest to anyone who has the high ambition to understand the current phenomenon of cults because it seems to provide crucial material that will help us understand better the causes of the cults and, perhaps, the result of their doings. And I have no doubt that many of the theories concerning what Jonestown tells us about American society and the cult phenomenon have much to commend them.

I cannot pretend to have read widely the many explanations that have been given about Jonestown. As a matter of fact, one of my frustrations in trying to think about and understand the life of those involved with People's Temple is a lack of any trustworthy accounts and information about them.[4] We can hope to have better descriptions in the near future about Jones and the people who trusted him so completely. It may well be, however, that such accounts will come not from those trained in the empirical methods of the social sciences but rather from those with a novelist's eye for ambiguity and pathos.

Yet the news reports and follow-up articles about Jonestown that have reflected theories and explanations are deeply informed by many of the assumptions enshrined and promulgated by social scientists and others who represent the intellectual orthodoxies associated with the contemporary university. Reporters for *Time, Newsweek,* the *Washington Post,* and the *New York Times*[5] may not be scientists, but they often write as people deeply informed by the social-scientific view of society. Thus their perception, as well as the ways they inform our perception of Jonestown, come theory-laden with the explanatory power and assumed wisdom of our science.

The explanation they provide of Jonestown, I think, looks something like this: Jonestown was possible only because Jim Jones preyed on the dispossessed and poor in our society. The people that made up People's Temple, with a few notable exceptions, were poor blacks and whites whom Jones was able to supply with a new sense of status and purpose. For these people are the losers in our society, and no fate is worse than theirs in a society that makes money success the primary determinant for one's own and others' regard. Jones was able to make these people feel like winners, like somebodies, because he gave them a coherent community and an explanation for why they had felt oppressed, the causal economic and societal forces that they now knew how to name as well as how to oppose. Like all significant religious leaders, Jones offered them a plan of salvation at once religious and political.

Thus People's Temple thrived on the rootlessness that many people seem to feel in our culture. Its members were people simply unable to exist without some belief, some cause, that would supply them meaning and purpose. Jim Jones offered such a cause and he showed he was serious exactly because he demanded extreme sacrifices from them. His demand that they turn over all their financial resources to the church was not itself an indication he was a scoundrel; in fact, by demanding sacrifices he indicated the substantial nature of the community.[6] Nor did his wish to be called "Dad" appear absurd; rather it was a profound indication that they had become part of a new family—and this time a family that would not betray them.

At a more profound level the willingness of the community to place trust in Jim Jones can be and has been interpreted as the inability of people to stand freedom. This explanation is meant to cut deeper than the mere claim that rootless people are tragically open to the kind of manipulation in which Jones was so adept. For rootlessness seems to indicate that we have a cultural problem that we need to rectify; but "inability to stand freedom" speaks more directly to the human condition. We assume we ought to be able to stand freedom, and if those who so uncritically followed Jim Jones could not stand it then the burden of proof rests on them rather than on our culture.

The fact that Jones fed on the economically and culturally deprived of our society is not sufficient to account for the ways he was able to convince some of them to kill and many to die. For that accounting we need theories of mass hysteria coupled with the isolation of Jonestown. It is no doubt true that Jones could never have persuaded so many to die if they had still been in San Francisco. Certainly the air of unreality created at Jonestown, as well as a sense of sharing the sacrifices and the deprivation necessary for survival there, created the possibility of a mass suicide that otherwise would have been impossible.

But such explanations, while no doubt containing some truth, are secondary to the undeniable reality of Jim Jones's personal power. I think there can be little question that in the last years of his life he was certifiably crazy. But there is also little doubt that he was an extremely powerful person with considerable insight and organizational skill. He was certainly charismatic, but it is also true that much of his power was based on the fact that he often spoke the truth. That is not to say that any intellectual sense can be made of his peculiar blend of Marxism and Christianity, but the intellectual incoherence of his views makes little difference. He obviously was a man who had not much use for theories. Rather, he simply used whatever seemed handy to articulate, for those that followed him, truthful claims about their existence and the injustice of our society.

Jones was right after all that we do live in a society of fear and hate; that is not news for anyone who had recently read the New Testament. The early Christians seem also to have thought that we always live in a world ruled by the powers of fear and hate. Yet Jones, unlike pastors in more established forms of Christianity, was able to present this view clearly and effectively to a group of people who had the experience to know it was true. Moreover, Jones held out a strategy designed to help them live in such a world. He offered an alternative community where love, not hate, would rule. Thus he claimed, "This is why we're here. It's for these children. It's all for them. We have to work, and work, and work, and we have to stay together for these babies! So that they can have a world full of love. A world where there is not hate! A world where there is social equality! A world with racial equality! A world with economic equality!"[7]

To be sure, this kind of idealism appears strikingly naive to those of us who think we have learned better. But Jones cannot so easily be dismissed. He did not just hold it up as an outcome to be realized in the future. He made it a present reality for many of those who followed him. People's Temple did become a place where blacks and whites discovered they could be brothers once they had both discovered who was their real enemy. People's Temple did provide people with their first experience of being responsible for someone else's life. People's Temple did offer the opportunity to experience the exhilaration of learning that you are capable of being loved and thus of loving.

Moreover, such love and community was not to be limited to those who participated in People's Temple as Jones was able to translate that experience into a program. He gave his people a cause, an adventure, a sense of being chosen. Because they had been blessed they now had the peculiar responsibility to witness and to transform the wider society into one of love and equality. Jones offered people something more profound than just meaning and status; he offered a mission.[8] The sacrifices they must make along the way were intelligible only in the light of such a mission—even the ultimate sacrifice that he required from them.

It seems easy after the event for us to think that the followers should have been able to spot Jones's paranoia and, perhaps, charlatanism. But I think that opinion is a failure to appreciate the genuine complexity of a figure like Jones. To be sure, he did use some of the tricks of any religious huckster; but they were incidental to his power over his people. Or it may seem that his increasingly bizarre

sexual practices and demands should have caused many to have
second thoughts; but again his demands did have a kind of rationality from within the world he had created. Even his use of blackmail
and physical threat made sense to a people who were convinced that
they were dealing with someone who had his hand on the pulse of the
very power of the universe.

Moreover, all attempts to dismiss Jones as a charlatan, someone
who was seeking his own interest in a narrow sense, simply fail to fit
the facts. Jones, no doubt, was cynical about much he was doing and
about many of his followers. But he was a true believer. There is no
sign that he had any doubt about the ultimate righteousness of his
cause or of himself.[9] Indeed, if he had been blessed with some
disbelief it might have been enough to save 900-odd lives. But he did
believe that his message was true and that he was crucial to its truth
— so crucial that he could ask these hundreds of people to die rather
than continue living without him.

Yet the very recognition of Jones's power as the primary explanation for what happened at Jonestown only increases our difficulty
with any attempt to explain what happened there. Even if Jones was
the figure that made possible their revolutionary suicide, then how
do we explain such power? It seems to be a power correlative to our
horror of the suicides—that is, we know of no ready way to explain
either. Both seem inexplicable given our everyday assumptions
about how the world works, or at least should work.

I believe that we can account for the peculiar power Jones held
over his people only if we will recognize that he was making an
essentially religious appeal that did offer a way, such as every significant religion offers, to deal with distressing aspects of our existence.
Of course, since the mass suicide the more established forms of
religions in our society perhaps have tried as much as possible to
show that their genuine religion is not like that offered by Jones. But
in fact what is embarrassing about Jones, in spite of some clear
differences, is how close much of what he had to say parallels
normative Christianity.

Like the early Christians, Jones thought in cosmic terms about
the struggle in which he was engaged. It was a struggle between
light and darkness, between good and evil. Any people who would be

worthy of such a struggle must be converted entirely from their former way of life. They must be willing to sacrifice everything—wealth, security, family, life itself—if their lives were to be transformed. And like the early Christians they understood that such a task was fundamentally political. As one of Jones's followers rightly claimed, "Jones has always wanted to build a multiracial, peaceful, egalitarian society. Here we have the opportunity to create human institutions from cradle to grave, literally. Social change is really our focus. We don't see that religion and politics are separate."[10]

Moreover, we must remember that early Christianity was no less disruptive of family life than was Jones's Christianity. You must leave father, mother, wife, and husband, for now the Christian community is your true family. Even more radical was the early Christian assumption that some should be freed from all familial ties for service to the Kingdom. It is no wonder that many decent pagans saw Christianity as a threat to everything they held dear. For their sons and daughters to convert to such a religion was bound to ruin promising careers. Even though there is no question that Jones used the sexual ethic he developed for his own personal pleasure and also used intimidation for maintaining his church, it is also true that much of what he had to say about the family had precedent in Christian history.

It is not my purpose to try to show that Jones was an orthodox Christian; he certainly was not. Indeed, his very success is a judgment on the church and on our society for giving people so little religious substance that they could not recognize heresy when they saw and experienced it. Jones was successful because he was able to co-opt the general religiosity of people, legitimated by vague reference to Christian symbols, and to turn that religiosity into a powerful force by putting pieces together in a perverted manner. What is tragic is that no one was well-enough schooled in a normative tradition to challenge Jones's understanding of God or Jesus. A people who have lost any sense of how religious traditions are capable of truth and falsity can easily fall prey to the worst religious claims, having lost the religious moorings that might provide them with discriminating power. No one challenged Jones when he threw the

Bible away, saying that it got in the way of his followers' perception of him.

The discrimination to make such a challenge was perhaps too much to ask of those who followed Jones, but it is not too much to ask of those who stood religiously outside People's Temple. But alas, we live at a time when the more orthodox forms of Christianity refuse to pass judgment on any religious phenomenon on theological grounds for fear that such judgments might violate the norm of tolerance. Like all good secularists, Christians today do not condemn the beliefs of cults but rather criticize them only for practices that seem to violate people's autonomy.[11] After all, beliefs are a matter of personal choice, not subject to claims of truth or falsity. Only actions can be condemned and those only on a basis that is shared by our general culture.

So we lacked and continue to lack the resources to explain as well as condemn what was happening in People's Temple. For any explanation of People's Temple necessarily requires religious claims, since Jones's power and the ultimate sacrifice of those at Jonestown had a religious nature. Sociological and psychological factors may explain some of what went on there, but the fact that hundreds of people committed revolutionary suicide cannot be explained so easily. They killed themselves because they thought they should die for what they believed the truth. No doubt some were murdered, but many willingly and bravely died because they thought such a death was consistent with the truth they had learned and experienced through the ministry of Jim Jones.

From our perspective we think their deaths foolish because they did not have to die. After all, the murder of Congressman Ryan and the reporters did not mean the end of Jonestown or of People's Temple. Rather, it meant the arrest of Jim Jones and those who had perpetrated the act. But from the perspective of those who thought their very existence depended on Jim Jones, such jailing meant nothing less than the dissolution of the community that they now identified as their very life. To lose the community was equivalent to losing their life. So, like the martyrs, they chose spiritual life rather than spiritual death. Better to be dead in body than face the living death that would come with the destruction of People's Temple.

Suicide, Martyrdom, and Truth

Some may object that I have given a far too favorable interpretation of what happened at Jonestown. Jones, after all, was a seriously sick man who had successfully convinced his 900-odd people to go along with his madness. That is the long and short of it and nothing further needs to be said. To take their deaths seriously as revolutionary suicide makes it sound like those poor ignorant people might have known what they were doing and thus should be treated as worthy moral agents.[12] Better to explain their deaths psychologically than to open up the possibility that their deaths had any meaning.

Yet I have tried to assume the point of view of the people of Jonestown, tried to show that psychological and sociological explanations fail to do justice to the reality of their deaths. They rightly died for what they believed. They rightly described their act as revolutionary suicide, for their deaths were meant to protest a world that would not allow the existence of the kind of community they were trying to build. The kind of society they envisioned was revolutionary, at least in principle, for it would require of wider society a transformation that would be nothing less than revolutionary. The pathos of their death can be felt when we reflect on how distant from the vision that Jones had originally burned into their imaginations was the community they experienced at Jonestown under his leadership. But even the distance between fiction and reality cannot undo the reality of a group of people who thought their beliefs true and so were willing to die for them.

That fact is just the problem. For the beliefs for which the Jones followers died were in fact false. The people were not wrong to worship God, but the god they worshipped was false. Yet even false gods have their power and such power cannot be countered simply by denying their existence. Rather, false gods like false worship can be countered only by the true God and true worship.

The faith generated by Jim Jones was demonic because it was a faith not in God but finally in man. No surer sign of the demonic character of that faith was the followers' willingness to take their own lives. For the willingness to take their lives, and the lives of others,[13] manifests the assumption that they must insure their own existence. The Jewish and Christian prohibition against suicide is not based on the inherent sacredness of life but rather on God's sovereignty over all life. Our life is not for us to do with as we please, but rather we must learn to look on our life as a gift that is not ours to dispose of.

Nor do Christians and Jews think this prohibition a mere prejudice or opinion peculiar to them. Rather they think that the prohibition against suicide is a true statement about the way life should be lived in the presence of God. The prohibition against suicide is thus not just a normative recommendation but indeed a statement about the very nature of human existence as bounded by the power of God. Those, therefore, who would contemplate and indeed even practice suicide as did those at Jonestown must be judged worshipers of a false god.

That judgment does not mean they are not martyrs, but that they are not martyrs to the true God. Rather they are martyrs of a society which no longer believes that issues of truth and falsity pertain in matters religious. They, like many, thought it better to believe something rather than nothing. Their mistake was to take such belief seriously, not realizing that religious devotion is in the society's outlook primarily a personal matter. In a more profound sense, however, they cannot even be martyrs. They were merely passive victims. They were victimized not just by Jim Jones, but by a society and by religious institutions that supply no means to discern the demonic, much less bestow the power to deal with it.

Our society often piously applauds those who seem to be self-sacrificial. Those at Jonestown were such to a degree that few of us would approve. But their mistake was not that they were willing to give their lives for what they believed but that what they believed was so wrong. In the absence of substantial beliefs their sacrifice became an end in itself, legitimating all the smaller but very demanding sacrifices that made them part of People's Temple in the first place. Their sacrifice, unlike that of Jewish and Christian martyrs, was demonic because it served not the true God of life but powers that we think we avoid by denying their existence.

Jim Jones was right that without ideals we live alone and die rejected. He offered ideals that promised community, something worth sacrificing for, and death among friends. But the means he used to form such a community should have been a sure sign that what People's Temple served was not the truth. Our tragedy is that there was no one internal or external to that community able to challenge the false presuppositions of Jones's false ideals. Our continuing tragedy is that our reactions to and our interpretation of the deaths of Jonestown reveal accurately how we lack the convictions to counter the powers that reigned there.

Notes

1. For a fuller account of these themes see my *A Community of Character: Toward a Constructive Christian Social Ethic* (Notre Dame: University of Notre Dame Press, 1981).

2. For an attempt to argue why Christians have rightly thought suicide to be immoral see my *Truthfulness and Tragedy: Further Investigation in Christian Ethics* (Notre Dame: University of Notre Dame, 1977), 101-115. This essay was written with Richard Bondi. For the most complete historical account of martyrdom, see N.H. Frend, *Martyrdom and Persecution in the Early Church* (New York: New York University Press, 1967). Frend quite rightly identified the issue of martyrdom as fundamentally political. Thus he says: "The problem which the Christian posed to the Empire was fundamentally the same as that posed by Judaism, namely the reconciliation of the claims of a theocracy with those of a world empire. In the West, the problem continued to dominate history in one way or another for fifteen hundred years, until obscured by the new ecclesiology of the Reformers. Lyons (one of the first mass Christian martyrdoms), however, set the stage, for there the claims of the state and the pressure of popular opinion confronted in the starkest term the claims of Christian confession and witness." Thus the claim of revolutionary suicide, at least in principle, is not unlike Christian and Jewish martyrdom insofar as each involves profound political conflicts.

3. The deaths of Masada are often mentioned as a counterexample to this prohibition, but it is by no means clear that the undeniable heroism of the defenders of Masada is justification for their final act. Indeed, most orthodox Jewish thinkers continue to condemn this act as suicide.

4. Besides the newspaper and weekly newsmagazine accounts of Jonestown, I have had to rely almost entirely on Charles Krause, *Guyana Massacre* (New York: Berkeley Publishing Co., 1978) and Philip Kerns and Dough Mead, *People's Temple, People's Lamb* (Plainfield: Logos International, 1979). None of these sources provide the kind of information one would like to have about the actual people who made up People's Temple, how the Temple was organized and run, what were the primary beliefs of the people, and the like.

5. The primary reports on Jonestown are in *Time* and *Newsweek*. In addition there is Winfrey. Carey Winfrey, "Why 900 Died in Guyana," *New York Times Magazine,* (February, 1979), 39-50. Also

of interest is Michael Novak, "Jonestown: Five Columns," (Washington, D.C: American Enterprise Institute Reprint, 94, 1978).

6. There is no doubt that Jones acquired great wealth through the Temple, but there is no indication that he was interested in using that wealth for his own personal enhancement. Jones did not desire money, but power. And the power he wanted was not the everyday kind we are familiar with but the power to determine the meaning of other people's lives.

7. Kerns and Mead, 41.

8. Novak perhaps rightly suggests that the clue to what was wrong with People's Temple lay in its utopian optimism. In contrast, he argues that Christianity, while sharing many of the ideals of utopians, is not utopian. Instead, "the God of Christianity and Judaism permits his people to wander in history in a wilderness. The sufferings, loneliness, anguish, and misery he permits them to share are fathomless. The Jewish-Christian God is no *deus ex machina,* no Pollyanna, no goody-two-shoes. He obliges each individual, in the darkness, to exert his or her own inner liberty and choice. He is the God of liberty. He exacts enormous and wearying responsibilities. The God we turn to on Christmas is not a God made in our measure, nor is he a function of our needs, personal or social. He does not rescue us from our responsibilities, mistakes, or betrayals. He offers no escape from the toils of history, chance, and contingency. He transcends our purposes and needs. Many cults today, political and pious, offer an easier messianism, a happier salvation, a more utopian political and social hope. The God of Jews and Christians obliges us to struggle and to suffer, even when there is no hope. There is no valid escape from freedom, even in despair; such is the anti-messianic messianism of Christmas" (6). While Novak is right in his contrast, it is not clear that People's Temple is easily or rightly described as utopian. The people seem to have understood that they were in a struggle that would not be over soon.

9. I think we simply do not know enough about Jones at this point to speculate about his understanding of himself. He obviously believed in his ideals, at least at one time. The influence of Father Divine on him in many ways seems to have been decisive, but that does not mean that he ever doubted the truth of what he was saying. He may have been a man who, recognizing he held no substantial beliefs of his own, asked greater and greater sacrifices of his people in hopes that they would not notice the thinness of the religious claims at the basis of his church.

And in an even more ironic twist, the more people he convinced of the righteousness of his cause, the more he convinced himself.

10. Krause, 69.

11. One of the ironies of our contemporary situation is that many of the charges against the cults as practicing brainwashing, made by Christians, is exactly the kind of charge that could be and was made against Christian conversion. Even so, some cults may well be engaging in practices that are coercive. But the issue is finally not whether the means of converting are coercive, but whether what they are asked to believe and do is true. The form of conversion that should be characteristic of Christians cannot in principle be coercive since Christians believe the only thing that should convince another of the truth is truth itself.

12. One of the most disturbing aspects of reactions to Jonestown is the inherent racism and class prejudice implied. The assumption is that if these people had just been better educated and well off they would not have fallen for this kind of cheap and trashy religion. There is no empirical or moral basis, however, for such an assumption.

13. One of the most overlooked aspects of Jonestown has been the failure to understand the connection between the murders and the suicide. For the murder of Ryan and others was a sign of the community's insecurity in their beliefs. Indeed it is my conviction that anytime a religion must resort to violence to secure its beliefs that is a sure sign that something has gone wrong with its claim to worship the God of truth and peace. Unfortunately Christianity provided Jones with many past precedents for the violence he used to protect his community. The use of violence is a sure sign that the community trusts not God, but themselves.

6. THE REALITY OF THE KINGDOM: AN ECCLESIAL SPACE FOR PEACE

with Mark Sherwindt

The Kingdom at the Mercy of Idealistic Theology: The Recent History

"Theology has yet to digest the radical change from the ethical to the eschatological understanding of the Kingdom of God."[1] So writes Wolfhart Pannenberg in his attempt to provide a theology that ingests the significance of the kingdom of God as the central reality of the Christian proclamation. If Pannenberg is correct in his claim that theology has hardly begun to appreciate the systematic significance of the eschatological focus required by the language of the kingdom, this is even more so the case in theological ethics. What at once seemed such a promising resource for ethical reflection threatens to dissolve in a sea of scholarly qualifications and ethical generalities that offer little direction for the practical life of Christian men and women and/or the role of the church in society.

The discovery in the nineteenth century of the centrality of the kingdom of God in the preaching of Jesus, a discovery that certainly was correct, seemed to have offered a fresh perspective on Christian ethics. Protestant ethics in particular gravitated toward this new-found ideal of the "kingdom" because of its traditional commitment to formulating a scripturally based ethic. In their search for such an ethic, however, Protestants often settled for biblical themes or concepts such as the law-gospel dialectic or *agape*. While theologically suggestive, such biblical themes and concepts were not easily translated into concrete ethical norms; such concrete norms that were formulated were not easily traced to or demonstrably derived from Scripture. Thus, Protestant attempts to provide concrete ethical analysis often fell back on some kind of "natural law" ethic which, however, lacked the more explicit rigor of Roman Catholic natural law discourse. The emergence of focus on the concept of the kingdom of God seemed to promise a way to move beyond this difficulty, for this biblical concept provided everything that was needed, from global vision to concrete specificity of conduct, for the development of a Christian ethic.

Moreover, there was the added advantage that the "kingdom ideal" synthesized both practically and conceptually the relation between personal and social ethics. The social and political character of the very image of "kingdom" serves as a reminder that any Christian ethic that is not first of all a social ethic is less than Christian. Early proponents of the social gospel were grasped by the political and social character of the kingdom ideal, and the force of their exhortatory fervor was to invoke more than the call to individual conversion, it was to provoke Christians to social action and change aimed at "Christianizing" the institutions of societal life. They looked to the kingdom of God for more than an "ideal"; they looked for a concrete and realistic portrayal of the just society. Thus, with neither ambiguity nor equivocation Walter Rauschenbusch could maintain:

The Kingdom of God is humanity organized according to the will of God. Interpreting it through the consciousness of Jesus we may affirm these convictions about the ethical relations within the kingdom: (a) Since Christ revealed the divine worth of life and personality, and since his salvation seeks the restoration and fulfillment of even the least, it follows that the Kingdom of God, at every stage of human development, tends toward a social order which will best guarantee to all personalities their freest and highest development. (b) Since love is the supreme love of Christ, the Kingdom of God implies a progressive reign of love in human affairs. We can see its advance wherever the free will of love supersedes the use of force and legal coercion as a regulative of the social order. This involves the redemption of society from political autocracies and economic oligarchies; the substitution of redemptive for vindicative penology; the abolition of constraint through hunger as part of the industrial system; and the abolition of war as the supreme expression of hate and the completest cessation of freedom. (c) The highest expression of love is the free surrender of what is truly our own, life, property and rights. A much lower but perhaps more decisive expression of love is the surrender of any opportunity to exploit men. No social group or organization can claim to be clearly within the Kingdom of God which drains others for its own ease, and resists the effort to abate this fundamental evil. This involves the redemption of society from private property in the natural resources of the earth, and from any condition in industry which makes monopoly profits possible. (d) The reign of love tends toward the progressive unity of mankind, but with the maintenance of individual liberty and the opportunity of nations to work out their own peculiarities and ideals.[2]

The kingdom of God provided for Walter Rauschenbusch not only a glimpse of God's future, but also the vision and a program for concrete change in human history. The kingdom of God ideal was productive of guidance sufficient to direct Christian social action, or, as Rauschenbusch put it elsewhere, to articulate "the program of Christian revolution: the kingdom of God on earth."[3] However, the conceptual relation between the image of kingdom and the concrete social and political recommendations remained unclear. The practical exhortation to move beyond the individual to the social was clear enough; conceptually, however, within this call to form the just society through christianizing political and economic institutions, the relation between individual regeneration and social sanctification was not addressed. The question of the role of the church did arise. Clearly the church served as model and as forward flank in the social gospel's call to action. Yet, an ecclesiology which clarified the differing character of the social relation in which the individual stood in the church and over against the world receded from focus. Church and world alike stood under the identical challenge to create a Christian social order through political democracy and fraternal socialism. Further, an ecclesiology which addressed the relations of continuity and discontinuity between the Church of Christ and the kingdom of God went undeveloped and without critical analysis.

Rauschenbusch's "program" was soon challenged on numerous grounds. His understanding of the kingdom was criticized for its naivete; his uncritical appropriation of liberalism's faith in social progress was regarded by many "realists" as far too simplistic, lacking in appreciation for the complexity of social change and the ambiguity of all attempts to secure more nearly just social arrangements. Yet, such criticisms are not the most important for our purposes; for what is most decisive about such views is that Rauschenbusch and his imitators lacked any sense of the eschatological character of the kingdom. They thought of the kingdom as an ethical ideal that required only our willingness to bring it to completion. Therefore the tension occasioned by the kingdom from their perspective was that between an ideal and its incomplete realization.

As a result they failed to see, as Pannenberg suggests, that the kingdom is not to be established by men but by God alone. The biblical scholars thus took the ethical stress out of the kingdom, at least in any direct way, as they demonstrated that the kingdom texts in the New Testament envisage cosmic revolutions and changes

> far beyond anything conceivable as a consequence of man's progressive labor. God will establish his Kingdom unilaterally. Therefore Jesus, and John the Baptizer before him, only announced the Kingdom of God, exposing every present condition under the light of the imminent future. This future is expected to come in a marvelous way from God himself; it is not simply the development of human history or the achievement of God-fearing men.[4]

This focus on the divine agency involved in the cosmic drama wherein heaven and earth are radically transformed undermined claims for the decisive significance of human progress aimed at societal reformation, at least in terms of ushering in the kingdom of God.

Moreover, the original ethical interpretation of the kingdom of God seemed to overlook another conceptual problem, namely, that there was no clear connection between the scriptural account of the kingdom of God and the moral ideals advocated in its name. Thus, it was (and is) claimed that the essence of the kingdom was love and/or justice; yet, such ideals or norms were not clearly derived from the notion of the kingdom itself. In fact, even if to our embarrassment, the very language of the kingdom does not call to mind categories of liberal democracy but of religious theocracy. Rauschenbusch recognized that the kingdom ideal was in the Old Testament that of "a righteous community ordered by divine laws, governed by God's ministers, having intercourse with the most High, and being blessed by him with the good things of life."[5] For Rauschenbusch, however, Jesus transformed this ideal by universalizing and spiritualizing it so that political democracy was seen as the result of as well as inherent to Jesus' insistence on the inherent value of each individual personality.[6] In this way, leaving Scripture far behind, Rauschenbusch was able to transform the theocratic image of the Kingdom of God into the democratic ideal of the brotherhood of man.

Rauschenbusch's assumptions in this respect are clearly just that —assumptions. Scripturally there seems to be no good grounds to associate the kingdom of God with any form of political organization and/or to assume that it is best characterized by any one set of ethical ideals such as love and justice. As a platitude it may be unobjectionable to claim that God's kingdom must surely be one of love and justice, but that does little to help one understand what is the meaning and content of love and justice. Indeed, when the content of such ideals is spelled out, as we see in the case of Rauschenbusch, we begin to suspect that the language of the kingdom is being used to underwrite ethical commitments and political strategies that were determined prior to the claims about the centrality of the kingdom for Christian ethics. In other words, apart from vague generalities about the social and political commitments of Christians required by the kingdom language, the concentration on the kingdom of God does not avoid the problem that the content of any Christian ethic must be derived from extra-biblical sources.

Pannenberg is particularly interesting in this respect, since he, more than any other contemporary theologian, promises to shape his theological program in terms of the eschatological vision required by Jesus' preaching of the kingdom. In most of his theological expression he has been extraordinarily successful. Yet, when he turns to assessing the ethical significance of the kingdom he sounds surprisingly like Rauschenbusch. Thus, even though he maintains that the "kingdom of God is that perfect society of men which is to be realized in history by God himself," he also insists that it is not some formalistic idea but the utterly concrete reality of justice and love.[7] But nowhere does Pannenberg tell us why justice and love are the defining marks of the kingdom; nor does he tell us what kind of justice or love are the kingdom's marks, or what social expression they are to take. Rather, we are offered generalities such as,

> love is the final norm of justice. Love is equipped to be the measure of justice because it is not an abstract principle. Love is a dynamic reality producing, in an ongoing process, new forms of human unity; each form surpasses its predecessor and anticipates its successor.[8]

What Pannenberg does not do is help us know by what criteria we are to determine which forms of unity in this "dynamic process" are to be identified as God's work for the upbuilding of the kingdom. Rather, in a manner much like Rauschenbusch, he puts forward an account of love that involves the respect for the other person that he assumes to be commensurate with the development of politics that stresses the notion of self-government and the sovereignty of the people.[9] One might well agree with Pannenberg's insights concerning love and justice, their relation to freedom and equality, and the moral significance of democracies, but it remains a question whether his commitment to the language of the kingdom in ethics makes any difference at all for his understanding or support of these ideals, norms, and strategies.

The problem here as well as with Rauschenbusch is that of abstracting the kingdom ideal from the concrete community which it presupposes. Focus must be brought to bear not only on the eschatological fulfillment of the promise of the kingdom, but on the concrete ecclesial community established in its name. The kingdom of God is the hope of the people whom God has called out among all the nations. The question of ecclesiology, therefore, precedes strategy for social action. Without the kingdom ideal, the church loses its identity-forming hope; without the church, the kingdom ideal loses its concrete character. Once abstracted from the community it presumes the kingdom ideal can be used to underwrite any conception of the just society.

Jesus and the Kingdom

Such criticism, however, may be unfair as it leaves out a crucial element in the recovery of the eschatological nature of the kingdom, namely, the centrality of Jesus for determining the nature and content of the kingdom. For the stress on the kingdom's eschatological reality has gone hand in hand with the insistence that the proclamation of the kingdom's presence now and in the future cannot be separated from him who proclaims the kingdom. Thus, Pannenberg maintains that

> Jesus insisted upon the present and radical relevance of God's coming Kingdom. He identified love as its ultimate norm, and, by exemplifying the love of God in his own life and death, Jesus proved to be the expected *christos*, the Messiah of God, who shall establish God's kingdom on earth. The dignity of Jesus as the Christ, as the Messiah, is a result of the way he represented and still represents for all of humanity the Kingdom of God as already determining and transforming the present by creative love. All the words and formulas of Christology have truth to the degree they express how the future of God's Kingdom became determinative for the present of Jesus' life and, through him, for the history of mankind. In Jesus' radical devotion to the Kingdom of God, the Kingdom became present in him. In him the Kingdom is present to all men.[10]

Put starkly, Jesus himself is the meaning and content of the kingdom.

Such an emphasis was not absent, however, from those who interpreted the kingdom in less straightforwardly eschatological terms. Thus for Rauschenbusch there could be no kingdom without the person of Jesus.

> The fundamental first step in the salvation of mankind was the achievement of the personality of Jesus. Within him the Kingdom of God got its first foothold in humanity. It was by

virtue of his personality that he became the initiator of the Kingdom.[11]

For Rauschenbusch, therefore, Christianity was built up, not so much on doctrine, but on the person of its founder. For in Jesus was provided

> a perfect religious personality, a spiritual life completely filled by the realization of a God who is love. All his mind was set on God and one with him. Consequently it was also absorbed in the fundamental purpose of God, the Kingdom of God. Like the idea of God, the conception of the Kingdom was both an inheritance and a creation of Jesus; he received it and transformed it in accordance with his consciousness of God. Within his mind the punitive and imperialistic elements were steeped out of it, and the elements of love and solidarity were dyed into it. The Reign of God came to mean the organized fellowship of humanity acting under the impulse of love.[12]

Rauschenbusch's commitments to liberal forms of christology are apparent from such quotes; yet, his suggestions in this respect should be neither ignored nor easily dismissed. In spite of his language of "a perfect religious personality," his insistence on the centrality of Jesus as crucial for determining the meaning of the kingdom is correct. Indeed in many ways it is not much different from the position of Pannenberg indicated above. It is the position of both theologians that the kingdom cannot be reduced to an ethical ideal and that moral norms cannot be known separate from the life and death of Jesus Christ. The issue between them is how best to understand what it means to claim Jesus as the form and content of the kingdom. For if, as Perrin argues (in *Jesus and the Language of the Kingdom*), the "kingdom of God" fundamentally involves a claim about God's activity in history on behalf of his people, then what we as Christians know of God's activity is known by looking at the life and death of Jesus Christ.

Theologically and ethically the significance of Jesus for determining the meaning and content of the kingdom implies that history assumes an importance that cannot be ignored as it often is by other forms of ethical reflection. For the particularity of Israel, Jesus, and the Church must be taken up constitutively into what those who proclaim Jesus as Lord and Christ regard as true and good and right. The kingdom does not start with nature, with the notion that the perfection implicit in creation be reformed by divine assistance; rather, the kingdom starts as the hope of a people called by God, which for Christians is defined by the life and death of the crucified Christ. The universal scope of the Kindom is rooted in the universal scope of God's reign. What we can know of this God and his kingdom is always given through the history of Israel filtered through the light of Jesus' cross.

It is the persistent claim in the Gospels that Yahweh continues to prove himself King through the work of Jesus. For through Jesus we see God's constant rule over nature and history as they are reclaimed by his good order. Jesus does not simply proclaim the coming of the kingdom, but he manifests its presence through his exorcisms and healing ministry.[13] Thus, as Gray suggests,

> in the mission of Jesus there is no question but that the Reign of God was central. This is not simply the order in which the highest moral ideals are finally realized with the impulses of the Divine authority and grace. What Jesus proclaimed and authenticated, by what he did and by what he was, was the irruption into history of the effective order of the Divine King with its power to transform the situation, to release new energies, as in the healing works of our Lord, to break the domination of forces which held men bodily and spiritually in thrall, as in what Jesus' contemporaries understood as the casting out of devils, the implication of which was so pointedly stated in Jesus' declaration of the strong man despoiled in the famous Beelzebub controversy (Mk. 3:23ff, Mt. 12:25ff). The present impact of the effective Reign of the Divine King in the gospel cannot be overemphasized.[14]

That the kingdom is present in Jesus is known not only by Jesus' power to renew our nature and spirit, but also in the rehabilitation of his people. The kingdom of God is a category which presumes and creates a people. God, through Jesus, has acted and is acting to vindicate his people, so that a remnant might remain faithful to him. Among God's people the poor, the oppressed, the underprivileged play a particularly prominent role, as their reversal of fortunes proclaim that all is not well with the world. Yet, it is not their poverty, not their oppression, nor their earthly powerlessness that make these persons paradigmatic citizens of God's kingdom; rather, their unencumbered reception of God's forgiveness and grace sets them apart as God's people. God's people have learned to be forgiven, and as such they are a people for whom patience and prayer are a possibility.

In the Beatitudes we see nothing less than the order of God's kingdom, the charter of his commonwealth, as we are treated to a vision of life that can occur only when a people have been formed who know who the true Lord of the world is. However, such a people is possible only because they have learned to be forgiven. For crucial to being a people capable of praying to Yahweh that his will be done on earth is that they have learned it is not necessary to try to justify themselves before such a Lord. They have learned that their King is a gracious King ready to forgive those able to be forgiven. By being able to be forgiven by God we learn how to forgive each other. That such a forgiven and forgiving community is possible is but an indication that God's rule is no utopian ideal, but a present reality that we are required to live out. There is no question of our "building" the kingdom, but of our willingness to trust that the kingdom was present in Jesus, is present in the Church by the power of the Holy Spirit, and will be fully manifest in the second coming. Thus, we are bold to pray:

> Our Father who art in heaven, hallowed be thy name, thy kingdom come, thy will be done, on earth as it is in heaven. Give us this day our daily bread; and forgive us our trespasses, as we forgive those who trespass against us; and lead us not into temptation, but deliver us from evil.

The Peaceful Space: The Ethics of the Kingdom

Even if focusing on Jesus as the presence of the kingdom as well as the ground of hope for the future fulfillment of the kingdom restores some ethical content to the notion of the kingdom, it is still not clear what implications the emphasis on the kingdom ought to have for our actual behavior and/or how we think about Christian ethics. For clearly it is a mistake to try to make the kingdom into a set of ideals, as Pannenberg comes very close to doing, which it is our responsibility to try to realize in society. The tension of the kingdom is not that caused by unrealized ideals; it is a tension between faithfulness and unfaithfulness.

Yet it is the intention of this chapter to claim that the eschatological nature of the kingdom as embodied in the ministry of Jesus does have immediate ethical implications. It does so not in the sense that the image of "kingdom" means that Christians should favor monarchy over democracy or vice versa, but in the sense that we are a people who have become part of a peaceable kingdom that has been made possible by the life and death of Jesus Christ. It is not our task to make the "world" the kingdom; but it is our task to be a people who can witness to the world what it means to be so confident of the Lord of this world that we wish for no more than our daily bread. It is not as if we are the kingdom, or that the Church is even the beginning of the kingdom but that as a people Christians can begin to point to the fact that the kingdom has been and is present in our midst.

Thus, within a world of violence and injustice Christians can take the risk of being forgiven and forgiving. They are able to break the circle of violence as they refuse to become part of those institutions of fear that promise safety by the destruction of others. As a result, some space, both psychological and physical, is created where we can be at rest from a world that knows not who is its king.

Such rest, however, is not accomplished by a withdrawal from the world, nor is it a rest in which there is no movement. For to be a part of God's kingdom means that we have found ourselves in the ongoing story of God with his people. That story provides us rest exactly because it trains us with the skills to face the dangers and threats of this existence with courage and patience. Rest is possible because we find that the kingdom is not a static space or way of being, but a journey that we have been graciously offered the opportunity to undertake. To be part of that journey means that we must be a particular kind of people formed by a particular set of virtues.

In this light we can read with fresh eyes as St. Paul tells us that the works of the flesh, the works of the world, are plain:

> Immorality, impurity, licentiousness, idolatry, sorcery, emnity, strife, jealousy, anger, selfishness, dissension, party spirit, envy, drunkenness, carousing, and the like. I warn you, as I warned you before, that those who do such things shall not inherit the kingdom of God. (Galatians 5:19-21)

This is not a list of petty moralisms, but a list of those forms of behavior that manifest our distrust and fear that there is no Lord, no God, whom we can trust as the good creator of this world. This is, therefore, not a matter of "personal" ethics, but an indication of the kind of character that is unacceptable in a community that not only witnesses to but manifests God's peace. In contrast to this is the community that knows that the

> fruit of the Spirit is love, joy, peace, patience, kindness, goodness, faithfulness, gentleness, self-control; against such there is no law. And those who belong to Christ Jesus have crucified the flesh with its passions and desires. (Galatians 5:22-23)[15]

That the fruit of the Spirit is such is not accident as we can risk being peaceful in a violent world, risk being kind in a competitive society, risk being faithful in an age of cynicism, risk being gentle among those who admire the tough, risk love when it may not be returned, because we have the confidence that in Christ we have been reborn into a new reality.

The Kingdom and the Church

Theologians presently are, and for some time have been, uncomfortable with making strong claims of some kind of identity between the church and the kingdom of god. For some the church has been a category of discomfort, even to the point of virtual silence. For others, the strong relation between the kingdom and the church has been singularly prominent to the point of constructing an ecclesiology which resembled in form, if not also to some extent in content, the revolutionary cadres of Leninist Marxism.[16] We rightly feel uncomfortable with such strong claims, but not because a strong relation between the concrete church and the kingdom of God ought not to be drawn. Rather, we are uncomfortable because neither the church nor the kingdom of God are what these liberation-theological colleagues claim them to be. We also rightly feel uncomfortable with those who would contend that the kingdom of God is exhausted in the life of the church, for we cannot help but ask in light of our experience of ecclesial life whether this is all there is.[17] Of course, there is more to the kingdom of God than the church. This more, however, is not grounded in metaphysical fiat, but in the stories of God preserved in our own traditions, which commend us to be ever watchful for the time when "God has put all things in subjection under his feet . . . when all things are subjected to him . . . that God may be everything to everyone." (1 Corinthians 15:27, 28)

From the perspective we have been developing, the church as that community formed by Jesus' story is not incidental for understanding God's kingdom. For, following the Pauline admonitions above, the virtues that form and are formed within the church are in fact a foretaste of the kingdom. To be sure, the church is not the kingdom, but neither is the life Christians share together something less than the kingdom's inbreaking. For the hope necessary to sustain the journey and pilgrim alike is in fact the first fruits of the kingdom, which we know to be God's will for the whole of creation.

Notes

1. Wolfhart Pannenberg, *Theology and the Kingdom of God*, edited by Richard John Neuhaus (Philadelphia: Westminster, 1977), 52. When Pannenberg seeks to explore the "systematic significance" of the eschatological focus required by the language of the kingdom of God, his own project directs him to a discussion of metaphysics and the "ontological priority of the future" to suggest how such a focus revolutionizes Christian thought. This chapter presumes that such a direction is unhelpful for two reasons. First, we question whether even metaphysically the ontological priority of the future makes sense. This involves the issue of how that which is an abstraction of what is not even existent (the not yet, the future) can be regarded as preeminently concrete (presupposed as the ground of every existent being, and of being itself). Secondly, and more importantly, such a metaphysical direction is misguided to the extent that ethical discourse is by definition practical, having to do with what is contingent. Thus, to move the discussion of the "ethical" significance of the eschatological focus of the language of the kingdom in the direction of the abstract and theoretical is counterproductive.

2. Walter Rauschenbusch, *A Theology for the Social Gospel* (Nashville: Abingdon, 1978), 142–3.

3. Walter Rauschenbusch, *The Righteousness of the Kingdom* (Nashville: Abingdon, 1968), 110.

4. Wolfhart Pannenberg, *op. cit.*, 52. Rauschenbusch was not so naive in this regard as many have claimed. In *A Theology for the Social Gospel*, he writes, "The Kingdom of God is divine in its origin, progress and consummation. It was initiated by Jesus Christ, in whom the prophetic spirit came to its consummation, it is sustained by the Holy Spirit, and it will be brought to its fulfillment by the power of God in his own time. The Kingdom of God, therefore, is miraculous all the way, and is the continuous revelation of the power, the righteousness, and the love of God" (139).

5. Walter Rauschenbusch, *The Righteousness of the Kingdom*, 80.

6. Ibid., 81.

7. Wolfhart Pannenberg, 76.

8. Ibid., 81.

9. Ibid., 121.

10. Ibid., 81.

11. Walter Rauschenbusch, *A Theology for the Social Gospel*, 151.

12. Ibid., 155.

13. Norman Perrin, *The Kingdom of God in the Teaching of Jesus* (London: SCM Press LTD, 1975), 76. It is of particular import that we stress God's reign over nature as well as over history. The peace which we share with one another is of the very same character as the peace which we as citizens of God's kingdom share with all of creation. This sheds new light on the relevance of issues such as vegetarianism and ecology as serious ethical issues for Christians.

14. John Gray, *The Biblical Doctrine of the Reign of God* (Edinburgh: T & T Clark, 1979), 319.

15. We would like to express special appreciation to Dr. James Tabor, University of Notre Dame, for helping us understand better Paul's use of the kingdom of God.

16. For further treatment of this matter, read Juan Luis Segundo, *The Liberation of Theology* (Maryknoll, New York: Orbis, 1976) in conjunction with Dennis McCann, *Christian Realism and Liberation Theology: Practical Theologies in Creative Conflict* (Maryknoll: Orbis, 1981).

17. Thus, a stark contrast is drawn between our parsing of the sense of incompleteness in our experience of ecclesial life and our expectation of the kingdom and Pannenberg's approach where the metaphysical claim of the ontological priority of the future serves as the fundamental substantiation of the distinction between church and kingdom. See *Theology and the Kingdom of God*, 78.

7. THE REALITY OF THE CHURCH: EVEN A DEMOCRATIC STATE IS NOT THE KINGDOM

Richard Neuhaus' "Christianity and Democracy" is important not only because it is well put, but because in it Neuhaus embodies the project of American theologians to forge a strong link between Christianity and American democracy.[1] Some may criticize the document for what appears to be its conservative tone, but such criticism fails to go to the heart of the matter. For I suspect such critics continue to share Neuhaus' basic claim that the church has a stake, and it is a theological stake, in making American democracy a success. But that is just the presumption I wish to question.

To do so not only involves complex theological and social questions, but it is also a personal challenge. For the understanding and defense of democracy, America's place within the international arena, and the theological appeals of "Christianity and Democracy" draw deeply from the wisdom of Reinhold Niebuhr. At one time I was so firmly convinced of the rightness of Niebuhr's perspective, that I would not only have signed "Christianity and Democracy" but done so enthusiastically. Therefore, that I find myself in such disagreement with this document requires me to explain to myself why my views have changed so radically.

The explanation for such a change no doubt has psychological dimensions, but those are not of immediate interest for the purposes of this response. Rather the change has to do with my increasing conviction of what is required if, as "Christianity and Democracy" puts it, "the first political task of the Church is to be the Church." For I do not think the church is being the church when it thinks "a choice must be made" between America and that bearer of totalitarian alternative, the Soviet Union. Nor do I think the church is being the church if it thinks and acts as if "America has a peculiar place in God's promises and purposes." Exactly when the church thinks it must put its spiritual and moral resources behind that kind of understanding of the world it loses its ability to be a "zone of truth-telling in a world of mendacity."[2]

The emphasis on the status and role of the church is the basis for my dissatisfaction with Niebuhr. Niebuhr simply provided no place for the church as a political alternative to the ways of nations and empires.[3] It is to "Christianity and Democracy"'s credit that in contrast to Niebuhr the significance of the church has been emphasized at the beginning of the document. But then it proceeds to offer an account of the moral status of democracy that draws deeply from the presuppositions of a Niebuhrian "realism." As a result there is a tension in the document that is resolved by a failure to carry through the claims about the church in the beginning of the statement. It is my conviction, however, that the tension should be resolved in the other direction. No state will keep itself limited, no constitution or ideology is sufficient to that task, unless there is a body of people separated from the nation that is willing to say "No" to the state's claims on their loyalties.

From a Niebuhrian perspective such an emphasis on the church as a political alternative to the politics of nations and empires must necessarily appear as politically naive. At best it is a form of Christian radicalism that, while morally impressive at certain times, is basically politically irrelevant, but at its worst is politically immoral insofar as it fails to face the necessity of having to make judgments between lesser evils. Yet nothing I hold compels me to assume that we live politically in a night where all cats are grey. Indeed I agree with many of the judgments of "Christianity and Democracy" about our current international situation. I do not believe that the American social and political system is as repressive as that of the Soviet Union. Nor do I have any illusions about the foreign policy of the Soviet Union as I assume they will take what they can get.

Moreover, I think "Christianity and Democracy" rightly stresses that the kind of totalitarianism represented by the Soviet Union has a virulent quality that is a modern political phenomenon. For the "monism" that attempts to absorb or replace all "intermediate institutions," such as church, family, economic relations, into an all encompassing state is but the working out of individualistic social and political theory. The only place I would fault the analysis offered by "Christianity and Democracy" in this respect is its failure to see this "monism" is but the mirror image of liberalism—a liberalism that ironically is most fully institutionalized in America.

For example, "Christianity and Democracy" praises democratic governments, and in particular America, because we have institutionalized the limited state. The state is understood only as one important actor in society that does not replace the role or authority of other institutions such as the church, education, or the family. This form of government is insured by such basic rights guaranteed by law as assembly, speech, elections, and assured transfer of power. Thus democracies respect not only rights of individuals but other institutions which are necessary to keep the state limited. In effect "the rights of the individual" have become the secular equivalent to the church as the means to keep government in its proper sphere.

But this interpretation of our political ideals fails to see that there is a fundamental tension between our commitments to the rights of the individual, preservation of "intermediate associations," and the ability to retain a limited state. Indeed the very language of "intermediate associations" already betrays liberal presuppositions that distorts the moral reality of such institutions as the family. For whatever else the family is it is not another voluntary association. The very means used to insure that the democratic state be a "limited state"—namely the rights of the individual—turn out to be no less destructive for "intermediate institutions" than the monistic state of Marxism. For it is the strategy of liberalism to insure the existence of the "autonomy of cultural and economic life" by insuring the freedom of the individual. But ironically that strategy results in the undermining of "intermediate associations" because they are now understood only as those arbitrary institutions sustained by the private desires of individuals.

What "Christianity and Democracy" fails to note is that the modern bureaucratic states, American and Soviet, are both creatures, to be sure in many ways quite different creatures, of liberalism. It is now an old, but still compelling, insight that the irony of the American conservative is that the social policies they support in the name of the freedom of the individual necessarily result in the growth of the state. The state becomes the only means we have to perform those functions that liberal values and strategies destroy. There is therefore a kind of monism working its way out in America. Though it is less immediately coercive than that of the Soviet Union, it is the monism of the freedom of the individual. The Russian lives in a social system that claims to achieve freedom by falsely investing all authority in the power of the Party; the American lives in a social system that tries to insure freedom by trying to insure that each individual can be his or her own tyrant.

Yet even if that is the case I am still willing to say that on a relative basis I prefer America to the Soviet Union. Such a preference partly has to do with my appreciation of the cultural heritage of each society. For part of the virtues of America derive from the inheritance of social and moral presuppositions from the past that have successfully qualified some of the excesses of pure liberalism. Of course the Soviet Union also contains anomalies that cannot be accounted for in terms of straight Marxist theory that no doubt make such a society livable. However, I cannot deny that, as a Christian, I am thankful that God has seen fit to confront me with the peculiar sorts of challenges we call America. However, such a judgment may well say more about the limits of my appropriation of Christian convictions than it does about the relative merits of America and the Soviet Union.

However, my refusal to support "Christianity and Democracy" is not based on what I take to be its deficient account of democracy as a social system. A deficiency, I might add, that I think was also characteristic of Niebuhr's often extraordinarily vague account of democracy. Nor is my disagreement based on the rather restrained approval given to market economics, though I think many theoretical and empirical questions involved in that approval require more justification than was given. The attempt to justify market economies because they are good for democracies surely must deal with the challenge to that assumption developed by C. B. Macpherson. For Macpherson has mounted a strong historical and theoretical argument that democracy as a society for the enhancement of people's developmental powers was essentially transformed and distorted by the growth of market economies that legitimated the extractive power of property in the name of insuring the freedom of the individual.[4]

Rather my disagreement with "Christianity and Democracy" results from its failure to understand that a state that is democratic nonetheless remains a state that if given the opportunity will be anything but limited. Indeed I fear that the theological legitimation given to democracy, and in particular American democracy, by Neuhaus' document fails badly to meet the challenge of our current situation. For that legitimation fails to supply us with the discriminating moral and intellectual skills we need to recognize when the state, and in particular the democratic state, has become less than limited. There is no state we should fear more than the one that claims to be "limited."

When you begin by defining democracy as limited you therefore lose the necessary critical purchase needed to recognize that democratic states, whatever their relative virtues, are nonetheless states. Or put differently, the problem with the claim that "democratic government is limited government" is far too formal. We have no idea what empirical marks in fact indicate when the state may have overreached the limits. Democracies after all can be just as tyrannical in their claims on the loyalties of their citizens as totalitarian alternatives. Indeed the tyranny may be all the more perverse because we have freely given the state the right to command our conscience.

The misleading description of the democratic state as limited is but the other side of the equally formal claim that the first task of the church is to be the church. For apart from a sense of the church as necessarily inclusive we are not provided with a compelling account of the empirical form such a church should take. To be sure the church is seen as the community that bears the message that every "early sovereignty is subordinate to the sovereignty of Jesus Christ," but we lack any clear sense what the empirical correlative of that affirmation might be if the church is to make that message a concrete challenge to the powers that be. The church, we are told, should maintain a "critical distance" from all kingdoms of this world, but we have little idea of what basis and how that critical distance should be embodied. Instead "Christianity and

Democracy" is so concerned to justify Christian support for liberal democratic regimes against the totalitarian alternative it seems to imply that democracies, and in particular American democracy, have a special relation to God's kingdom in a manner that the necessity of that "critical distance" has been qualified. It thus provides us with a Lutheran justification of the limits of the political and yet maintains a Calvinist sense that God's will for the development of human freedom is to be found in the American experiment.[5]

The church may well be free to preach the gospel in America, but that by no means insures that the state that is allowing the church to so preach is a "limited state." After all Hitler never prevented the church from worshiping freely. Indeed in many ways the church was given special privilege in Nazi Germany, but such privilege did not make it freer. It is perhaps correct that regimes should be judged by their willingness to allow for the freedom of the church to worship and preach the gospel—to let the church be the church—but it makes a good deal of difference what kind of church and what kind of preaching it is that is allowed to be so free.

I simply do not believe that the "guaranteed right of the freedom of the church" insured by democracies in itself should lead us to think that democratic societies and states by being democratic are any less omnivorous in their appetites for our loyalties than non-democratic states. Indeed exactly because we assume that democracies protect our freedoms as Christians we may well miss the ways the democratic state remains a state that continues to wear the head of the beast. For example, democratic societies and states, no less than totalitarian ones, reserve the right to command our conscience to take up arms and kill not only other human beings but other Christians in the name of relative moral goods. In the absence of this kind of concrete criteria of what Christian convictions entail, I do not see how "Christianity and Democracy" helps us know when and how to recognize the subtle ways that democratic states tempt us to lead less than free lives as Christians.

It may be objected that pacifism is a far too stringent criterion as no state can meet or ought to be able to meet that standard. But if that is the case, then I must ask those who would serve "limited states" in the name of relative goods where their loyalty to God's kingdom might in some decisive way qualify that service. For as "Christianity and Democracy" points out "as a universal community, the Church witnesses to the limits of the national and ideological loyalties that divide mankind. Communal allegiance to Christ and his Kingdom is the indispensable check upon the pretentions of the modern state. Because Christ is Lord, Caesar is not Lord. By humbling all secular claims to sovereignty, the Church makes its most important political contribution by being, fully and unapologetically, the Church." Yet it seems that universality should be qualified in the name of our service to democratic nation states as we can be called on to kill Christians from totalitarian states in the name of the relative goods of our "open societies." But then in what sense is the Church our first loyalty? Or, what kind of unity is it that would have us eat at the same table to which we have been invited by a crucified savior only to be told at the end of the meal that the peace of that table does not mean we cannot kill one another for the goods of the nations in which we find ourselves living?

I do not see how loyalty to democracy in this sense is any less tyrannical. Rather it suggests that the democratic state is no less a state and it will respect the "freedom" of the church only to the extent that it can count on that "freedom" to underwrite its ends as a nation that knows not that Christ is in fact Lord. This is particularly the case when we legitimate, as "Christianity and Democracy" does, the assumption that it is the church's task to choose sides between the totalitarian and non-totalitarian states. Once we are told we must choose sides in this manner then I do not see in what sense democracy remains a limited loyalty on the Christian's conscience. For democracy has in fact become an end in itself that captures our souls in subtle ways we hardly notice. We thus stand ready to kill in order to preserve America against her enemies—enemies who are necessarily defined as totalitarian and thus anti-Christian. And yet we persist in thinking we belong to a church that is free so that it can recognize and resist the power of the beast. We thus fail to see that such a church has in fact become a captive to and in America.

In fact I think it is simply incorrect to claim that the overriding conflict of our century is between totalitarian and democratic social systems. That was certainly Reinhold Niebuhr's view of the matter as his vision was determined by the Cold War strategies following World War II. But I do not see how it is possible even on empirical grounds to sustain that vision of our international situation. There are too many other actors on the world stage to so easily character- ize our current international situation. To be sure many developing nations are oppressive, but certainly the category "totalitarian" is insufficient to characterize the many different forms of societies and governments that are aborning in our world—many of which are American allies and clients. I suspect the great challenge of the church is to learn to exist in these newly developing societies without imposing on them the habits of mind that have too long been nur- tured at the knee of societies that learned too well how to co-opt the church to their purposes in the name of freedom.

The overriding conflict of our time is not that between democra- cies and totalitarianism, not between those who are for human freedom and those that seek to repress it. Rather the overriding conflict of our time is the same as that from the beginning for it is the conflict between those that would remain loyal to God's king- dom and those that would side with the world. And the world is exactly those people and institutions claiming that Christians too must be willing to choose sides and kill in order to preserve the social orders in which they find themselves. As Christians when we accept that alternative it surely means that we are no longer the church that witnesses to God's sovereignty over all nations, but instead we have become part of the world.

That I reject "Christianity and Democracy" 's analysis of our situation and alternatives does not mean I wish to deny that there is a linkage between Christian faith and human freedom. But it does mean, I suspect, that I have quite a different understanding of the nature and status of freedom. As Christians we seek not to be free, but to be faithful disciples of our Lord who would not employ violence to avoid death at the hands of a state. Just as that oppressive regime could not prevent his authorization of God's kingdom so neither as Christians do we believe any worldly power can stop us from living true to God's peaceable kingdom. It is of course true that they can kill us, but they cannot rob our death, any more than they could rob Jesus' death, from its service to God.[6] In that lies our freedom to see the world as it is rather than as it would like to be seen. In that commitment lies the possibility of the church to be a "zone of truth-telling in a world of mendacity." For nowhere is that lie more powerful than when it takes the form of the nation state which tries to make us believe that God's kingdom depends on the false ideals that it promises to secure through coercion and violence.

So by all means let the church be the church. But let us remind ourselves that it is not first of all a strategy for insuring the existence of the limited state. Rather the call for the church to be the church means that the church is the only true polity we can know in this life. For the church, because it is a polity that fears not the truth, is also a community that has the courage to form its citizens virtuously. Thus the challenge before us is to be a patient and hopeful people who are able to live truthfully between the times. Only by being such a people will we be able to resist the false choices—such as choosing between America and the Soviet Union—that would have us take sides in a manner that divides the Christian people from each other and their true Lord.

Notes

1. Richard Neuhaus, "Christianity and Democracy: A Statement of the Institute on Religion and Democracy," *Center Journal*, 1, 3 (Summer, 1982), 9–25.
2. All these are phrases from "Christianity and Democracy." Though this essay is a response to "Christianity and Democracy," I think the reader will be able to follow my remarks without being familiar with Neuhaus' text. However I urge the reading of "Christianity and Democracy" not only to test the fairness of my interpretation but because Neuhaus has said explicitly what many continue to assume without defense.
3. Though this claim needs much more adequate defense I think it is right. "Christianity" as a belief system was important to Niebuhr, but the church as a significant social alternative simply did not play a methodologically significant role in his conception of Christian ethics. Though often seen as a critic of Western presumption there was a side of Niebuhr that was extremely world affirming. Indeed he could speak in *The Nature and Destiny of Man, II* (New York: Scribner and Sons, 1949) of the task "of reorienting the culture of our day" (205). The very structure of *The Nature and Destiny of Man* is meant to show how there can be a synthesis of "Biblical religion" and the Renaissance to sustain such a "reorientation."
4. C. B. Macpherson, *Democratic Theory: Essays in Retrieval* (Oxford: Clarendon Press, 1973), 120–42.
5. This same kind of tension is manifest in Richard Neuhaus' most recent book, *The Naked Public Square: Religion and Democracy in America* (Grand Rapids: Eerdmans, 1984). In this book Neuhaus is willing to use the phrase "Christian America" which certainly seems to go beyond a Lutheran justification of the limits of the political realm.
6. I suspect the most compelling sense of what it means to be victimized is when a person is made to die in a manner that makes that death impossible to claim as their own. Christians' ultimate power is to be a people who refuse to let the world determine the meaning of our death. Such power requires the existence of a community which has the capacity to remember those who have died rather than betray that faith.

8. ON SURVIVING JUSTLY: ETHICS AND NUCLEAR DISARMAMENT

Beginning with the End

I am going to begin by telling you how the analysis that constitutes the main portion of this chapter comes out—that is, I am going to begin with the end. My conclusion is that culturally we lack a coherent morality to sustain the current antinuclear enthusiasm on the part of many. By typifying and analyzing what I take to be the four main moral positions underlying the antinuclear movement—that is, the pacifist, just war, survivalist, and sovereign-states deterrence—I will try to support this conclusion.

In another, more substantive sense, I am going to begin with the end. For I want to show that the challenge of nuclear weapons involves theological issues that require a theological response—a response, however, that our culture lacks the resources to develop. In particular I will contend that the ethical confusion underlying the proposals for nuclear disarmament is at least partly due to false eschatologies. Put differently, the peace sought by many is too often equivalent to order while lacking a sufficient sense of what a just peace entails.[1] For a peace based on insufficient eschatology cannot help but be an abstract ideal that lacks concrete embodiment in the lives and habits of an actual community. Moreover without such a community our strategies for nuclear disarmament as well as the moral resources on which they draw cannot help but offer short term solutions and false consolation.

Before I begin analyzing the four moral positions, I need to make two general points. The first is to remind you that they are types—that is, they are ideal characterizations that may fail to depict accurately the complexity of any actual position. For example, my last two types—the survivalist and sovereign-state deterrence—can both be interpreted as forms of just war logic since each is a way to work out the criteria of proportionality. The differences I locate between these types are more a matter of classifying different kinds of rhetorical appeal than strict logic.[2] Yet I hope to show that such differences are illuminating as they represent significant moral and strategic alternatives.

Second, the analysis I offer necessarily involves moral and strategic considerations not easily separated. Any one moral position may have several strategic alternatives, but it is just as likely that agreement on strategic alternatives may mask deep moral differences. That such is the case means that the analysis I provide oversimplifies at some points. However, I hope the attempt to locate the complex relation between moral and strategic considerations will compensate for this obvious problem.

There is a more profound problem with the task I have set for myself in this chapter. Why bother trying to make explicit the various ethical positions underwriting the antinuclear movement since no more is claimed by the participants in that movement than that they are a political coalition? They do not presuppose that they share a common moral position nor do they need one to sustain the movement. But I think such a response is insufficient since the diverse ethical commitments are by no means compatible. Unless our differences are uncovered, moreover, the movement risks losing its power once it is no longer able to command the attention of the media.

But this puts me in a rather odd position, especially since I am a pacifist. For it almost seems immoral to do what I propose as it may have the result of making the political task of disarmament more difficult. My only defense is to retreat to the questionable assumption that the unexamined life is not worth living. But let us not forget the classical words of Peter Devries, "The unexamined life may not be worth living, but the examined life is no bowl of cherries either."

Pacifism

I will not discuss the pacifist responses to nuclear disarmament at any length since pacifism, at least in principle, does not make any particular claims about nuclear war that it does not make about any war—except that if war is bad, nuclear war is worse. Pacifism needs to be discussed briefly, however, as a necessary backdrop for helping us understand the logic of the just war position and how the latter differs from survivalism. By pacifism, which obviously has many different forms and types, I mean any position that involves the disavowal of violence as a means to secure otherwise legitimate ends.

The pacifist claims the issue raised by nuclear weapons is not one of being killed but of unjust killing. For example, as Ed Laarman has suggested,

> For Christians, the first issue raised by nuclear or any other kind of war should not be, "Am I ready to die?" but "Am I ready to kill?" Christians in the United States should be more troubled by American missiles pointed at the Soviet Union than by Soviet missiles pointed at them. While this may be existentially hard to achieve, it is clearly required by our confession. As Christians, we believe that it is more important for us to be faithful to God the Father and our Lord Jesus Christ than it is simply to survive. The central question for Christian citizens in this instance is whether the use and possession of nuclear weapons is consistent with our Christian commitment.[3]

Though pacifist and just war positions are often seen as opposites, they share the assumption that the first question about violence is whether or how I should be ready to kill. Moreover the just war perspective, like that of the pacifist, places the burden of proof on those who would take up violence, rather than those who would refrain from it. As a result, the pacifist and just war positions have a "moralistic" cast that the other two positions lack. Both the pacifist and just war advocate approach these issues already armed with certain moral presuppositions that challenge the resort to violence. The question of the legitimacy and use of nuclear weapons is thus answered by determining the degree to which they conform to predetermined moral presuppositions. The significance of this will be most clearly seen once the just war position is contrasted with that of sovereign-states deterrence.

Before leaving the pacifist option, however, I need to qualify my claim that the pacifists have nothing particular to say about nuclear warfare that they do not also say about any warfare. There are some pacifists who justify their position in consequential terms, calling attention to the bad results of violence. Undoubtedly they could make their case more strongly with reference to nuclear war. Pacifists of this sort might share presuppositions with the survivalist inasmuch as the latter has a stake in showing that nuclear warfare, unlike other forms of war, threatens the very existence of the human species. Viewed in this way war becomes the ultimate form of irrationality.

A pacifism of a more theological sort—for example, a pacifism based on the conviction that any resort to violence betrays one's relation to God even if it otherwise might have good results—makes no particular judgment against nuclear warfare that is not an extension of the general negative judgment about all violence. That such is the case, moreover, reminds us that it makes a difference how and what kind of religious convictions are used to inform the various typological positions I have isolated. For example, while they share a certain approach to the question, the pacifist is more likely to make more direct theological appeals than the advocates of just war positions. In the hopes of commanding the conscience of many, the latter has a stake in justifying his or her position in terms of appeal to some account of natural law. In contrast, the survivalist tends toward apocalyptic appeals though such appeals do not necessarily require theological presuppositions. The sovereign-states deterrent advocates, as we shall see, share a natural affinity with various forms of Augustinianism and/or realism.

Just War and the Limits of Nuclear War

My partial treatment of the just war position in relation to pacifism already suggests its complexity. Contrary to the assumed or asserted clarity of the just war criteria, complex questions concerning the status and content of the just war position remain outstanding. On the surface the just war position appears straightforward enough. For example, we have become used to characterizing the criteria of the just war as: (1) declared by a legitimate authority; (2) has a just cause; (3) that there be a reasonable hope of success; (4) proportionally more good than evil comes from the war; (5) the war be fought

with a just intention; (6) noncombatant immunity; (7) the object is
not to kill the enemy but to incapacitate them, therefore prisoners of
war are treated respectfully; and (8) unnecessary suffering is
avoided.[4]

But this simple list is deceptive because each of these "criteria" is
ambiguous. What is legitimate authority? What does it mean to
"declare" war and how do we distinguish "defensive" from "offensive" wars? Who are noncombatants in the age of democracies? Do
all the criteria have to be met to make a war just or only some of
them? If the latter, which ones? Is there a lexical order among the
criteria and if so what is its basis? And why these criteria and not
others? Where did these come from and from what paradigm of
legitimate violence do they draw their justification? For example, is
the just war position developed from a paradigm of self-defense or
from one of defense of the innocent?[5] (Interestingly this also has
implications for the theological appeals required since the latter
paradigm is more likely to require special theological assumptions
not thought necessary for self-defense. But then the latter may well
involve assumptions about the status of survival not easily reconciled
with some of Jesus' teaching concerning the secondary status of
regard for self.)

Even more important than these questions is the status given to
the just war position. The questions raised in the last paragraph are
overly formal if the just war position is interpreted not as a deductive
set of rules, but rather as an ongoing discussion of a civilization
which limits the extent of the destruction caused by wars. From this
latter perspective, the just war is more appropriately described as a
tradition that can be expressed only as a theory if, as James Johnson
insists, "care is taken to express this theory generally and with a
degree of open-endedness. That is, room must be left for particular
interpretations of the general provisions of the theory and for development of its ideas to cope with new experiences of reality."[6]

When just war is understood in this fashion nuclear weapons are
not automatically ruled out simply because they seem to violate the
principle of noncombatant immunity. Since the purpose of just war
thinking is not to determine in a legalistic manner what is or what is
not a just war, but rather to make war as nearly just as it can be,

there is no clear distinction that can be drawn between just and unjust weapons. Again, as Johnson reminds us,

> Moral values are perceived by individuals and cultures in the encounter with history, and persistence of the ideas of noncombatant immunity and the authority to initiate war over so long a time argues as strongly as possible that these represent deeply held values in Western culture. The weakness of weapons limitation is that it does not draw directly on some such deeply held value, but rather proceeds indirectly from others; for example one way to protect noncombatants is by restricting weapons used in the presence of noncombatants to those most capable of being used discriminatingly against combatants. Weapons limits represent a means, not an end; the categories of noncombatant immunity and right authority instead point to ends perceived as valuable by Western culture generally.[7]

Thus the often made, but seldom analyzed, claim that nuclear weapons have made just war thinking irrelevant fails adequately to understand the purpose of just war thought. On the contrary, it has made such thinking all the more relevant. By drawing on the just war tradition we are forced to find and develop ways to conduct even nuclear warfare less unjustly—e.g., the development of the neutron bomb.[8] For again, as Johnson reminds us,

> There is a kind of implicit impetus in the just war tradition to conceive of strategies and tactics, to invent and deploy weapons that are less massively destructive of persons and their values than those already at hand. It is thus, for example, an implication of just war tradition that an alternative should be found to tactical nuclear weapons intended for use against land forces. Use of such weapons besides risking escalation to a general nuclear interchange, would cause immediate and long-term damage to noncombatants that is hard or impossible to justify.[9]

Interesting as these issues are for an interpretation of the just war position, for my purposes it is more important to locate the moral logic underlying the just war tradition. As I have already noted, just war thinking necessarily draws on pacifist presuppositions for its rationale—that those who resort to violence bear the burden of proof. Equally important is how that proof is supplied, for it is not prima facie evident that the justification for the resort to violence does or should draw on the alleged "right to self-defense." Indeed, there is evidence that the strongest accounts of just war thinking are based on the duty to aid the innocent. From this perspective it can be seen that morally the just war tradition is first of all much more a matter of social theory about legitimate authority than simply a casuistical attempt to justify the use of violence to protect one's own person.

Thus Paul Ramsey calls attention to the fact that Augustine refused to justify Christian participation in war on grounds of self-defense. Since it is better to suffer evil than to do it, Christians must be personally ready to die rather than defend themselves if such defense requires that the aggressor be killed. Here the rationale for the just war is not self-defense, but defense of the innocent. Consistently Ramsey argues that such a defense of the innocent must be made impersonal through the office of the state.[10] Such impersonality is exactly what allows the limited form of response since the state has reason, and indeed is required, to use no more force than is necessary to prevent the attacker from destroying the innocent. Indeed it may be one of the most important insights of the just war position to limit the right to make war to but a few "sovereigns," for otherwise we have no way to limit the individual's destructive capacity. This distinction between individual and state makes it possible, at least in principle, for one to be personally a pacifist and yet, in the interest of limiting the violence necessary to protect the innocent, support a state policy of just war.[11]

So one might well offer a defense of certain forms of nuclear strategies on the grounds that the state has a duty to those it is pledged to defend when threatened by the nuclear weapons of the other side. Of course such a defense would require these strategies be shaped as much as possible by a commitment in accordance with just war thinking. However, when such a commitment significantly affects policy making, it often encounters new difficulties. For example, a discriminating nuclear strategy might well require that our nuclear weapons be counter-force targeted rather than counter-city. The problem with that strategy, however, is it increases the likelihood of nuclear war since it tempts the other side to think that they might be able to wage nuclear war in which they might be a relative "winner."

But perhaps such difficulties, and the objections they encourage to just war theories, fail to do justice to the moral integrity of the just war position. For remember that just war logic, at least as I have depicted it, does not draw on survival as an overriding value to justify its logic. It assumes neither the survival of the individual nor the nation as an end in itself. Survival must be subordinated to the moral obligation to protect the innocent, of which the nation is only the means. Thus it might be possible to develop a just war nuclear strategy—for example, a counter-force targeting—that increases the danger of nuclear war, but that is not in itself a decisive moral consideration for those committed to a just war tradition. For it is inherent in their position that war must be subject to political ends beyond survival. As we shall see, therefore, just war thinkers share the concern with sovereign-state deterrence advocates to subject the nuclear buildup to rational political objectives.[12]

The integrity of the moral logic of the just war position in this respect seems to me unassailable. What must be asked, however, is whether it is capable of commanding the necessary political support. For in an interesting way once the implications of the just war position are spelled out the possibility of a society sustaining the moral ethos necessary to support such a war seems as unlikely and utopian as a nation taking a pacifist stance. For example, are the American people ready to support a nuclear policy that is more nearly just if that means destabilizing a system of mutually assured destruction in a manner that increases the likelihood of nuclear war? The commitment necessary for a nation to sustain a just war strategy is almost as demanding as that necessary to sustain a consistent pacifism.

Returning to those who interpret the just war position in a more formal manner, they are not without resources when it comes to the issue of nuclear war. Even if they judge that nuclear weapons are inherently indiscriminate, they might still argue that such arms can be possessed as a bluff and thus serve as a deterrent. The bluff position assumes it is immoral to use nuclear weapons; yet it allows us to possess those weapons as a threat against the enemy provided we have no intention of ever carrying it out. Indeed, even if we are attacked, we must resolve not to return in kind. The only proviso is that the enemy must remain uncertain whether we are bluffing or not.

One problem with such a strategy is that the enemy must be unsure whether you are really so moral you would not return in kind. Indeed the resolution not to use our weapons requires the leader of a just war nation to act as if he or she is not bluffing. But such a position confuses our professed commitment to democratic polity since citizens cannot know if their leaders are or are not willing to refrain from using these weapons. Thus such a strategy by its very nature excludes the possibility of public debate necessary to sustain a just war strategy.[18]

The final problem with the bluff position, or the possession-but-no-use strategy, is it does nothing to help stabilize, and may even make more unstable, our current weapons balance. In order to sustain a peace based on the existence of our ability to annihilate one another, we are constantly forced to counter the supposed strength of the other side. But since we are never sure how the strength of the other side should compare to ours, we are in the position of having to add to the nuclear arsenal in the hope of finding a position from which we can begin to disarm ourselves. But if we ever approached such a position (e.g., if we knew how to develop an unfailing laser defense system), it would only contribute to the danger since the other side could never let such a system be deployed. And so it goes . . .

The Survivalist

In contrast to pacifists and the just war advocates, the survivalists do not begin with an established theory about if and when life can be taken justly. Rather survivalists are so impressed with the destructive power of nuclear weapons and a sense of horror with the prospect of their use they conclude nuclear war must be excluded at all costs. Their concern is not whether nuclear weapons can be used in a discriminating manner, but whether the very existence of such weapons does not threaten the existence of the human species. It is extremely important that we understand why the issue of human survival is so central for them.

The survivalists do not begin with any commitment to pacifism. They, at least in principle, assume and accept the possibility of conventional war (though as we shall see they think nuclear war has now made that impossible). But if one accepts war as a possible means to settle disputes among nations, then why single out nuclear weapons as particularly wrong? Are they not but another stage, admittedly an extraordinary stage, in mankind's attempt to secure weapons of war that are effective? Hence survivalists must show the essential discontinuity between conventional and nuclear weapons. They do so by condemning nuclear weapons not because they cannot be used in a discriminating manner but because they threaten the existence of the globe. So survivalists have an interest in maintaining that nuclear war will be total war since otherwise they would have no basis for singling out nuclear weapons as deserving particular condemnation.

Jonathan Schell has developed this position well in his *The Fate of the Earth*. After a painstaking analysis of the unimaginable destructive power of nuclear weapons, he concludes:

Bearing in mind that the possible consequences of the detonations of thousands of megatons of nuclear explosives include the blinding of insects, birds, and beasts all over the world; the extinction of many ocean species, among them some at the base of the food chain; the temporary or permanent alteration of the climate of the globe, with the outside chance of "dramatic" and "major" alteration in the structure of the atmosphere; the pollution of the whole ecosphere with oxides of nitrogen; the incapacitation in ten minutes of unprotected people who go out into the sunlight; the blinding of people who go out into the sunlight; a significant decrease in photosynthesis in plants around the world; the scalding and killing of many crops; the increase in rates of cancer and mutation around the world, but especially in targeted zones, and the attendant risk of global epidemics; the possible poisoning of all vertebrates by sharply increased levels of Vitamin D in their skin as a result of increased ultraviolet light; and the outright slaughter on all targeted continents of most human beings and other living things by the initial nuclear radiation, the fireballs, the thermal pulses, the blast waves, the mass fires, and the fallout from the explosions; and considering that these consequences will all interact with one another in unguessable ways and, further- more, are in all likelihood an incomplete list, which will be added to as our knowledge of the earth increases, one must conclude that a full-scale nuclear holocaust could lead to the extinction of mankind.[14]

Of course this is the worst-possible-case scenario, but Schell argues that we have no reason to think that a nuclear exchange once begun would lead to any other results. And in the absence of any knowl- edge to the contrary it is immoral to continue to possess such weapons.

But why is it immoral? According to Schell it is because "we have no right to place the possibility of this limitless, eternal defeat on the same footing as risks that we run in the ordinary conduct of our affairs in our particular transient moments of human history."[15] We have no right to prevent the possibility of a common world which encompasses our past, present, and future. And it is just that world which is the source of all value. The creation of "a common world is the use that we human beings, and we alone among the earth's creatures, have made of the biological circumstances that, while each of us is mortal, our species is biologically immortal. In fact, it is only because humanity has built up a common world that we can fear our destruction as a species."[16] And such destruction is unthink- able for "there are no ethics apart from service to the human com- munity, and therefore no ethical commandments that can justify the extinction of humanity."[17] Therefore the question the peril of extinc- tion puts before the living is: "Who would miss human life if they extinguished it? To which the only honest answer is: Nobody."[18] That very fact is enough to sustain the judgment that nuclear weapons must be eliminated because anything that threatens the very value of value itself is inherently immoral.

But it is not sufficient to eliminate nuclear weapons, according to Schell, for their existence has in fact brought an end to war itself. With "the invention of nuclear weapons, it became impossible for violence to be fashioned into war, or to achieve what war used to achieve. Violence can no longer break down the opposition of the adversary; it can no longer produce a victory and defeat; it can no longer attain its ends. It can no longer be war."[19] As if this were not enough, Schell argues further that nuclear weapons have not only ended the possibility of war, but war's necessary correlative, the nation-state. For there is an insoluble connection between war and sovereignty, and the price we pay for our insistence on dividing ourselves into sovereign states is the peril of extinction.[20]

Thus, those who tell us that we must have nuclear weapons to prevent their use are deceiving themselves and us. We deploy them not for protection, but to protect national sovereignty and, "if this aim were not present, they would be quickly dismantled." Yet to call into question the status of national sovereignty has a further implication, for it means that there is no way we can disarm nuclear weapons without disarming conventionally. Conventional arms continue to insure for some nations the ability to employ the science, which cannot be destroyed, to build nuclear weapons. Through this chain of reasoning Schell reaches the extraordinary conclusion that has become the most quoted passage of this important and widely read book:

> But if we accept both nuclear and conventional disarmament, then we are speaking of revolutionizing the politics of the earth. The task we face is to find a means of political action that will permit human beings to pursue any end for the rest of time. We are asked to replace the mechanism by which political decisions, whatever they may be, are reached. In sum, the task is nothing less than to reinvent politics: to reinvent the world.[21]

As we approach the year 2000 we must expect a good deal of apocalypticism; yet it is a bit surprising when it comes in the pages of the *New Yorker*[22] and in the rhetoric of nuclear terror. For

Schell's depiction of our situation certainly has an apocalyptic tone and his solution, if it can be called that, utopian. But neither his description nor his solution are to be belittled for that. After all, Christians are a people who follow a savior who was clearly apocalyptic and made utopian appeals. Rather the problem with Schell's position is not its apocalyptic tone, but our inability to assess his claims. For his argument against nuclear weapons is valid only if his empirical claim is valid—namely, that the use of nuclear weapons will lead to the destruction of the human species. He may well be right about this, and he certainly provides us with some graphic illustrations of the power of nuclear weapons, but we have no way of knowing whether in fact he is right—at least we can have no way of knowing until it is too late. The moral significance of this point cannot be ignored, for it illustrates what happens when the moral issue raised by nuclear weapons shifts from the problem of discrimination to that of the survival of the human species. (Moreover there is the further problem of knowing whether *all* humans must be destroyed for Schell's case to be made good. One feels a bit like Abraham bargaining with God over Sodom—what about a hundred, ten, etc.)

However, a more profound problem with Schell's apocalyptic account is not that it is apocalyptic, but that it is apocalyptic humanism. It can properly be asked if human survival is the ultimate good, or whether, without humanity, there will be nothing left to value. Certainly there are religious traditions that can respond with a resounding yes when asked if there will be anyone to value anything if mankind is destroyed. Moreover the survival of the human species as an end in itself has moral implications about the relation of humanity to the animal world that certainly needs to be analyzed if not questioned. Schell simply does not tell us why we should make morally normative the philosophically questionable, but scientifically useful, designation of "species."

Schell's reliance on the status of the human species as the determinative moral factor reveals the deep gulf between himself and pacifism and the just war position. The latter assume that, even if it threatens the very survival of the human species, one must not do evil that good may come—for example, murder another human being. Such an assumption draws on profound theological convictions about how God would have us care for this creation that constitutes a theocentrism quite different from that of Schell.[23]

It is interesting to note that Schell does appeal to the example of Christ in support of his views. He tells us Christ stated that

> religious faith that is divorced from the love of human beings is empty and dangerous. For example, He said, "If thou bring thy gift to the altar, and there rememberest that thy brother has aught against thee; leave there thy gift before the altar, and go thy way; first be reconciled to thy brother, and then come and offer thy gift." We who have planned out the deaths of hundreds of millions of our brothers plainly have a great deal of work to do before we return to the altar. Certainly, the corpse of mankind would be the least acceptable of all conceivable offerings on the altar of this God.[24]

But would it? It is surely correct to say the murder of the human species would hardly please God, but that is not to say that our death, indeed the death of the human species itself, would deny his ultimate love for us. Schell's humane concerns can cause us to ignore that he subordinates to survival all other values that we think make our living and our dying worthwhile.

The significance of this point is nicely displayed by Paul Ramsey's argument in *War and the Christian Conscience* against Arnold Toynbee and others who had suggested it would be better to negotiate with the Soviets from a position of weakness than to continue to risk nuclear annihilation. In response Ramsey reminds us that as Christians we always know the world will end, and "knowledge of an end by nuclear destruction in twenty-four hours has no more inherent power to render present life meaningless than does an end for natural cosmic reasons two billion years from now. Liberty and justice can only be preserved by forces which today can be used only at the risk of vastly destructive nuclear war."[25] Moreover, we must take that risk, for, according to Ramsey, "On their way to the heavenly city, the children of God make use of *pax-ordo* of the earthly city and acknowledge their share in responsibility for its preservation."[26] Because Christians have their hope in the heavenly city they need not adopt a nuclear pacifism based on fear or death, even the death of the human species. In his *Just War* Ramsey further suggests that because our secular age no longer has the confidence that we have an ultimate destiny, wars have become more danger- ous. We spiritualize our politics; that is, we make absurd claims that wars can be fought for peace, and as a result increase the terror of war. Indeed we must recognize that coercion is the mother's milk of this earthly order and that any justice achieved will not eliminate but depend on this fact. Thus we will be more able to discipline our warfare once we recognize that wars can only be pursued to secure a relative balance of violence that allows for some justice.[27]

Finally Schell's position has been criticized because of his utopi- anism. Theodore Draper says,

> This [Schell's book] is a travesty on thinking about nuclear war. It is also the most depressing and defeatest cure-all that has ever been offered. If we have to "reinvent the world" to control nuclear war, the chances of saving the human race must be somewhere near the vanishing point. Deterrence is child's play compared with what Schell demands of us. His prescription is a disguised counsel of despair. It gives up the struggle against nuclear war in the world as it is in favor of chanting and shouting for a world that does not exist. Utopians are like that: they hold out the vision of a feast to starving people who are never permitted to eat any of it.[28]

Schell, in *The Fate of the Earth,* is certainly utopian, but that does not mean he is wrong. At the very least it seems to me he has helped us to locate some of the fundamental ethical issues entailed by calls for nuclear disarmament. The morality of nuclear deter- rence does raise profound theological issues concerning the status of humanity and the status of our moral commitments that cannot, as Schell has shown, be avoided. If we are to disarm, and disarm justly, it may well mean that we will have to take larger risks than Schell is willing to envision. The peace we pursue must not be any peace, but a peace based on truth and justice. The problem with Schell's utopi- anism is not that it is utopian but that the peace he envisions may not be just.

Sovereign-States Deterrence

The position I here call sovereign-states deterrence seems at first to be the exact opposite of Schell's. It has little or no use for his moral fervor. Indeed many of the advocates of this position deny all moral commitments. They disavow all moral claims since they assume that we must begin thinking about the nuclear situation not as it should be but as it is. They thus pride themselves on being "realistic" rather than allowing their thinking to be clouded with legalistic distinctions between killing and murder, or sentimental concerns about the "fate of the earth."[29]

What is often overlooked both by advocates and critics of sovereign-states deterrence is that their disavowal of morality involves substantial moral conviction. For their "realism" is based on the assumption that we do better to face limits and try with humility and imagination to do the best we can within those limits. For them, the fundamental limit that we must accept for thinking about war, and in particular nuclear war, is the nation-state system. For all its obvious failures, the nation-state system provides the best means we have for securing a relatively just international order. Advocates of this type do not assume that individual nations themselves are just, but rather that the nation-state system is the best means we have to secure what justice and peace are possible in this world. Such justice and peace no doubt will always be less than the idealist desires; nevertheless it is better than the violence legitimated by those who would have us kill in the illusion of eradicating war from our lives.

Fundamental to the sovereign-states deterrence position is the rejection of what Michael Howard, in his brilliant book, *War and the Liberal Conscience,* has described as the liberal theory for wars.[30] According to Howard, the liberal conscience, which began as early as Erasmus, simply refused to accept war as a rational endeavor. Impressed by the horror of war, the liberals assume that war was the result of some hidden conspiracy or intellectual or moral failure that could be corrected. Interestingly the various reasons the liberals gave for the existence of war and the strategies they suggested for its elimination are employed by those who currently call for the reduction, if not elimination, of nuclear weapons.

For example, Howard suggests that liberals allege wars "occurred because they were a way of life among a militarized aristocratic ruling class and would die out when this was replaced by what St. Simon called *les industrieux*."[31] Hence, war could only be eliminated when republican and democratic principles were extended to all the nations, or at least to the nations of Europe. But exactly the opposite took place, for the rise of democracy went hand in hand with the rise of the violence in war. Ironically, authoritarian regimes have greater freedom to fight limited wars since they do not need to use ideals to convince a reluctant populace that they should support and fight for something from which they would receive little personal benefit. The modern scale of war, and perhaps the modern scale of weaponry, are correlative to our democratic convictions and institutions.

Another liberal theory was that if wars did not result from aristocratic habit, they must be the result of vested interests, the distorted perceptions of a governing class and their capitalist interest—particularly arms manufacturers. But this theory seems not to hold up when twentieth-century war is considered. It remains a matter of debate to what extent it may be the case with regard to the advanced weapons systems of today. Yet as we shall see, one of the main interests of advocates of sovereign-states deterrence is to subject economic and technological interest in weapon development to political control.[32]

Finally, liberals blamed the diplomats and their manipulation of the balance of power for the existence of war. Now certainly it is the case that clumsy diplomacy and ruthless power-politics can result in wars, but what the liberal has ignored, according to Howard, is that power-politics are the politics of not being overpowered. Indeed, many liberals were prepared to fight wars of self-defense, but it is the business of the diplomat to make it unnecessary to fight such wars, or to insure that

> . . . if they do come, their country should not be confronted by a coalition so overwhelming, and be left so bereft of help, that it fights in a hopeless cause. To transcend this necessity and create a genuine world system of collective security has

been the aim of liberal statesmen throughout this century. But such a system demands a degree of mutual confidence, a homogeneity of values and a coincidence of perceived interests such as did not exist even in the limited society of inner-war Europe. We are a long way from creating it in the culturally heterogeneous world we inhabit today.[33]

Underlying the liberal search for the cause of war from the perspective of sovereign-state advocates is a fundamentally mistaken assumption—that war is irrational. According to Howard, what the liberal has failed to see, and I take this to be the essential assumption of the sovereign-states deterrence advocates, is that

War is an inherent element in a system of sovereign states which lacks any supreme and acknowledged arbiter; and the more genuinely those states by reason of their democratic structure embody indigenous and peculiar cultural values and perceptions, the less likely are they to sacrifice that element of sovereignty which carries with it the decision, if necessary to use force to protect their interest. To this extent surely Mazzini was right: in order to have internationalism, one must first create nations; and those peoples who have already achieved cultural self-consciousness and political independence can all too easily forget the claims of those who have not. Where Mazzini and his imitators were at fault was in assuming that, because the creation of nation states was a necessary condition for peace, it would also be a sufficient one.[34]

At the root of the liberal thinkers' confusion about war, Howard argues, lies the habit of seeing war as a distinct and abstract entity. "War is simply the generic term for the use of armed force by states or aspirants to statehood for the attainment of their political objectives."[35] Thus from the perspective of sovereign-states deterrence, war is not something we should seek to eliminate, but rather is part and parcel of our way of life. The only concern is how it can best be used.

Contrary to Schell, sovereign states advocates hold that nuclear weapons are but one development among others in the continued state of war that exists between nations. Like all weapons, they are created to serve the purpose of advancing our particular nation's ends. Such weapons do exist to preserve a peace of sorts, but it is a "peace" that is the name for the accommodations that at any one time benefit all parties to a lesser and greater extent. Insofar as nuclear weapons serve that end they are not inherently immoral.

From the perspective of the sovereign-states deterrence advocate, we must be smart in our violence. As a result they tend to side with those who would have us subject our nuclear weapons and policies to political ends—that is, we must make them serve purposes and interests. In particular they are concerned that technology is now determining the politics rather than being under the control of a rational foreign policy. This point of view was classically stated by Henry Kissinger in 1974 (although subsequently disavowed) when he said, "What in the name of God is strategic superiority? What is the significance of it politically, militarily, operationally at these levels of numbers? What do you do with it?"[36]

Indeed what bothers advocates of sovereign-states deterrence about the current talk of a policy of a "winnable" nuclear war is that because it has no political purpose, it is extremely dangerous. Winnability, according to Theodore Draper, "presupposes that a nuclear war could go on 'over a protracted period' without unacceptable and uncontrollable destruction of the countries waging it. It assumes that 'favorable terms' would have some human meaning after such a nuclear conflict."[37] For Draper such a scheme has only one saving grace: "it is so grotesque and mindless that it is inconceivable that the American people will not rebel against it and make Congress refuse to accept it."[38]

But then what should be our strategy? According to Draper we must make mutually assured destruction the object of our nuclear policy. Having accepted that we must quit asking, "How much is enough?" Likewise we must stop relying on negotiations to produce reductions.

Negotiations tend to register the progress of the arms race rather than to put an end to it. Any numerical change that leaves intact the ability of each nuclear superpower to destroy the other cannot change the fundamental strategic balance between them; the excess of the nuclear weapons is so great that a ceiling or reduction which does not get below the level of redundancy cannot significantly change the basic character of the problem. Anyone who expects a great power to give up an advantage in negotiations or not to get the best trade possible for it, is already living in Jonathan Schell's reinvented world. Unfortunately, we have only one real world, and it is not hospitable to illusions or fantasies. This way of thinking about nuclear war is a trap for the innocent and a boon to nuclear warriors.[39]

So Draper realistically advocates a policy of deterrence which seeks not to abolish nuclear weapons in the hope we will never have to use them. The crucial point for a deterrence policy is that any level of "nuclear weapons over and above what is necessary to have a devastating effect on the other side is no more than an exercise in redundancy."[40] The question of "Who is ahead" is simply meaningless or, worse, stupid. We do not need more; all we need is enough. The arsenal of nuclear arms should be fixed at some rational level by a calculation of needs of deterrence rather than by competition and rivalry. Such a procedure would free the United States to set its own foreign policy rather than react constantly to the Soviets. Therefore some form of unilateral actions makes all the sense in the world.

As I have already pointed out, while sovereign-states deterrence advocates make no exaggerated moral claims, they are clearly morally motivated. Their attempt to make nuclear policy serve political ends is a moral policy because politics always entails moral assumptions. While sharing some strategies with certain just war positions, sovereign-states deterrence fundamentally differs from them since it sets its nuclear strategy not by prior criteria which determine legitimate violence but by what is good for the sovereign-states system. Thus a sovereign-states deterrence position does not in principle deny the right to have nuclear weapons on grounds of the principle of discrimination; nor does it prevent us from aiming our weapons at civilian populations if this would result in a more stable relation between the two superpowers; nor would the sovereign-state deterrence position require the moral gymnastics of the bluff position for it is certainly committed to the use of the weapons. We threaten, and our threat is real. Indeed, people in charge of our government would be immoral not to use the weapons to prevent an attack or retaliate.

But I suspect at this point we also encounter some of the deepest difficulties in the sovereign-states deterrence position. It is not clear that we are morally prepared as a population to sustain the realism it demands. Put differently, the ability to sustain a just-nation deterrence policy requires the citizens of a nation to view themselves as individuals who must be willing to use nuclear weapons for limited moral ends and purposes, such as preserving the values inherent to the nation-state system. Such a position is certainly coherent, but what the sovereign-states deterrence advocates have failed to do is show us how it can be lived as an ongoing project—that is, as a position requiring the killing of millions—without its destroying any sense of what makes life a morally worthy enterprise.

On a more practical level, the problem with the sovereign-nations deterrence position is that, like the just war position, it is beset with instability. Calculating "deterrence" turns out to be an extraordinarily difficult matter. It certainly helps to ask "What is enough?", but determining that is not simple.[41] For the issue is not simply the destructive weapon itself, but how and where it is to go. Thus we are in the ironical position that weapons and delivery systems that may promise us more security threaten instability and a greater likelihood of nuclear war. What could be more utopian than Draper's assumption that the Pentagon will be open to a significant reduction in nuclear weapons?

Finally, there is the problem of nuclear proliferation. It is one of the virtues of the sovereign-state deterrence system that it attributes no special moral status to one nation more than to another. But just to the extent that it legitimates each nation pursuing its enlightened self-interest, it has little reason to deny to other nations the possession of nuclear weapons. Thus it appears, to employ Garrett Hardin's image of the commons, that what is good for each nation might well result in our having no commons at all and in which the more fortunate cows would be killed outright rather than left to starve to death.

Ending with a Beginning

At the risk of ending with a whimper rather than a bang I must now ask where has this analysis gotten us. In some ways it seems to have made our situation worse for it seems we lack, as I suggested at the beginning, a coherent moral response that unambiguously requires nuclear disarmament. Or in other words those positions that entail such disarmament are based on questionable moral convictions that we would be hesitant to apply in other aspects of our lives. We thus seem left with our nuclear arsenals not knowing how to live with them and not knowing how to rid ourselves of them.

Moreover we fear this situation may be profoundly pathological. As Schell suggests:

> When one tries to face the nuclear predicament one feels sick; whereas when one pushes it out of mind, as apparently one must do most of the time in order to carry on with life, one feels well again. But this feeling of well-being is based on a denial of the most important reality of our time, and therefore is a kind of sickness. A society that systematically shuts its eyes to an urgent peril to its physical survival and fails to take steps to save itself cannot be called psychologically well. In effect whether we think about nuclear weapons or avoid thinking about them, their presence among us makes us sick, and there seems to be little of purely mental or emotional nature we can do about it.[42]

I think Schell is right about this—nuclear weapons do make us sick but not just in a psychological sense; they make us morally sick. More accurately, however, these weapons manifest that the moralities that form our existence are insufficient insofar as they presuppose survival as the overriding good. Ironically there is a deep kinship between Schell and the sovereign-states deterrence advocates as both draw deeply on our fear of death as individuals, nations, and species for support of their position. But it is exactly such fear that is the basis of our creation and possession of the bomb.[43]

It is the peculiar wisdom of the just war tradition to relativize the value of survival and to ask us to die and, more importantly, kill for the limited moral good embodied by the sovereigns that currently take the form of the nation state. Thus the advocates of just war, at least in principle, acknowledge the finite status of our values for which we should be willing to die. Such a view obviously draws on profound eschatological assumptions concerning how we are to live in this time between the times.

That just war advocates presuppose such an eschatology, moreover, reveals a still more profound commonality between them and the pacifist. For the Christian pacifist agrees that life cannot be an end in and of itself—there are many things for which we should be willing to die rather than lose these goods. For example, we should be willing to sacrifice much, perhaps even our lives, rather than abandon the innocent to violent destruction. Such protection after all is not simply a formula for achieving a safe society but essential for the achievement of justice.

Where the pacifist differs with the just war advocate is whether killing can ever be compatible with the achievement of genuine justice. Indeed just to the extent that just war theory can provide a rationale for the possession and perhaps use of nuclear weapons, it may be a sign of the questionable nature of all justice based on violence. Or put differently, it may reveal the profound unreality of the kind of realism that results from a just war perspective. For what values, however significant, could ever legitimate the use of these weapons which seem to offer no promise of being subjected to moral limits or purpose? Of course that same question, I think, finally challenges the possibility of war itself.

It has not been my intention in ending in this fashion to suggest our situation is hopeless unless we have a return to God and/or ccept a pacifist stance. No one should believe in God as a means to challenge nuclear war any more than anyone should become a pacifist as a strategy for preventing war. Rather we should only believe in God if God in truth is the beginning and end of our existence; we should only take up the way of nonviolence if we believe that is the way of God with the world.[44] Neither a massive return to belief in God nor nonviolence would solve the nuclear dilemma. All I have tried to show is how the absence of each illumines why we have come under the power of our own creation.

Notes

1. For a fuller development of this point see chapter 9.
2. I am grateful to James Childress and John Howard Yoder for helping me see this point.
3. Edward Laarman, "Nuclear Deterrence and the Bluff," *The Reformation Journal* (June, 1982), 15.
4. I draw this list from James Childress' fine essay, "Just-War Theories: The Bases, Interrelations, Priorities and Functions of Their Criteria," *Theological Studies,* 39 (September, 1978), 435–41.
5. See, for example, Paul Ramsey's still very important discussion of this in *War and the Christian Conscience* (Durham: Duke University Press, 1961), 34–59.
6. James Johnson, *Just War Tradition and the Restraint of War* (Princeton: Princeton University Press, 1981), XXII.
7. Johnson, 167.
8. John Connery has recently argued along these lines in his "The Morality of Nuclear Warpower," *America* (July 17, 1982), 25-28. He quotes John Courtney Murray's claim that "since nuclear war may be a necessity, it must be made a moral possibility. The possibility must be created. To say that the possibility of nuclear war cannot be created by human intelligence and energy, under the direction of a moral imperative is to succumb to some sort of determinism in human affairs." However the bishops of the American Catholic Church in their recent Pastoral are increasingly inclined to deny any moral legitimacy for the planning or possessing of nuclear weapons.
9. Johnson, XXXV.
10. Ramsey's important discussion of Augustine in *War and the Christian Conscience* has often failed to be appreciated in this respect. For Ramsey saw quite clearly that just war is as much a theory of state craft as it is an instrument for casuistry. This is perhaps clearer in his *The Just War* (New York: Scribners, 1968).
11. Johnson, 47–49.
12. Thus Ramsey argued in *War and the Christian Conscience:* "The Great Deterrent leaves us without a link between force and purpose. We needed them and need now some substitute for the kind of warfare that can in no sense be an extension of national policy; and this can mean the creation of the possibility of limited application of power. The more this is understood, the better. The risks involved in this are the risks of walking the earth as men who do not deny that they know

the difference between murder and war or between warfare that is justified and that which exceeds all limits. The risks are the risks of seeing to it that war, if it comes, will have some minimal national purpose connected with it" (166).

13. I owe this point to Laarman, 15–19.

14. Jonathan Schell, *The Fate of the Earth* (New York: Alfred Knopf, 1982), 93.

15. Schell, 95.

16. Schell, 118–19.

17. Schell, 132.

18. Schell, 171.

19. Schell, 191. It is interesting to note that Schell accepts a presupposition of the "realist" who insists that war must serve political purpose.

20. Schell, 187.

21. Schell, 226. In his most recent book Schell provides a more "realistic" account of how the world might move from deterrence to an abolition agreement. It is interesting however, that his account clearly continues to presuppose the existence of the nation state system. See his *The Abolition* (New York: Alfred Knopf, 1984).

22. Schell's book was originally published as a three-part essay in the *New Yorker*.

23. It is interesting to compare Schell's position with that of James Gustafson in his recent *Ethics in a Theocentric Perspective,* Vol. I (Chicago: University of Chicago Press, 1982).

24. Schell, 134.

25. Ramsey, *War and the Christian Conscience,* 193.

26. Ramsey, 205. While I am sympathetic with Ramsey's basic point that our thinking about the morality of war cannot be based on survival and fear one can still maintain as a Christian that the how of survival is not unimportant. It may be true that God intends to kill us all in the end, but that does not mean how we live in between the time is unimportant.

27. Paul Ramsey, *The Just War: Force and Political Responsibility* (New York: Charles Scribner's Sons, 1968), 42–69.

28. Theodore Draper, "How Not to Think About Nuclear War," *New York Review of Books,* XXIX, 12 (July 1982), 38.

29. Systematic statements and developments of this position are not easily found but I associate it with people like McGeorge Bundy, George Kennan, and Solly Zuckerman. I have used the thought of Michael Howard below even though his book does not explicitly deal with the

nuclear question because it states more candidly the essential moral presuppositions behind this position.

30. Michael Howard, *War and the Liberal Conscience* (New Brunswick: Rutgers University Press, 1978).

31. Howard, 130.

32. Interestingly Solly Zuckerman, who is otherwise a realist, continues to lay the blame for the nuclear arms race on the scientist. Thus he says, "The basic reason for the irrationality of the whole process is the fact that ideas for a new weapon system derive in the first place, not from the military, but from different groups of scientists and technologists who are concerned to replace or improve old weapons systems—for example by miniaturising components—or by reducing weight/yield ratios of nuclear warheads so that they can be carried further by a ballistic missile. At base, the momentum of the arms race is undoubtedly fueled by the technicians in governmental laboratories and in the industries which produce the armaments." *Nuclear Illusion and Reality* (New York: Viking Press, 1982), 103. On the basis of such an analysis it would seem that perhaps the best thing we could do would be to kill the scientists who are working at these projects. On a more serious level, however, I suspect that Zuckerman is right at least to the extent that the issue becomes one of the imagination—for it is not simply new weapons systems that lure us deeper into suicide but our failure to envisage peace as a genuine alternative.

33. Howard, 132.

34. Howard, 133.

35. Howard, 134.

36. Quoted by Alan Geyer in his *The Idea of Disarmament: Rethinking the Unthinkable* (Elgin, Illinois: The Brethren Press, 1982), 71. Geyer's book is an eloquent and well-argued position for the possibility of disarmament.

37. Draper, 40.

38. Draper, 40. Where Draper gets this rather touching faith in the American people is not revealed. In this respect he seems to be as utopian as Schell.

39. Draper, 41–42. Draper is generally in agreement with the proposals advanced by Zuckerman.

40. Draper, 42.

41. Again see Geyer for some very useful suggestions in this respect.

42. Schell, 8.

43. David Novak, in a yet unpublished paper, "The Threat of Nuclear War: Jewish Perspectives," suggests that the idolatry embodied in nuclear weapons is first of all revealed by our assumption that we now have the power to destroy ourselves. Novak rightly reminds us that God alone reserves that power for himself.

44. For the best analysis of the nuclear dilemma from this perspective see Dale Aukerman, *Darkening Valley: A Biblical Perspective on Nuclear War* (New York: The Seabury Press, 1981). Aukerman says: "Humanly considered, there seems so little prospect of stopping the rush toward nuclear annihilation. But communities of disciples will not, because of this, be immobilized or impelled into frantic activism. World War III is not inevitable. The God of Scripture continues to make His offer of rescue in utter seriousness and His is a sovereignty of surprises. A group of disciples, listening together in prayer, will be able to discern forms and acts of witness God wants of them" (205).

9. AN ESCHATOLOGICAL PERSPECTIVE ON NUCLEAR DISARMAMENT

One is unsure how to account for or to understand ethically the growing consensus in the world and, in particular, in America that nuclear weapons be eliminated or at least their proliferation halted. Certainly we have much to thank Ronald Reagan for in this respect since no doubt the knowledge that we have someone in the White House who seems more than ready to use these weapons has contributed to an awakening of their unimaginable destructiveness. Yet there is a peculiar moral ambiguity about the movement against nuclear weapons. I suspect the ambiguity lies in this: the moral presuppositions that give the movement its greatest political clout are those that are the most problematic from a theological point of view.

In order to illumine why that is the case I want to direct our attention to an aspect of the nuclear disarmament question that has largely been overlooked, namely, the eschatological dimension. For the moral claims made against and for the existence of nuclear weapons make sense only as they draw on profound assumptions about how we should understand our history. After all, "eschatology" is but the word we use to remind ourselves that "there is no significance to human effort and, strictly speaking, no history unless life can be seen in terms of ultimate goals. The *eschaton,* the 'Last Thing,' the End-Event, imparts to life a meaningfulness which it would not otherwise have. This is what we mean by eschatology: a hope which, defying present frustration, defines a present position in terms of the yet unseen goal which gives it meaning."[1]

But exactly what seems so frightening about our current nuclear policies is that they seem to threaten the very possibility of sustaining a hope that can give meaning to our current efforts. Thus Jonathan Schell's crucial argument against nuclear weapons is the threat they pose to the possibility of continued human life on this planet. He argues that there can be "no ethics apart from service to the human community, and therefore no ethical commandments that can justify the extinction of humanity."[2] Therefore the question

160

the peril of extinction puts before the living is: "Who would miss human life if they extinguished it? To which the only honest answer is: Nobody."[3] According to Schell that fact alone is enough to sustain the judgment that nuclear weapons must be eliminated. For him anything that threatens the very value itself is inherently immoral.

Is Schell right to claim that the destruction of the human species means the end of all value and worth in the universe? He seems to presuppose a definite eschatological perspective, but it is one that knows no end—at least in the sense of a temporal end that signals the finite character of our existence. For he argues that the end that should determine what we do and not do must involve the simple recognition that "our species is biologically immortal."[4] Schell presents us, therefore, with a clear case of humanistic eschatology that attempts to secure the eternality of our existence through our ability to control and master our history—exactly the same eschatological presumption that leads to our having nuclear weapons in the first place.

Some may challenge this interpretation on the grounds that Schell really has no eschatology since he does not presuppose that there is an end to history. We are not participants in a history that has an end, but rather all we have is a purpose that keeps us going—namely, to insure the biological immortality of the human species. But why should we do that according to Schell? Drawing on Hannah Arendt he argues that to be human requires the creation of a common world which seeks to transcend our individual lifespans by insuring an "earthly immortality" carried by the ongoing human stream.[5] But ironically that seems to deny our very character as historic beings as we are denied of an ending that any good story requires—we have no end except to be unending.

Because Schell's eschatology is so attenuated his position cannot help but be apocalyptic. Since the only end he can envision is an unending one, nuclear weapons are singled out as inherently immoral because they threaten the end to our "immortality." And "life without the hope for human survival is a life of despair."[6] In a peculiar way Schell is thus the mirror image of those Christians who cannot resist speculating about the imminent end of the world and, perhaps, even cooperating to bring it about. Both theologically are presumptuous since they fail to understand that the Christian expectation of the end can be hopeful only because we know that it is God's future and his decision that will bring it about. If all that stands between us and despair is the prospect of the indefinite continuation of the human species, we indeed live in a hopeless world.

In a sense if Schell did not have the threat of nuclear weapons, he would almost have to invent it. For without such a threat our existence would lack a necessary sense of adventure. Perhaps we have created and seek to eliminate nuclear weapons at the same time because we have no other means collectively to make our lives interesting. Thus the basic problem is one of imagination for we must learn to envision a world of peace where our Promethean presumption about our power to possess or eliminate nuclear weapons is challenged.

Christians, exactly because their hope is grounded in God, must learn to wait patiently by refusing to let the danger of nuclear weapons tempt us to buy security through apocalyptic threats. Such a waiting does not mean we withdraw from the struggle by wallowing in self-indulgent despair. Rather our waiting must be a time of activity that seeks to present to the world the excitement of God's peace. Thus it must be a waiting that imaginatively opens forms of watching that are otherwise unavailable.

From the perspective of this kind of Christian hope, however, Schell's position is not so different from those who favor the attempt to maintain order through some form of nuclear strategy. Like him they assume that the ultimate end is the perpetuation of the human species but they differ with regard to the best means to accomplish that task. Unlike Schell they see little chance of "reinventing" the world. Indeed we cannot be free, as Schell suggests, of the nation-state system of which war is but a necessary correlative. For war "is simply the generic term for the use of armed force by states or aspirants to statehood for the attainment of their political objectives."[7] Nuclear weapons are but one development among others in the continued state of war that exists between nations. Such weapons help preserve the peace as long as we remember that peace is the name for the political accommodations at any one time that generally benefit all parties in the nation-state system to a lesser and greater extent. The answer is not to eliminate such weapons, but to be smart in our use of them. From this perspective the opponent of the proliferation of nuclear weapons can argue, for example, that we do not need more of them than is necessary to stop our enemy from attacking us first. Since at present we have more than a sufficient number, something should be done to reduce our stockpiles.

Those who argue in this manner assume, like Schell, that our task is to survive. They usually refrain, as he did not, from making quite as grandiose claims about the eternal destiny of the human species, but they assume that it would be difficult to live in a world that might have an end, for such an end would make all our current hopes false. The only way we can ensure our survival, however, is by refusing to be tempted by apocalyptic prophecies and utopian solutions and to use the resources we have, i.e., the nation state, to sustain what peace we have to insure our survival.

Thus, at least in these two prominent strategies, the antinuclear movement draws on a profound eschatological assumption about the continued necessity of our survival if the world is to have meaning. The possibility of eliminating or at least of controlling nuclear weapons thus seems to depend on our willingness to exploit politically this deep conviction. It is our task to ensure that the history of the world comes out all right. And at the very least that means we must act to ensure the continued survival of the human species.

Corresponding to this eschatological perspective is a very definite meaning of the word "peace." For the peace sought is the peace of order that first looks to insure the survival of ourselves and of those closest to us. Of course we do not desire to kill anyone else in the process of ensuring our survival, but the stress is still put on our own survival. Thus, what bothers us most about the threat of nuclear weapons is not that we may be implicated in the murder of million of Russians but that we may well be killed if a nuclear exchange occurs between the United States and Russia.

The eschatology of the New Testament and its corresponding sense of peace, however, stand in striking contrast to who of those who assume that our history has no meaning if our purpose is not to insure the survival of the human species. There can be no question that many of the early Christians anticipated an end to human history and many of them assumed that such an end was imminent. That they did so is not surprising for, as A. E. Harvey has observed, the Bible makes an implicit claim to tell the "story of the world, starting from the very beginning and looking forward to the very end. In this, it obeys a convention, or perhaps we should rather say a necessity, which lies on every story-teller. A story needs an ending. A point must be reached at which one can feel that certain issues are resolved, a certain finality has been achieved . . . It is an essential device for making sense of our experience. Unless we postulate an end towards which our efforts are tending, or which will relieve us from our suffering, our life becomes meaningless and even unendurable."[8]

Harvey suggests that to a people schooled on this view of the world the notion of an imminent cosmic cataclysm does not appear so strange. Thus Jesus'—or at least the early church's—apocalyptic expectations are not as bizarre as they first appear. Indeed from what we have just seen of Schell, the necessity of giving meaning to the present by viewing it in the light of an imminent future is something that is still very much with us. Ironically the nuclear threat has put us in a unique position from which we can perhaps better understand the attitude of the early Christians. Thus Harvey notes "it has been known for a long time that the earth cannot sustain life indefinitely. The cooling down of the sun, the effects of the second law of thermodynamics, set a limit to our existence of some 200,000 years. But this prospect is so far removed from our human time scale that it can have no influence on the choices and policies which we adopt in our day to day life. On the other hand, a nuclear catastrophe could be upon me in the lifetime of ourselves, our children or our grandchildren. Moreover, it will not come to pass by pure accident or inexorable natural laws. It will occur, if at all, through the decisions and errors of men; indeed many competent observers would say that it can be averted only by a significant change of heart in our leaders and their constituencies. But this, of course, is precisely what was being said in the time of Jesus. Only repentance on a national scale would avert God's judgment in the form of a cataclysmic end to civilization. The time scale was short: but the issue would depend on the moral choices of men."[9]

But some of you may by now have begun to lose patience with all this talk of eschatology and in particular with these last apocalyptic notes. Christian biblical scholars and theologians have spent the last century trying to explain Jesus' and/or the early church's apocalyptic pronouncements in a manner such that we do not have to take them seriously. It seems particularly inopportune to raise them in relation to the issue of nuclear disarmament since they can only further complicate this already complex issue. After all, the world did not come to an end during the generation of the people who knew Jesus, and Christians, like other folk, have had to try ever since to live in a world which seems to go on indefinitely.

But quite to the contrary, Christians are a people who believe that we have in fact seen the end; that the world has for all time experienced its decisive crisis in the life and death of Jesus of Nazareth. For in his death we believe that the history of the universe reached its turning point. At that moment in history, when the decisive conflict between God and the powers took place, our end was resolved in favor of God's lordship over this existence. Through Jesus' cross and resurrection the end has come; the kingdom has been established. Indeed it had to come in such a fashion for it is a kingdom that only God could bring about.

Unless this is assumed the demands to forgive our enemies push us beyond what we normally think to be humanly possible as long as we assume that the world in which we exist will go on indefinitely. But decisive to Jesus' message is that the old world has passed away and a new moral order has therefore been made possible. "Jesus' message has power, not in spite of, but because of its promise of a future which is not ideal or utopian, nor a mere variation for the better on what we know already, but is both radically new and able to be envisaged on a human time scale, 'in our generation.' Faithful and eager attention to such a future introduces a new dimension into the present; for the present becomes, not a mere working out of consequences of the past, but a transition to an altogether different future. The present is transformed by the discovery of possibilities which were not apparent until it was seen in the light of the future."[10]

Christian pacifism only makes sense within this perspective precisely because it is not a pacifism that guarantees a world without war. The pacifism of the Christian is not to be judged by its observable results—though it certainly seeks results. Rather " 'Peace' describes the pacifist's hope, the goal in the light of which he [or she] acts, the character of their action, the ultimate divine certainty which lets their position make sense."[11] Christians are thus a peaceable people not because through such peace we can promise the ongoing existence of the world, but because we believe nonresistance is the way God has shown that he deals with the world and it is the way to which he therefore calls us to be faithful.

The peace to which Christians witness cannot be equated with any peace that derives from our desire for survival, whether that be personal, national, or species survival. A peace based on survival cannot help but be idolatrous and unjust as it necessarily tempts us to accept the lesser evil in the name of security and order. But as I suggested earlier, it seems that it is just that kind of "peace" that provides the greatest resource for seeking to find politically effective means to call halt to the nuclear arms race.

This presents a particular challenge to the Christian pacifist, at least of the eschatological kind with which I identify, for the Christian pacifist desires as much as anyone to prevent the possibility of nuclear war. Yet we cannot pretend that every human good, or indeed the good of the human species itself, hangs on that goal. For the peace we desire is the peace of God that comes from the recognition that it is not our task to make history come out right—either through the possession or dispossession of nuclear arms. Rather, we believe that history has already come out right and just because it has we can take the time in a world threatened by its own pretentions of control to seek patiently a truthful peace. That is a peace that derives not from our fears but that is based on the profound confidence that God has shown us the way he would have his world governed. We can take the time to watch exactly because we know the Master of the universe will end the story justly.

Of course this does not mean that the Christian pacifist cannot and should not join in political coalitions with others in the hope of stopping the nuclear arms race. But if we do so we must remember at least part of our vocation is to help clarify the moral issues at stake. For example, we can perhaps point out that just war criteria at least offer morally a more compelling case than those based on survival since the just war position presupposes that the issue is one of legitimate killing and not simply survival. For although it is seldom noticed, just war is a pacifist position to the extent that it assumes that the burden of proof is on those who would use violence rather than those who would refrain.

For the just war tradition continues to draw on the eschatological presuppositions of the Christian pacifist. In principle advocates of the just war position must be willing to lose rather than to employ means that would entail the indiscriminate killing of noncombatants. That kind of capitulation surely suggests that the just war position, insofar as it is shaped by our obligation to protect the weak, draws on profound eschatological presuppositions which are not easily reconciled with the assumption of those who maintain that survival is a worthy moral end necessary to sustain the purposefulness of our current endeavors. (Moreover, I suspect if the logic of the just war position were more candidly stated, it would appear as politically presumptuous as the pacifist. For a just war would require extraordinary moral resources on the part of the citizenry of a country in order to give the leaders moral and political permission to prepare to fight a war justly. For example, would the American people be willing to bear the financial burden that could not but accompany the significant buildup of our conventional forces necessary to free Europe of nuclear weapons? I doubt it.)

It has not been my intention to provide a moral "solution" to the nuclear arms race based on pacifist principles. Indeed I do not think any such solution is possible. Instead I have tried to broaden the more strictly ethical questions about nuclear disarmament to show how our moral positions inextricably presuppose an eschatological framework. That I have taken the time to do that can only be justified by the fact that we believe that even in the face of nuclear destruction God has given us the time and patience to be a peaceable people.

Notes

1. John Howard Yoder, *The Original Revolution* (Scottdale, Pennsylvania: Herald Press, 1971), 56.
2. Jonathan Schell, *The Fate of the Earth* (New York: Knopf, 1982), 132.
3. Schell, 171.
4. Schell, 119.
5. Schell, 118.
6. Schell, 184.
7. Michael Howard, *War and the Liberal Conscience* (New Brunswick, New Jersey: Rutgers University Press, 1978), 134.
8. A. E. Harvey, *Jesus and the Constraints of History* (Philadelphia: Westminster Press, 1982), 71–72.
9. Harvey, 74–75.
10. Harvey, 97.
11. Yoder, *The Original Revolution,* 56.

10. SHOULD WAR BE ELIMINATED?

On Getting the Problems Right

As noted in the two previous chapters large numbers of people are now convinced that we should eliminate all nuclear weapons. In their recent pastoral letter the Roman Catholic Bishops of America seem virtually to have joined these ranks. Still more people, while they do not call for the complete destruction of nuclear weapons suggest that we should drastically reduce the kind and number of our nuclear stockpile. This latter group includes such highly respected persons as George Kennan and Robert MacNamara, the sort who cannot be accused of political naivete. As yet, however, these many voices have precipitated no change in public policy and they seem unlikely to do so in the near future. Indeed we are told that the peace movement threatens the peace, as peace can only be guaranteed through strength which means more, not less, nuclear missiles. And so the stockpiles continue to grow.

Why do we seem caught in this dilemma? Why, when all admit that nuclear weapons threaten our very existence as nations if not as a species, do we seem so unable to free ourselves from their power? Some suppose that people want peace, but our leaders, inspired by some nefarious motive, do not. Such explanations are far too simple; the problem is much more recalcitrant than a change in leadership can solve. We all, leaders and followers alike, seem caught in a web of powers that is one of our own making yet not under our control. We say we want peace, but we seem destined for war.

Why is this the case? Why do all our attempts to think morally about war seem often so futile in the face of war's irresistible inevitability? In spite of its horror and destructiveness, its insanity and irrationality, might it be that we have overlooked the fact that war has a moral purpose? Could that be the reason why no matter how compelling the logic against nuclear weapons, we still seem defeated by those who say, "All that may be quite right, but . . . ?" What are the moral presuppositions that make that "but" seem so powerful?

169

In order to try to understand these kinds of questions I am going to propose a thought experiment which may help us reconsider our assumptions about war and its place in our lives. The experiment is to provide the best negative answer I am able to the question: "Should war be eliminated?" We tend to think such a question absurd. After all, it is not a question of "should" at all, but "can." We all know we should eliminate war; the problem is we cannot. Asking if we should eliminate war is like asking if we should eliminate sin. Of course we should, but the problem is that we cannot. Therefore to ask such a question is to start us off in the wrong direction.

While admitted that there may be aspects of the question bordering on the absurd, I hope to show that by pressing it seriously we may be able to illumine why war is such an intractable aspect of our existence. Moreover, by insisting on using the language of *should* I want to force us to consider what is at stake morally by the very fact we describe some forms of violence as war. Too often those concerned to make moral judgments about war, whether they be pacifists or just war theorists, assume that the description *war* is unproblematic—the only question is how to eliminate or control war. Yet that is exactly what I am suggesting cannot be assumed.

It may be objected that just war theory in fact does presuppose the kind of analysis of war I am suggesting. Rather than being a theory about the criteria necessary to determine if or how a war may be fought morally, the just war is an attempt to understand war as a moral enterprise. I have no reason to deny such an interpretation of the just war theory. Moreover, if in fact that is what just war theory is about, then the moral description of war I will try to develop can be seen as an attempt to make candid implicit assumptions entailed by just war thinking.

Ethical reflection about war, therefore, does not begin by asking what makes a war more or less just. Rather a morality is already implied by the very fact we call it war. For war is not simply another name for violence.

We must begin, therefore, by asking: Do we know what we mean by calling something a war? Certainly war entails violence, but yet the very description *war* seems to propose a different moral evaluation than violence. At the very least, *war* denotes purposive human activity which *violence* does not always imply. Perhaps that is why normal categories dealing with killing do not seem to apply in war. For example, we are taken aback by the suggestion that war is but legitimized murder on a mass scale. Our resistance to calling war murder indicates we assume it has a moral legitimacy, or at least it is not morally illegitimate as is murder.

Indeed some who argue currently against nuclear weapons do so in defense of war as an important moral institution. From their perspective war is being ruined by modern weapons of mass destruction. They deny that "nuclear war" is appropriately so called because war presupposes that good can be done through its prosecution. Thus George Kennan challenges "the thesis that these devices, the so-called nuclear weapons, are really weapons at all—that they deserve that designation. A weapon is something with which you try to affect the purposes and the concepts on an opponent; it is not something with which you blindly destroy his entire civilization, and probably your own as well."[1] We might say that Kennan, and others who argue like him, are trying to eliminate nuclear war in order to make the world safe for war. But we must ask if their position is coherent, for once the moral presuppositions underlying their acceptance of war are made candid, it may be the case that nuclear weapons are but a new development in the institution of war.

If it is so important to save war as a significant moral option, we need an account that makes explicit war's moral status. In spite of all calls for peace, such an account might show us that if war were eliminated we would be morally the worse for it. By this I do not mean merely that we would miss the extraordinary individual heroics often associated with war, or lose the kind of comradeship war creates between soldiers and citizens.[2] It is undoubtedly true that war often provides the occasion for our most impressive moral behavior, but these good results are not contained within the very fabric of war itself. The issue is not whether war occasionally can have good results, but whether war, with all its horror, destructiveness, and brutality, is an institution that nonetheless serves moral purposes which we should not will to be without.

This is the issue I seek to address although I honestly must say I am skeptical if any response can be coherent. In particular I fear any abstract account of *war* risks lapsing into a false idealism. What we need to talk about is not war, but this or that war. Philosophical analysis of the kind I propose has the dangerous tendency to console by offering explanations for what is essentially inexplicable.

So why pursue it? First, I hope by proceeding in this manner we will be able to get beyond some of the current rhetoric about nuclear war and deal with the basic issue of war itself. The current debate about nuclear weapons in a disturbing fashion is beginning to resemble the conflict over abortion. Both sides have arguments and responses to which the opponent does not listen. By directing our attention to war rather than simply the morality of nuclear weapons, I hope to raise new questions which will perhaps prevent our discussion from ending in a shouting match. I do not intend to solve the moral problems raised by nuclear deterrence strategy; rather my purpose is to try to help us understand morally how we have arrived in a situation where our so-called safety can be insured only if we are willing to will countless deaths and destruction. I want first to understand, not judge or offer solutions.

Second, by developing a moral case for war I hope to illumine the ambivalence Christians often exhibit about war. That ambivalence is at the heart of *The Challenge of Peace: God's Promise and Our Response.*[3] The kind of ambivalence with which I am concerned is not the bishops' unwillingness to condemn forthrightly all forms of deterrence. Rather I wish to call our attention to the even more fundamental ambivalence concerning war itself. For in spite of the bishops' avowal that Christians are fundamentally a people of peace, they affirm that Christians can participate in war as a legitimate moral endeavor. I hope to show, in spite of the bishops' assertion that war is always the result of sin (a fact they continue to presume, and it is a presumption consistent with the natural law basis of the just war tradition), that war is a morally positive institution.

Finally I want to develop as strong a case as I can for war because I am a pacifist. Too often pacifists try to win easy victories against those who support war by stressing war's irrationality and horror. The problem with such strategy is, in spite of war's obvious irrationalities and horrors, it somehow is beside the point. It is so, I think, because it ignores the powerful moral presupposition that sustains war's viability in spite of its brutality. The significance of the pacifist's refusal to cooperate with war can only be appreciated by understanding why war has such a hold on our moral imagination.

Moreover, by proceeding in this way I hope we will also be able to better understand the theological disagreements between pacifist and just war thinkers.[4] For by developing a positive case for war I hope to show that pacifist and just war thinkers draw on quite different assumptions about eschatology. Both entail assumptions about how history should be told and the Christian role in it. By suggesting how war determines our history we can better understand why Christians cannot allow that history to define their existence. Pacifism, therefore, is not just an attitude about war, but it entails the belief that God, through Jesus Christ, has inaugurated a history that frees all people from our assumption that we have no moral alternative to war.

War in a Catholic Perspective

The suggestion that Christians have a moral ambivalence about war leads us to suppose that some explicit theological justification of war might be at work as well as the more generally accepted moral ones. Investigation of two significant documents, Pope John XXIII's *Pacem in Terris* and the recent Pastoral Letter of the American Roman Catholic Bishops, *The Challenge of Peace: God's Promise and Our Response,* shows this to be the case. In the following treatment of them it is not my intention to try to give a complete analysis, but rather to try to make explicit each document's understanding of war. For though each says much about the ethics of war neither tries to explain what they understand war to be. By attending to how they make their ethical case I hope to show that their implicit understanding of war is more positive than their ethical pronouncements about war would lead one to believe.

I have chosen these documents because they are representative of a church's position rather than that of an individual thinker. Moreover they bring to bear elements, some conflictual, from a Christian tradition that has developed the most sophisticated moral analysis of war. While the documents urge peace, they nonetheless continue to maintain war as a moral possibility, if not a duty, for Christians. I hope my criticism of these documents will expose these assumptions as well as generate some of the conceptual tools we will need to understand war in a more positive light.

Pacem in Terris was promulgated in 1963 and brought a new emphasis on peace by a church that had in the past generally been associated with the just war tradition.[5] In *Pacem in Terris* the just war theory is subordinated to a wider vision of peace. Thus John XXIII argues, "There will never be peace among men unless peace resides in the soul of each man—unless each person preserves within himself the order commanded by God" (165). That order is to be found in the natural law which can be known by all people. Its most basic principle is "that every human being is a person naturally endowed with intelligence and free will. Thus man has rights and duties flowing directly and conjointly from his very nature. These rights and duties are universal and inviolable and therefore inalienable" (9).

Every human right, the right of life, truth, conscience, family, work, private property, assembly, political participation, is connected with a corresponding set of duties. Since we are social by nature a well-ordered society is one where "every natural right of a man and the duties of others to acknowledge and foster that right is recognized" (30). In such a society authority is primarily a moral force as order is maintained by an "appeal primarily to the conscience of individual citizens . . . , to the duty of each one to work willingly for the common good of all. Since all men are naturally equal in human dignity, no one has the power to force compliance on another, except God alone, Who sees and judges the unseen thought of men's hearts" (48).

Thus the encyclical assumes an organic view of society where each nation contains elements of the common good by safeguarding the personal rights and duties of individuals (60). Society, and the state which serves it, is peaceful since by definition it seems there can be no conflict between rights if everyone is allowed to pursue those rights fairly. The more we cooperate the less we will need to resort to violence.

This basic assumption is then applied to international affairs. Each state has "reciprocal rights and duties and the relations between States should be harmonized in truth, justice, active cooperation, and liberty. For the same natural law which governs the relations between individual men must also regulate those between states" (80). Thus the relations between States must be governed by truth. Truth calls for the elimination of every form of racism and recognition of the inviolable and immutable principle that all states are by nature equal in dignity. Each state therefore has the right to exist, to make progress, to possess the means for its development, and to bear the principal responsibility for bringing about and expanding its own progress and growth. Truth also demands that each nation have the right to its good name and to due honor" (86).

It may be that the advantages each state seeks to acquire will lead to disagreements but those should be settled not by force of arms but by "appraisal of the arguments and attitudes of the opposing sides, a mature and objective weighing of the facts, and an equitable adjustment of the opposing views" (93). Peace, therefore, cannot be based on the stockpiling of weapons, but on mutual trust. "Justice, right reason, and an appreciation of the dignity of man urgently demand that the arms race stop; that weapons on hand in the various countries be reduced through parallel and simultaneous action by the parties concerned; that nuclear weapons be banned; and that all men finally come to an agreement on a suitable disarmament program with an effective system for mutual control" (112).

It is easy to accuse *Pacem in Terris* of naiveté, but I think such an accusation overlooks the substantive assumptions embodied in the encyclical. These assumptions are all the more powerful because they are widely shared. Like the encyclical, many assume that war is the result of a failure to give persons their rights to pursue their interests. If each of us is satisfied in himself we would be at peace with one another; in like manner nation states would be at peace having nothing to gain by aggression. War is not so much wrong, therefore, as it is plain irrational.

Yet the view that peace results from cooperation between free individuals is seriously flawed. Flawed not because we are more fundamentally depraved than the encyclical assumes, though I certainly think it is far too optimistic concerning human good will, but because the kind of violence embodied in the institution of war is not due to the pursuit of our interests at the expense of others but rather, as I hope to show, results from our moral commitment to the good of others. That the encyclical fails to confront this reality of war causes, I think, its calls for peace to appear flaccid. We thus dismiss it as but another idealistic call for peace in a world constituted by war.

Pacem in Terris, however, is not only a vision peculiar to the Catholic Church, but it also articulates a view of peace that is the working assumption of many schooled by the Enlightenment. It may seem odd to suggest that the Catholic Church, the great enemy of the Enlightenment, has now become its most prominent advocate, but I think this is what has happened. For the working assumption of the encyclical is something like this: There is a fundamental symmetry between establishing and maintaining a just constitution within a state and in establishing and maintaining a just relationship between states.[6] If we could instruct just states of autonomous moral agents then we could secure peace between them, reserving war for protection against unjust aggressor states.

The Challenge of Peace begins by asserting, quite contrary to these Enlightenment assumptions, that the Christians' longing for peace is based in the Gospel rather than natural law. The bishops suggest that there can be no question that Jesus was on the side of peace against war.[7] Indeed Jesus not only taught peace but, as the full demonstration of the power of God's reign made present in his life and work, Jesus gives a peace beyond what is possible for relations between autonomous nation states (51). "Jesus gives that peace to his disciples, to those who had witnessed the helplessness of the crucifixion and the power of the resurrection (Jn. 20:19, 20, 26). The peace which he gives to them as he greets them as their risen Lord is the fullness of salvation. It is the reconciliation of the world and God (Rom 5:1-2; Col 1:20); the restoration of the unity and harmony of all creation which the Old Testament spoke of with such longing. Because the walls of hostility between God and humankind were broken down in the life and death of the true, perfect servant, union and well-being between God and the world were finally fully possible (Eph 2:13-22; Gal 3:28)" (51).

Nevertheless, the bishops go on to say, the peace and reconciliation Jesus left with the early Christians "were not yet fully operative in their world" (53). They assert on the one hand that "Jesus Christ is our peace, and in his death-resurrection he gives God's peace to our world," (54) but on the other hand, it is false to suppose that Jesus or the scriptures provide us with a "detailed answer to the specifics of the questions which we face today. They do not speak specifically of nuclear war or nuclear weapons, for these were beyond the imagination of the communities in which the scriptures were formed. The sacred texts do, however, provide us with urgent direction when we look at today's concrete realities. The fullness of eschatological peace remains before us in hope and yet the gift of peace is already ours in the reconciliation effected in Jesus Christ" (55).[8]

Thus the Christian must live between the vision of the reign of God and its concrete realization in history. Any ethical response to war must be worked out in the light of this tension. Christians may take different stances about war as they move toward the realization of God's kingdom in history, but all Christians will "find in any violent situation the consequences of sin: not only sinful patterns of domination, oppression or aggression, but the conflict of values and interests which illustrate the limitations of a sinful world" (61). Therefore pacifism is a legitimate response by Christians to war, but it is not that which the bishops take. For while their letter is addressed "principally to the Catholic community, we want it to make a contribution to the wider public debate in our country on the dangers and dilemmas of the nuclear age".[9] Therefore the ethical basis of the Pastoral must be one that is not based on specifically Christian presuppositions.

In order to develop a position capable of providing such guidance the bishops, in spite of their analysis of the New Testament, turn to the just war theory. That theory, they argue, is built on the fundamental assumption that "governments threatened by armed, unjust aggression must defend their people. This includes defense by armed force if necessary as a last resort" (75). We therefore have a "fundamental right of defense." Even more strongly put, the bishops quote Pius XII who argued that "a people threatened with an unjust aggression, or already its victim, may not remain passively indifferent, if it would think and act as befits a Christian. Their defense is even an obligation for the nations as a whole, who have a duty not to abandon a nation that is attacked" (76).

Thus while recommending nonviolent means to fend off aggression, the bishops candidly suggest "we must recognize the reality of the paradox we face as Christians living in the context of the world as it presently exists; we must continue to articulate our belief that love is possible and the only real hope for all human relations, and yet accept that force, even deadly force, is sometimes justified and that nations must provide for their defense" (78).[10] For it is an essential presupposition of Catholic teaching about war that "every nation has a right and duty to defend itself against unjust aggression" (p. iii).

For my purposes it is not necessary to pursue the bishops' detailed account of the just war theory, its implications for nuclear weapons, and their arguments against deterrence. The crucial issues have already been joined by their willingness to underwrite the presumption that the state has the right and duty to defend itself and yet maintain that, in principle, peace should be possible in our world. Once the former presumption has been granted, and it is not clear why they grant it, it is not easy to see how what they say about the Gospel's commitment to peace can be anything more than an unrealizable ideal.

Of course it may be asked what is wrong about having such an ideal. Given the fact that we live in a war-ridden world, it would seem to be a good idea at least to keep the goal of peace ever before us. But I am not so sure that is the case. For such an ideal might well encourage us, if war is not only a necessary but morally necessary part of our lives, to self-deceptive explanations for our involvement with war. It may well be war is "the result of sin and a tragic remedy for sin in the life of political societies," but even as such war can serve moral purposes.

Perhaps what we need to learn from this is that, while it sounds right to say war is due to sin, such claims are of little interest. For such a description does not help us understand what war is and why it seems such an inevitable part of our lives. Therefore I will try to give an account of war that goes beyond such broad categories in the hope that by it we will better understand why the bishops cannot bring themselves to deny war as an institution integral to the nation state.

For there seem to be two different views of war in *The Challenge of Peace* that reflect the two different ethical perspectives of the Pastoral—the one based on the Gospel, the other deriving from natural law assumptions. From the perspective of the former, war is the unambiguous sign of sin and can never be called a good. From the perspective of the latter, war can sometimes be a good, indeed a moral duty, necessary to preserve human community. While not strictly incompatible it is not clear how one can hold both at once.

This is particularly true if one continues to maintain, as the Pastoral does, there can be no incompatibility between nature and grace, reason and revelation (17). For if just war is based on natural law, a law written in the conscience of all men and women by God, then it seems that war must be understood as the outgrowth of legitimate moral commitments. If war, however, is the compromises we make with sin then it is not clear on what grounds, given the gospel ethic depicted by the Pastoral, Christians can participate in war. That is, it is not clear if one presumes that Christians should avoid intentionally cooperating with sin.

How Cooperation Results in War

Many, impressed with the universality of violence, attribute war to some fundamental aspect of human nature. The difficulty with such "explanations," however, is they tell us little about the specific activity we call war. As Kenneth Waltz suggests, while human nature no doubt plays a part in bringing about war, it cannot "by itself explain both war and peace, except by the simple statement that man's nature is such that sometimes he fits and sometimes he does not."[11] In other words to say that war is the result of some aspect of human nature is at once to say too much and too little. Too much is said because it is unclear what possibly could count against such a claim. Too little, because concentration on the "primary" cause of war directs our attention away from an analysis of the relation between states. Attempts to explain war by appeals to human nature mistakenly assume that war has *a* cause.

As I suggested at the beginning, war is not simply violence in a magnified form. Rather, it is an institution which arises among peoples who can claim sufficient commonality to transform violence into power. As Hannah Arendt reminds us, power is an instrument of rule and thus is the mitigation of violence.[12] Power implies the ability of people to cooperate so that explicit violence is not needed. Violence is that to which individuals, whether they be particular persons or foreign states, resort in order to challenge the legitimacy of power.[13] When power breaks down, violence is often the result. Therefore, according to Arendt, power is indeed the essence of all government, but violence is not. While we might call war violent, its essence is not violence, for in a moral sense it is the enemy of violence.

War is an institution that occurs uniquely between agents of power. Currently we call such agents "nation states" though war is by no means limited to that particular institution. War, for example, can occur between people who have not organized themselves into nations as we know them. War must be a continuing possibility between nation states (or other communities), since there neither is nor does it seem there ought to be a system of law, of power, enforceable between them. Communities exist on the basis of shared public concern. Each state must judge its own interests and purposes in terms of its particular history and situation. As a result, to accept war is not to accept violence or anarchy; it is to accept commonality and cooperation.

In his now classic, *Man, the State, and War: A Theoretical Analysis,* Kenneth Waltz develops the moral assumptions behind this account of war by calling attention to Rousseau's analysis of the nature and the cause of war. According to Rousseau, persons were originally dispersed sufficiently to make cooperation unnecessary. But numbers increased and contact with other humans posed the alternatives: cooperate or die. Rousseau illustrates this with the simplest example: "Assume that five men who have acquired a rudimentary ability to speak and to understand each other happen to come together at a time when all of them suffer from hunger. The hunger of each will be satisfied by the fifth part of a stag, so they 'agree' to cooperate in a project to trap one. But also the hunger of any one of them will be satisfied by a hare so, as a hare comes within reach, one of them grabs it. The defector obtains the means of satisfying his hunger but in doing so permits the stag to escape. His immediate interest prevails over consideration for his fellows."[14]

The example, while obviously overly simple, conveys a significant but often overlooked point. Unlike most who link conflict casually to some imperfection of our nature—particularly of our reason— Rousseau tries to show that the "sources of conflict are not so much in the minds of men as they are in the nature of social activity."[15] Conflict arises not from our individual selfishness, though we may be selfish, but from the nature of cooperation whereby one person's immediate interest and the general long-term interest of the group are not the same. Yet the long-term interest can be served only when all individuals concerned forgo their immediate interest. Yet it is not merely that each must forgo an immediate interest, but each must trust the others to do so as well. As Waltz points out, "The problem is now posed in more significant terms. If harmony is to exist in anarchy, not only must I be perfectly rational but I must be able to assume that everyone else is too."[16] But that is exactly what I cannot assume.

If the rational choice is to forgo the immediate good to cooperate, then rationality entails the acceptance of the possibility of coercion whereby the dissenting individual is forced to serve the common good. This is the moral importance of power; without it we could not justify our pursuit of the common good which in turn justifies all our attempts at cooperation. From such a perspective society (and resulting states) is a remarkable moral achievement. For a state is a unit created by establishing habits of trust through which the citizen is encouraged to submit to a general will for the good of the whole. Whether the state is organic or only the name of some power that has so established itself so that its decisions are accepted as decisions for all it is nonetheless a force for order. Compliance is rationally fortified by two considerations: one does have the power to change the decision; and one judges that in the long run it is to his or her advantage to cooperate with the state's decision and work for change in the accepted ways. According to Rousseau the better the state the more prominent the second consideration.[17]

The distillation of a cooperative venture into a state allows for the further possibility of cooperation/conflict between states. Here unity is particularly important. For questions of foreign policy call for choices that are supported by the state as a whole. If a state is to have a foreign policy it must be able to speak at times with a single voice. War, therefore, is a particularly important time as, in war, states are most likely to be able to generate nearly unanimous backing. The unity of the nation, in fact, is partly derived from antagonism generated by international contact. Thus individuals participate in war because they are members of states and because only states can make war on other states.[18]

War is thus not to be immediately judged as good or evil any more than the man who pursues the hare. Contrary to the assumption of *Pacem in Terris* Rousseau has tried to show that even if all states were good states, that is, states which work to procure the uncoerced consent of their citizens, we would not necessarily have a world of peace. For the will of any one state is only a particular will in relation to another. The absence of any authority above states to prevent or adjust conflicts means that war is inevitable. Abstractly put, "that among particularities accidents will occur is not accidental but necessary."[19]

Theoretically, we can imagine two alternatives to war: (1) impose an effective control on separate states or (2) remove states from the sphere of the accidental; that is, to define a state that is not particularly constituted. The former possibility is fraught with its own dangers; the extent of the power necessary for such control is frightening to us. The latter is impossible since states by their very nature are formed and "maintained by nothing better than chance."[20] Indeed our greatest danger comes when some states forget their particularity and claim universality and thus the right to determine the affairs of other states.[21]

The startling simple implication of Rousseau's analysis is that war occurs because there is nothing to prevent it. As we cannot presume all individuals will comply uncoerced with the common good of the state, so we cannot assume states will subordinate their ends. If we seek cooperation we must accept the possibility of war. Of course Rousseau's account does not purport to tell us how one or the other war is caused; surely in each case a wide range of circumstances and purposes is at work. Particular wars may be more or less justifiable, but war *per se* is never justifiably excluded as a possibility. War just is; it is neither good nor bad.

Perhaps from this perspective we can appreciate the ambiguity we often feel about war as an institution. We do not generally seek war; we think of it as something we choose when we have no other choice. Even though war is clearly human activity, we tend to conceive it as an external agent, a fate that we had not willed but which we cannot but follow. It is just in the "nature" of things. War is finally no one's fault; it is an unsolicited yet unavoidable consequence of our shared activities. War in this sense is simply beyond good and evil.

Should War Be Eliminated?

Rousseau has suggested that war is an unavoidable by-product of our cooperation. While in itself morally ambiguous, as a by-product of cooperation, its elimination would mean as well the extinction of cooperation. Therefore we should not seek to eliminate war.

But there are perhaps other reasons why war should not be eliminated, which are related to this, yet distinguishable from it. These point to the moral purpose served specifically by war. We do not live in a world of a common morality. What goods we share are those that come to us through the achievement and sacrifices of our forebears. Our goods are inseparable from our histories and our histories can only be preserved as they are associated with states pledged to protect them. While no one wishes war, it may in some cases be the only way to preserve these goods.

Indeed in war we learn to sacrifice ourselves for these goods. No morality is worthy that does not require sacrificing even our life.

War, also, teaches us to preserve the common life, even to kill for it, precisely because the common life transcends the life of the individual. Indeed to refuse to kill for the state would be to dishonor those who have given their lives for the morality that the state is pledged to protect. So when threatened the good state cannot but ask us to be willing to kill in the name of the good we have achieved.

Indeed the very achievements that we are often called upon to protect through the means of war are those that in the past have been achieved through war. We must pursue war exactly because not to do so dishonors those who have made us what we are through the sacrifices they have made in past wars. This is not simply to make the point that engagement in war breeds extraordinary camaraderie, although that is surely true. Rather it is to say, with Hegel, that it is only in time of war that the state achieves its true universality. For only then are "the rights and interests of individuals established as a passing phase."[22]

Yet I do not think Hegel has put it quite right, for it is not a matter simply of our individual interests being qualified in times of war for the greater good. Rather war reaffirms our history by offering us the opportunity to be worthy of our history by making similar sacrifices. We fight wars because our ancestors have fought wars. Wars provide us a way to realize our continuity with our ancestors, to locate ourselves within their continuing saga, and in the process, to give to that saga an otherwise absent coherence over time.

There is no question that war makes marvelous history to read. We like to read about war, I think, not simply because there are sometimes good and bad guys, winners and losers, but because war, unlike most of our lives, seems to be more coherent. To be sure, in the middle of a battle the participants seldom know what is going on or what they are doing, but looking back on the confusion, an order emerges that often reassures us that, whether we won or lost, we still have a damn fine story to tell. Not only to tell but to be. It is a particular story to be sure, and perhaps we tell it with a good deal of bias, but it is nonetheless ours.

In that respect I sometimes think there is a deep commonality between baseball and war. I am hesitant to make such a suggestion as it seems so frivolous if not immoral. War is too serious for such comparisons. Yet just as baseball seems to be played not for the playing itself but for the gathering of statistics so that we may later tell the story, so wars seem to be fought so that we are able to place ourselves within a framework that gives us a place to be. We fear destruction, but even more we fear not having a niche within an ongoing history. War is our ultimate comfort in a world without a history for it provides us with a story. To be sure it may be a hard and even gruesome story, but such a story is better than no story at all.

I am not suggesting that we fight wars in order to have a story to tell. Rather the stories that we learn to tell as peoples inextricably involve war as one of the major characters in the story. That this is the case perhaps helps us understand further why it is almost impossible to exclude war as an imaginative possibility from our lives. For if war is no longer a possibility we fear we will lose the ability to locate ourselves in a worthy story or as participants in the ongoing life of a people.

In summary, I have suggested that war is to provide for as well as sustain the particular goods of particular peoples in a divided world. War is not anarchy existing between states, but rather it is anarchy's enemy insofar as it allows corporate entities, such as the nation states to perpetuate their own particular shared goods; to preserve their histories and moralities. Conflict in the international arena may not only arise as societies protect their histories but as they attempt to share them as well. Indeed it sometimes appears that nations with the most in common war the most frequently and bitterly, much as within families conflict is often bitterest. As the ties of cooperation are strong so is the possibility of conflict; for, as I have argued, the two are inextricably related.

Such is the best case I can muster for the moral viability of war. It is obviously an ideal account as the sheer stupidity, mendacity, and perversity that often gets us into war is missing. Moreover the presumption of nation states that their ambitions override all other interests, even those of the survival of the human species, is not taken into account. But the case I have tried to present is not meant to provide the discriminating judgments necessary to determine the wisdom of particular wars. Rather all I have done is to suggest why some find it so hard to exclude war as a moral possibility in human affairs. You can accept my analysis and still condemn particular wars as irrational, imprudent, or immoral. What you cannot do, if this account is right, is condemn a war on the grounds that all war is fundamentally immoral.

Peace, Justice, and the Viability of Pacifism

In the preceding sections I have done my best to give an account of war as a moral institution. But in what ways has it helped us understand why Christians so often say they are advocates of peace but accept the necessity of war? Does it, for example, help us to understand why the bishops, in *The Challenge of Peace,* acknowledge the nonviolent character of the Gospel while continuing to support Christian participation in war?

As we have seen, the bishops suppose they must accept war as an inevitability in this time between the times. The peace brought by Jesus is an eschatological peace. It is God's gift and cannot be the work of humankind. While God's peace may provide the individual with a sense of future union with God, it cannot be the working principle for present relations between nations; it is but an ideal in a complex and fallen world. Some in the name of God's peace may personally renounce the use of all violence, but they can by no means stand as an example for nations or, for that matter, all Christians.

The peace that is already ours in Christ is a religious not a political reality (55).[23] Committed as they are to this eschatological peace which is not just the absence of war but the peace that comes from justice, Christians cannot exclude the possibility of violence (68). So any pursuit of justice, any pursuit of a peace that is political, may require that Christians sadly use violence since "the struggles for justice may threaten certain forms of peace" (60).

For the bishops, St. Augustine gave the clearest answer to the question why Christians must resort to war even though they desire peace. Thus they tell us

Augustine was impressed by the fact and the consequences of sin in history—the "not yet" dimension of the kingdom. In his view war was both the result of sin and a tragic remedy for sin and the life of political societies. War arose from disordered ambitions, but it could also be used, in some cases at least to restrain evil and protect the innocent. The classic case which illustrated his view was the use of lethal force to prevent aggression against innocent victims. Faced with the fact of attack on the innocent, the presumption that we do no harm, even to our enemy, yielded to the command of love understood as the need to restrain an enemy who would injure the innocent. The just war argument has taken several forms in the history of Catholic theology, but this Augustinian insight is its central premise (81-82).

In a similar manner David Hollenbach has argued that for the just war theory the goods of peace and justice are interdependent. "Justice is regarded as the precondition of peace in the concrete political order. The pursuit of justice, even by force, can in some circumstances be the only way to fulfill the duty to promote both peace and justice."[24] Both Hollenbach and the bishops agree that the resort to war comes not from the counsel of Jesus, for to follow his nonviolent example would be to collapse the tension between the already and not yet of Christian eschatology. As long as we live in history there must exist an unresolved tension between justice and nonviolence. This tension requires the Christian to use violence in the cause of justice.[25]

The assumption that war can be a means for achieving justice, I think, entails a view of war very similar to the one I have developed. The bishops and Hollenbach assume a state has the responsibility to defend its people in the cause of justice. Yet what it means to "defend its people" is never made clear as wars are seldom fought to protect the physical survival of a people but rather for the achievement of this or that political advantage. Behind this question are complex questions about the justification of just war thinking. For we are sometimes told that just war theory is derived from the analogy of self-defense and at other times the primary paradigm that justifies the use of violence is the defense of the innocent. While these may not be incompatible they can make a great difference for how one understands the nature and role of state power to prosecute war.[26]

However if, as I have suggested, war is the means a people have to protect not just their existence but their interpretation of their existence, then war in a sense does not need a "justification." Perhaps that is why some prefer to talk not about just war, but of justified war.[27] The justice war protects is the cooperative achievement by a people that often has been the result of their forebears' waging war for limited moral goods.[28]

Aside from the individualistic analogy often employed, we are reminded in this context that just war theory is much more a theory of state action than a justification of individual response to attack. In other words the primary actor required by just war thinking is not the individual, but the state acting on behalf of its society. Here the theory can be correlated with my previous account. In a sense only the state has the right of self-defense for it alone has the responsibility of defending that history that makes a people a people. "The state" is the name we give to those charged with upholding the patterns of cooperation achieved by our society to preserve our particular shared goods. To preserve that cooperation and relative peace the state must be prepared to wage war against any who would threaten it. That is the "justice" that war protects.

This kind of interpretation of the "justice" of the state, I think, may be the necessary presumption to make clear why, in spite of a tacit affirmation of peace, the bishops continue to insist that nations have the right and duty to defend themselves against an unjust aggressor. But if this account is right, then I think the bishops need to be more candid than they have been about the status of peace. For I do not see how you can give nations the right to defend themselves and yet, at the same time, maintain that peace is not only the ideal but the normal state of affairs between nations. For are you not required to recognize that such a "peace" is but the justice dependent on the continued possibility of war?[29]

In this respect I do not see how the bishops can maintain, as they try to do, the right of some to be nonviolent. That they do so is, of course, extraordinary; imagine Roman Catholics ever hinting that pacifism is an option as appropriate for Christians as just war.

Yet surely an affirmation of pacifism cannot but seriously qualify the bishops' defense of just war as not merely the means of peace but also as the form just peace must take in this time between the times.

The bishops, however, are very careful in their support for the pacifist position. For they are very clear that their support is for the pacifist options for "individuals" (119). Moreover they suggest that this "new moment" determined by our possession of nuclear weapons has meant an increasing convergence between pacifist and just war positions. For "they share a common presumption against the use of force as a means of settling disputes. Both find their roots in the Christian theological tradition; each contributes to the full moral vision we need in pursuit of a human peace. We believe the two perspectives support and complement one another, each preserving the other from distortion" (120–121). At any rate, the bishops never propose, nor can they propose, pacifism as an option for statecraft.[30]

Hollenbach is even more adamant in his support of pacifism as an option for some Christians. Both pacifism and just war positions are necessary if

> the full content of Christian hope is to be made visible in history. Each of these ethical stances bears witness to an essential part of the Christian mystery. Each of them, however, is incomplete by itself. Within time it is simply not possible to embody the fullness of the kingdom of God in a single form of life or a single ethical standard. Thus if the Christian community is to be faithful to the full meaning of the paschal mystery as the inauguration of the kingdom of God, there must be a pluralism of ethical stances represented within it. I would conclude, therefore, that both the pacifist and the just war ethic are legitimate and necessary expressions of the Christian faith. The necessity of such pluralism in approaching the morality of warfare is a particular case of the more general theological truth that the kingdom of God cannot be fully expressed in any single historical way of living or hierarchy of values. Pacifism and just war theory are both historical syntheses of a particular

aspect of the Christian hope with an historical-political interpretation of how the basic values of justice and peace are
related to each other within time. The fact that these two
traditions have been present within the Christian community
for millennia has not been an accident but a theological
necessity.[31]

Thus those who adhere to just war need the pacifist to remind
them of the centrality of nonviolence that is too easily lost amid the
intricacies of public policy debates. Pacifists on the other hand need
the just war representatives to remind them of the centrality of
justice and that Christian responsibility can never be limited simply
by avoiding evil but requires the positive promotion of both justice
and peace.

It may seem terribly ungrateful for me as a pacifist to argue
against this unusual acceptance of the pacifist position, but I think
there are important reasons for doing so; or more accurately, I fear
that the approval of pacifism as a stance for individuals may seem to
put the bishops more firmly on the side of peace than they are. They
seem to support pacifism when in fact the structure of their argument ought to lead them to be more candid about their support of
war. If, as they maintain, it is not just a right, but a duty of a state to
defend itself through the force of arms, pacifists act irresponsibly
insofar as they absent themselves from the joint moral undertaking
which the state must perform.

Of course in times of peace it may be that the state has the
resources sufficient to give some the privilege to follow their conscience against war. Such a policy can make sense on a number of
pragmatic grounds since such people may make poor soldiers or to
grant them exemption from military service may result in taking
some of the moral heat off the military. Yet it is difficult to understand how a state can perpetuate such a policy when its existence is
being threatened if in fact, as the Pastoral argues, a people
threatened with unjust aggression "may not remain passively indifferent" (76).

In spite of the general statements about peace in the Pastoral, it
continues to assume that those who would take the pacifist stance,

even as individuals, bear the burden of proof. They bear the burden of proof because, the bishops presume, states are the bearers of our history, and nations (as I have argued) rely upon war or the possibility of war to sustain our history. Indeed the assumption that the state bears our history leads straight to the affirmation that war is not just a necessity caused by sin, but an institution morally necessary for the protection of the goods of a society. And if it is such then those who refuse to go to war have made a decisive moral mistake.

Although Hollenbach tends to interpret the difference between just war and pacifist positions primarily in strategic terms, he must as well give a secondary status to pacifism. The pacifist tradition "argues the nontheological part of its case against the just war on a competing historical-political interpretation of the relation between nonviolence and justice. It maintains the use of force inevitably contributes to an escalating spiral of both violence and injustice."[32] While the advent of nuclear weapons has certainly given new weight to this pacifist position, nonetheless it cannot "be made the basis for a political ethic for a pluralist society."[33] In contrast the just war is an attempt to consider how the "basic values of life, freedom, justice, etc., are related to each other in the light of our historical experience and our practical understanding of the political order."[34] Thus the ultimate problem with pacifists is that they are "prepared to tolerate injustice in the limit situation where justice cannot be attained by nonviolent means."[35]

Hollenbach's account, therefore, seems but another version of the suggestion that the pacifist is useful to remind those who are really concerned about justice that violence may finally be self-defeating, but pacifism cannot be a stance of the church. The crucial claim by Hollenbach is that pacifism cannot be made the political ethic for a pluralist society, that is, a society that has its being shaped and protected by war. For the "just war theory, the goods of peace and justice are interdependent, but justice is regarded as the precondition of peace in the concrete political order. The pursuit of justice, even by force, can in some circumstances be the only way to fulfill the duty to promote both peace and justice."[36]

The affirmation of pluralism, however, is not as free from cost as Hollenbach suggests. For it appears that by embracing both pacifism and just war theory he can provide the means to achieve justice in a pluralist society. He assumes such a society is so significant that the Gospel's command of peace can be qualified in the interest of the "justice" such a society represents.

I do not think, therefore, that Hollenbach can resolve the tension between pacifist and just war theories as easily as he suggests. He, and the bishops, want on the one hand to say the just war is the attempt to set down the "conditions under which exceptions to the general obligation to nonviolence might be made," and there is certainly some truth to that.[37] But on the other hand, they want to maintain that war is the character of our lives "between the times" as the failure to go to war cannot but result in injustice. From this latter perspective the just war theory is not just a theory of exceptions, but an attempt to limit the destructive potential of war once it is recognized as a moral necessity. As such just war, as a theory, denies pacifism; it does not attempt to make war impossible, but rather to make the moral necessity of war serve human purposes. As such it would seem that the bishops and Hollenbach should welcome the account I have tried to give concerning why war cannot morally be eliminated from our lives.

The Elimination of War: A Theological Imperative

By developing a moral case for war I have tried to help us understand ambivalence about war among Christians. We say we want peace yet we still hold out the possibility of war. I have taken *The Challenge of Peace* as a prime example of this ambivalence as the bishops, who strive to take the Gospel imperatives for peace so seriously, seem yet unable to free themselves from the assumption that Christians must still be willing to support war in the interest of justice. Such ambivalence takes form in eschatological appeals to our living between the times when our ideals must be compromised by the recognition of our sinful condition. Thus the bishops uphold the right, if not duty, of nations to defend themselves thereby underwriting the hold war has over our imaginations. While we all want to minimize war in general, we will not relinquish the possibility of war for our national communities. We do so not simply because we believe we live in a sinful world, but because we believe that our nations are the bearer of commitments and goods which justice compels us to defend even if such defense requires war. We wish for peace but plan for war; and we get it.

My analysis, I believe, pushes the bishops in the direction that they clearly want to avoid. To this it may be objected that I have treated the bishops unfairly as they give every indication that they wish to rid the world of war.[38] Quoting John Paul II, they say, "Today, the scale and the horror of modern warfare—whether nuclear or not—makes it totally unacceptable as a means of settling differences between nations. War should belong to the tragic past, to history; it should find no place on humanity's agenda for the future" (21). Surely by criticizing nuclear weapons the bishops do not mean to encourage war. Moreover they underwrite the concern to develop nonviolent ways for conflict resolution rejecting the argument that pacifists have no response to violence (221–230). Yet one must question how seriously such suggestions are to be taken as long as the bishops unwaveringly affirm that Christians can in times of stress resort to violence. As long as the bishops entertain the moral possibility of war I cannot see how they can avoid its actuality.

But did they (and do we) have an alternative? I believe we do. It is an alternative to which the bishops point in their sensitive portrayal of the peace brought by Jesus' life, death, and resurrection. Such a peace, as the bishops quite rightly note, is not simply the absence of war, but it is rather a peace that is itself an alternative to a world at war. As such it is not some ideal, but is an actual way of life among a concrete group of people. The bishops are quite right, it is an eschatological peace, but they are wrong to think it can be ours only on the "edge of history." Rather it means that we must see peace as a possibility amid a world at war.[39] The decisive issue is how we understand the eschatological nature of God's peace. The bishops stress the "already but not yet" as a way of legitimating Christian participation in war. But, as the bishops also indicate, to view the world eschatologically does not mean simply to mark the kingdom as yet to come for in fact the kingdom has been made present fully in Jesus Christ. That is why they rightly say Jesus' words requiring us to forgive one another, the requirement to love our enemy more than

all others, are not just ideals but possibilities here and now (45, 48).
Thus Jesus "made the tender mercy of God present in a world that
knew violence, oppression and injustice" (15).

God's "tender mercy" is not a sense of forgiveness that comes
after we have had to use violence for justice, though such forgiveness
certainly is not withheld, but rather his "tender mercy" makes it
possible to stand against the world's tragic assumption that war can
be the means to justice. To be sure, here a different understanding of
eschatology is at work than that of the bishops, but I believe it is one
that is closer to that of the New Testament. For the bishops seem to
have accepted the view that the early Christians were nonviolent
only because they had a mistaken apocalyptic idea that the world
was soon to end. When that end failed to arrive Christians reluc-
tantly took up the means of violence in the interest of justice. In fact
what we now know of the New Testament eschatology differs from
such a view. To be sure, the early Christians looked for God's reign
immediately to become a reality for all people, but that did not
qualify their dedication to live in that reign here and now.[40]

The eschatology of the New Testament rests not in the conviction
that the kingdom has not fully come, but that it has. What is
required is not a belief in some ideal amid the ambiguities of history,
but rather a recognition that we have entered a period in which two
ages overlap. As John Howard Yoder has observed "These aeons are
not distinct periods of time, for they exist simultaneously. They
differ rather in nature or in direction; one points backwards to
human history outside of (before) Christ; the other points forward to
the fullness of the kingdom of God, of which it is a foretaste. Each
aeon has a social manifestation: the former in the 'world,' the latter
in the body of Christ."[41]

The Christian commitment to nonviolence is therefore not first of
all an "ethic" but a declaration of the reality of the new age. Again
as Yoder puts it,

Non-resistance is thus not a matter of legalism but of discipleship, nor "thou shalt not" but "as he is so are we in this world"
(I Jn. 4:17), and it is especially in relation to evil that discipleship is meaningful. Every strand of New Testament literature

testifies to a direct relationship between the way Christ suffered on the cross and the way the Christian, as disciple, is called to suffer in the face of evil (Mt. 10:38; Mk. 10:38f; 8:34ff; Lk. 14:27). Solidarity with Christ ("discipleship") must often be in tension with the wider human solidarity (Jn. 15:20; II Cor. 1:5; 4:10; Phil. 1:29). It is not going too far to affirm that the new thing revealed in Christ was this attitude to the old aeon including force and self-defense. The cross was not in itself a new revelation; Isaiah 53 foresaw already the path which the Servant of Jahweh would have to tread. Nor was the resurrection essentially new; God's victory over evil had been affirmed, by definition one might say, from the beginning. Nor was the selection of a faithful remnant a new idea. What was centrally new about Christ was that these ideas became incarnate. But superficially the greatest novelty and the occasion of stumbling was His willingless to sacrifice, in the interest of non-resistant love, all other forms of human solidarity, including the legitimate national interests of the chosen people. The Jews had been told that in Abraham all the nations would be blessed and had understood this promise as the vindication of their nationalism. Jesus revealed that the contrary was the case: the universality of God's kingdom contradicts rather than confirms all particular solidarities and can be reached only by first forsaking the old aeon (Lk. 18:28-30).[42]

So in spite of the bishops' (and Hollenbach's) attempt to clear a space for the pacifist I cannot accept the terms of their acceptance. For pacifism and just war are not simply two ethical strategies for the achievement of God's justice in the world. Rather they draw on different assumptions about history and its relation to God's kingdom. The debate between pacifism and just war thinking is a theological issue of how we are to read and interpret history. I have argued that war is part and parcel of societies' histories, a necessary part which provides them with their sense of moral purpose and destiny. The problem with those histories is not that they are devoid of moral substance, but that they are not God's history. They are not the way God would have his kingdom present in the world. The

debate between pacifism and just war thinking is, therefore, a theological question of how we are to read and interpret history.

Christians believe that the true history of the world, that history
that determines our destiny, is not carried by the nation state. In
spite of its powerful moral appeal, this history is the history of
godlessness. Only the church has the stance, therefore, to describe
war for what it is, for the world is too broken to know the reality of
war.[43] For what is war but the desire to be rid of God, to claim for
ourselves the power to determine our meaning and destiny? Our
desire to protect ourselves from our enemies, to eliminate our enemies in the name of protecting the common history we share with
our friends, is but the manifestation of our hatred of God.[44]

Christians have been offered the possibility of a different history
through participation in a community in which one learns to love the
enemy. They are thus a people who believe that God will have them
exist through history without the necessity of war. God has done so
by providing the world with a history through the church. For
without the church we are but a scattered people with nothing in
common. Only through the church do we learn that we share the
same creator and destiny. So the world's true history is not that built
on war, but that offered by a community that witnesses to God's
refusal to give up on his creation.

This does not mean that our existence is constituted by two histories. There is only one true history—the history of God's peaceable
kingdom. Christians can admit no ultimate dualism between God's
history and the world's history. The peace we believe we have been
offered is not just for us but it is the peace for all, just as we believe
our God is the God of all. Thus we do not preclude the possibility
that a state could exist for which war is not a possibility. To deny
such a possibility would be the ultimate act of unbelief; for who are
we to determine the power of God's providential care of the world?[45]

Christians, therefore, offer a "moral equivalent to war" in William James' sense by first offering themselves. James rightly saw
that the essential problem for the elimination of war lies in our
imagination. Under the power of history created by war we cannot
morally imagine a world without war. But James' suggestion that we
find new contexts to sustain the virtues which arise in war is too

weak. What is required is not simply discovering new contexts to sustain martial virtues, but rather an alternative history. Precisely this God has offered through the life, death, and resurrection of Jesus of Nazareth. Such an alternative is not an unrealizable ideal. No, it is present now in the church, a real alternative able to free our imagination from the capacity of war.

For the imagination is not simply a container of images or ideas that we now entertain in preference to other images and ideas. Rather the imagination is a set of habits and relations that can only be carried by a group of people in distinction from the world's habits. For example nothing is more important for the church's imagination than the meal we share together in the presence of our crucified and resurrected Lord. For it is in that meal, that set of habits and relations, that the world is offered an alternative to the habits of disunity which war breeds.

In the practice of such a meal we can see that the morality that makes war seem so necessary to our lives is deeply flawed. For it is a morality that sees no alternative to war as the necessary means to sustain our particular loyalties. It leads us to suppose those loyalties can be protected, we think, only by eliminating the threat of the other, be it aggression or merely strangeness. But in the meal provided by the Lord of history we discover our particularity is not destroyed but enhanced by the coming of the stranger. In the church we find an alternative to war exactly because there we learn to make others' histories part of our own. We are able to do so because God has shown us the way by making us a new people through the life, death, and resurrection of Jesus Christ.[46]

From this perspective "Should war be eliminated?" is a false question. It is not a false question because the elimination of war is impossible or because war has a moral viability that means we should not eliminate it. Rather it is a false question because war has been eliminated for those who participate in God's history. The miracle we call the church is God's sign that war is not part of his providential care of the world. Our happy task as Christians is to witness to that fact.

But perhaps all this misses the point. To say the church is the carrier of a history other than the history of war sounds lofty, but in fact we know we do not live in such a history. We continue to live in a history determined by nation states where war shows no signs of abating. Even worse it is a world now threatened by nuclear annihilation. Do Christians, because of their commitment to peace, say that is too bad for the world and let others do their fighting for them? Or do they follow the Augustinian solution noting that the two histories are hopelessly mixed together on this side of the eschaton so we are required to use the means of violence to support the history of the world?

Once again we have arrived at a false alternative. Christian commitment to nonviolence does not require withdrawal from the world and the world's violence. Rather it requires the Christian to be in the world with an enthusiasm that cannot be defeated, for he or she knows that the power of war is not easily broken. Christians, therefore, cannot avoid, just as the bishops have not tried to avoid, attempting one step at a time to make the world less war-determined. We do that exactly by entering into the complex world of deterrence and disarmament strategy believing that a community nurtured on the habits of peace might be able to see new opportunities not otherwise present. For what creates new opportunities is being a kind of people who have been freed from the assumption that war is our fate.

Christian commitment to nonviolence is a way of life for the long haul. Exactly because we understand how morally compelling war can be we know what a challenge we face. That is why we offer the world not simply moral advice designed to make war less destructive, but rather a witness to God's invitation to join a community that is so imaginative, so rich in its history that it gives us the means to resist the temptation to give our loyalties to those that would use them for war. At Babel we were scattered, each having our own language and history, and even those who followed Jesus were scattered prior to his death, yet in his resurrection we have been gathered again to be part of God's history. In him we have our peace, by his grace we can be of good cheer since he has overcome the world (Jn. 16: 32-33).[47]

Notes

1. George Kennan, *The Nuclear Delusion: Soviet-American Relations in the Atomic Age* (New York: Pantheon Books, 1983), 243.

2. The classic account of this perspective on war is J. Glenn Grey's *The Warriors: Reflections on Men in Battle* (New York: Harper Torchbook, 1970). For a recent attempt to defend the vocation of the soldier, see Walter Benjamin, "In Defense of the Soldier, "*Christianity and Crisis* 43, 19 (November 28, 1983), 453-58; and my response in the same issue, "What Can the State Ask?"

3. *The Challenge of Peace: God's Promise and Our Response* (Washington, D.C., United States Catholic Conference, 1983). All references to the Pastoral will appear in the text and refer to the numbered paragraph.

4. It is often alleged, moreover, if one is a pacifist then one really has nothing to say of interest about war. For example, the Harvard Nuclear Study Group begins its "The Realities of Arms Control" with the claim: "In an imperfect world, few people have been willing to adopt pure pacifism, which means the refusal to defend one's self, family, country, or allies from any kind of attack. Those who are not pacifists must wrestle with many difficult choices about weapons, their existence, and their potential use. This has always been true. Warfare is as old as human history, and disarmament as a prescription for avoiding it dates back at least to biblical times." *Atlantic Monthly* 251, 6 (June, 1983), 39. The implication that pacifists simply have nothing to say about war or strategies of disarmament is a silent rebuke suggesting that pacifists simply do not face up to the hard issues. But the pacifist, no less than the just war advocate, must be concerned to find means to make war less likely and less destructive. After all, the pacifist refusal to participate in war does not mean that all wars are therefore morally on a par. Indeed it is even more a moral imperative for the pacifist to be concerned with issues of how disarmament can take place since the pacifist knows that calls for peace apart from an account of how such peace might take place cannot but appear as utopian.

5. John XXIII, *Peace on Earth* (Huntington, Indiana: Our Sunday Visitor, 1965). I am treating *Peace on Earth* not only because it provides the necessary background for understanding the Pastoral of the American Bishops. For the bishops' appeal to just war seems to presuppose the kind of reasoning suggested by *Peace on Earth*. Indeed Bryan

Hehir suggests that the Pastoral is an attempt to blend *Peace on Earth* with the methodology of the Second Vatican Council's "Pastoral Constitution on the Church in the Modern World." See his "From the Pastoral Constitution of Vatican II to the Challenge of Peace" in *Catholics and Nuclear War,* edited by Philip Murnion (New York: Crossroad, 1983), 71–86.

6. For an extremely helpful account of Enlightenment accounts of war and peace see W. B. Gallie, *Philosophers of Peace and War: Kant, Clausewitz, Marx, Engels and Tolstoy* (Cambridge: Cambridge University Press, 1978).

Of course one of the crucial issues that too often goes unanalyzed in most of the literature dealing with war is whether we know what we mean when we say *state.* Obviously a *state* is not the same as a people nor is it clear that a nation state corresponds to what was classically meant by a "state"—that is, a sub-unit for the government of a society. One wonders if the Enlightenment accounts of *state,* which seem to be accepted in *Pacem in Terris,* have any relation to what empirically counts for state in the modern world.

7. The bishops' account of war in the Hebrew scriptures unfortunately is not well developed. It is as if they admitted that war is seen as a valid mode of God's way with Israel, but fortunately we have the New Testament to balance that emphasis. If they had attended to such works as Millard Lind's *Yahweh Is a Warrior: The Theology of Warfare in Ancient Israel* (Scottdale, Pennsylvania: Herald Press, 1980), they would have been able to see a much stronger continuity between Israel and Jesus on the question of war.

8. There is an ambiguity in the bishops' position for it is unclear if the peace Jesus brought is not relevant for nuclear war because it is an eschatological peace or because Jesus did not speak explicitly about questions of nuclear war. I doubt the bishops would want to press the latter argument since there are many matters on which they want to speak authoritatively, such as contraception, on which Jesus did not speak explicitly.

9. Paragraphs 16 and 17 of the Pastoral give the most extended justification for the assumption that the pastoral should address the public policy debate on its own terms. Even with the presumption of the bishops, however, the matter is still fraught with ambiguity. For it is not clear if they want to enter the public debate because Catholics are "also members of the wider political community" and may thus be in positions of public responsibility about such matters; or if they want to

address all people of good will. If the latter, then it seems they are right to think they must presuppose a natural law starting point—that is, "a law written on the human heart by God"—that provides moral norms all can agree on irrespective of their faith. If the former, it is not clear why they cannot continue to speak theologically without resorting to natural law. The reason such issues are important is it is not clear the bishops can have it both ways. For at least they want in principle to claim that while the norms of natural law do not "exhaust the gospel vision," neither are such norms in fundamental conflict with the obligation of Christians to follow Christ. Yet they also suggest that just war may be the kind of thinking necessary in a sinful world and thus less than the full demand of, and perhaps even a compromise with, the Gospel. This formal issue is reflected by the political ambiguity of the Pastoral. For example, David J. O'Brien observes,

> The bishops are caught in a classic bind. If they ground themselves exclusively in the spiritual imperative of love and withdraw from the effort to influence the public consensus and public policy, they may indeed mobilize considerable support for a critical, prophetic witness within the church, even if it costs the church many members and opens the community to charges of public irresponsibility. At the other extreme, they may stand too closely to the prevailing framework of responsibility, looking at issues through the lens of decision makers, become sympathetic to their dilemmas, and accept only the limited alternatives that seem to be presently available. If they move one way they seem utopian, unrealistic, and irresponsible. If they move the other they appear to have lost their integrity as Christian leaders acquiescing in a situation they themselves have defined as unjust and immoral. "American Catholics and American Society," in *Catholics and Nuclear War*, 27.

10. In defense of the bishops on this point Dennis McCann says,

> Lest the bishops be dismissed as at best muddled and at worst hypocritical we must recognize that within the Catholic tradition moral questions have never been exhausted by referring to the real or imagined ethic of Jesus. Later developments within the Christian ethos, beyond the time of Jesus and the early Christians, are regarded as themselves part of the promised "gift of the Spirit." Without preempting the discussion of the bishops' "quasi-theological beliefs," here I must point out that when Catholic tradition adopted the paradigm of just war theory and

began to transform it according to its own agenda, the transition was not marked by tortuous equivocation but by a new sense of what "the call of Jesus" requires "in context of the world as it presently exists." The use of lethal force, in other words, came to be regarded as the most effective and the least unacceptable way "to prevent aggression against innocent victims." The paradigm of just war theory became morally necessary, as soon as Catholic tradition, following St. Augustine, admitted that war itself was not just the result of sin but also a "tragic remedy for sin in the life of political societies." "The NCCB Letter and Its Critics: An Ethical Analysis," in *Christian Perspectives in Nuclear Deterrence* edited by Bernard Adeney (Forthcoming).
Later McCann says such a position is justified by the trinitarian vision of the Pastoral as such a vision is obviously "larger than the words and deeds of Jesus of Nazareth. While such is and will ever remain the decisive moment of incarnation in history, that moment has meaning only in the context of the whole process. The mystery of God's Trinitarian presence thus is reflected in the overall pattern of meaning discerned in human life: we are to 'take responsibility for his work of creation and try to shape it in the ways of the kingdom.' " McCann, thus, seems to suggest that "just war" is a further development of the spirit, but surely that is an extremely doubtful claim. It may be that the trinitarian vision is larger than the words and deeds of Jesus, but I do not see how it can be claimed that vision is not in essential continuity with all that Jesus said and did. In truth the bishops seem torn between justifying just war as a necessary compromise for living responsibly in a sinful world or as, as *Peace on Earth* suggests, a position consistent with natural law.

11. Kenneth Waltz, *Man, The State, and War: A Theoretical Analysis* (New York: Columbia University Press, 1959), 29.
12. Hannah Arendt, *On Violence* (New York: Harcourt, Brace, and World, Inc., 1970), 36.
13. Ibid., 47.
14. Waltz, 167–68.
15. Ibid., 168.
16. Ibid., 169.
17. Ibid., 178.
18. Ibid., 179.
19. Ibid., 182.
20. Ibid., 183.

21. I think it is not accidental that the two most imperialistic states in the world today, U.S.A. and the USSR, are both founded on the universalistic assumptions of the Enlightenment.

22. Quoted by Michael Walzer in his *Obligations: Essays on Disobedience, War, and Citizenship* (New York: Simon and Schuster, 1970), 184.

23. In the light of the influence of liberation theology this claim seems a bit surprising; or at least one would have expected the bishops to provide a more elaborate defense. For if they wish to claim that the Gospel is political concerning matters of justice then I did not see how they can limit the Gospel's admonitions for peace to the "religious" realm.

24. David Hollenbach, *Nuclear Ethics: A Christian Moral Argument* (New York: Paulist Press, 1983), 22–23. I introduce Hollenbach's work at this point, as he has spelled out more fully the position the bishops have taken in the Pastoral. I do not want, however, to claim that his views are identical with that of the Pastoral.

25. Though the bishops and Hollenbach urge nonviolent forms of resistance in the interest of justice they always hold out the possibility of violence if nonviolence does not work. Yet they fail to give any indication how we are ever to know if nonviolence has not worked and thus we can turn to violence. I suspect behind their failure to press this issue is the assumption that war is of the essence of state action so the ability of a state to use nonviolence is extremely limited. They owe us an account, however, of how a Christian can do justice to the neighbor if we use the means that tell the neighbor that they are less obligated than we to love the enemy. For the "innocent" that we defend cannot be defended "justly" if the form of the defense belies our conviction, based on Jesus' way of dealing with the world, that the enemy is to be loved even as they attack. Peace and justice are not equal "means" for the building of God's kingdom, but rather the justice that required the forgiveness of enemies that makes peace possible is the kingdom.

26. Paul Ramsey has argued the strongest for the paradigm of defense of the innocent for justification of just war logic. I suspect that is why Ramsey places so much emphasis on the principle of discrimination as the overriding criterion for the justifiability of war. The bishops, unfortunately, seem to move uncritically from appeals to self-defense to defense of the innocent without noting how they make a difference for how one derives the various criteria of just war or their priority. The analysis of war I have provided, however, is meant to provide them a way out of this difficulty. For in effect they can say the justification of

just war for a nation state can be put in the language of self-defense because its larger intention is to defend the innocent within the state. Therefore the fundamental intention of just war at an individual level is defense of the innocent, but as a social policy it appears in the form of "self"-defense but the "self" is a public agent.

27. See, for example, Paul Ramsey, *The Just War* (New York: Scribner's Sons, 1968), 4–18.

28. That is why the criteria of discrimination may not be overriding for a state's prosecution of war since the task is to protect the past goods achieved by war. Therefore, from a just war perspective the bishops may be right to suggest that the principle of proportionality is just as, if not more, important than discrimination for determining the morality of nuclear warfare.

29. In his *The Just War: Force and Political Responsibility,* Paul Ramsey is admirably clear that the great task is to save war and politics for purposeful use by mankind. Therefore, the task is not to make war impossible, but to make it serve human ends through disciplining it through a politics formed by just war commitments. Therefore just war is commensurate with the assumption that war is not the exception in international relations but the norm. The bishops, however, drawing on the assumptions of *Pacem in Terris* seem to presume that war is the exception. I am simply suggesting that their position would be more consistent if they had followed Ramsey's lead.

30. Michael Novak, unlike the bishops, denies that pacifism, even of an individual sort, is required by the New Testament. The peace offered by Jesus is not the absence of war, but a form of knowing and being in union with God. It is a mistake, though one that is honored, to believe that we are called to imitate Jesus' nonviolence, as it is a misreading of scripture as well as the Catholic tradition. Novak argues we must "sharply distinguish between pacifism as a personal commitment, implicating only a person who is not a public figure responsible for the lives of others, and pacifism as a public policy, compromising many who are not pacifists and endangering the very possibility of pacifism itself. It is not justice if the human race as a whole or in part is heaped with indignities, spat upon, publicly humiliated, destroyed, as Jesus was. It is not moral to permit the human race so to endure the injustice of the passion and death of Christ." *Moral Clarity in the Nuclear Age* (Nashville: Thomas Nelson, 1983), 34. Novak's argument is to the point, but I think he has not pressed it consistently enough. For why does he not argue further that Jesus was wrong to allow himself to die

at the hands of such injustice? Or why not argue that at least the disciples should have come to Jesus' aid since Jesus' teaching should have convinced them that their overriding duty was to aid the innocent against injustice. One cannot but feel that those who defend so strongly the use of violence in the service of justice are finally trying to rescue Jesus from the cross. See, for example, Carol Oglesby, "Rescuing Jesus from the Cross," *The CoEvolution Quarterly,* 39 (Fall, 1983), 36–41.

It is not easy to characterize the difference between Novak's position and that of the bishops for it is not simply a difference about how to understand the facts and strategic alternatives. Rather it involves profound assumptions about the status of the just war theory as well as where one begins reflection on the ethics of war. Novak, unlike the bishops, does not assume that you can begin with the just war criteria and then ask in a legalistic way whether nuclear strategy conforms or does not conform to those criteria. Rather one must begin with an interpretation on the international situation which relativizes the status of the just war theory. Thus he says, "virtually all arguments about the prevention of nuclear war hinge on judgments concerning the nature of the Soviet Union and its nuclear forces" (49). Even apart from the question of whether Novak's account of the Soviet Union and his depiction of the international situation is correct, he has not given us more reasons for why we should begin our ethical analysis of nuclear war with the international context. Indeed, given Novak's account, it is extremely unclear why he bothers to treat the just war theory at all. For a more detailed critique of Novak's views, particularly his rather odd view of "intention," see James Cameron, "Nuclear Catholics," *New York Review of Books,* xxx, 20 (December 22, 1983), 38–42.

31. Hollenbach, 31.
32. Ibid., 43. Hollenbach, therefore, at least seems to suggest that pacifism might be a social policy.
33. Ibid., 43. Like the bishops, Hollenbach assumes that the church's social ethics must be one amenable to the non-Christian. Yet, he confuses that issue with the claims that Christian convictions must be capable of being construed in policy terms. The latter may be possible without those strategies being agreeable to non-Christians.
34. Ibid., 43. The problem with such claims is that such values are so abstractly put that we cannot be sure what institutional form they may assume. It may be that some who argue against nuclear war because it

threatens survival itself are right to remind us that values such as freedom can be idolatrous when they make our very survival problematic.

35. Ibid., 28.

36. Ibid., 23. Hollenbach's basic mistake is to think that justice and peace are the means to build the kingdom rather than the form of the kingdom itself.

37. Ibid., 37.

38. I may have been particularly unfair to the bishops by treating what is essentially a political document as if it should be conceptually coherent. Indeed, in many ways the document is stronger exactly because it is a hodge-podge of different positions representing the different viewpoints of the various bishops. Yet the bishops say they want to be true to the intent of the Gospel and as much as I am able, I want to help them do just that.

39. For a marvelous account of a spirituality of peace, see Rowan Williams, *The Truce of God* (New York: The Pilgrim Press, 1984). One of Williams' strongest themes is that peace is not simply what is left when social constraints have all vanished. Such a conception of peace he rightly criticizes as infantile, for the world created by such a peace is one where nothing happens and nothing is left to do. Rather the peace that is identified with Christian reconciliation is that which requires change and newness of life, not only of the heart, but in the structures of politics and industry (58).

40. For a fuller defense of this view see my *The Peaceable Kingdom: A Primer in Christian Ethics* (Notre Dame: University of Notre Dame Press, 1983).

In his "The Moral Methodology of the Bishops' Pastoral," Charles Curran suggests that "much New Testament moral teaching is influenced by the eschatological coloring of the times; that is, many thought that the end of history was coming quickly, and such an understanding obviously colored their approach to moral questions. However, our understanding of eschatology is quite different. It is our understanding that the end-time has begun in Christ Jesus but will be completed only in his second-coming." *Catholics and Nuclear War,* 47. While I doubt the simplicity of Curran's description of early Christian attitudes about eschatology, I still do not see why he thinks that makes a difference about how Christians are to understand the New Testament. For the early Christians did not think they refrained from violence because the end of history was soon to come, but rather they refrained from violence because, as Curran suggests, they thought the end time had come.

On cannot but feel an uneasiness on the part of many Catholic moralists about the methodology of the Pastoral. The "conservatives" cannot but be worried about the implications for other questions of the moral life. For if you are willing to appeal to the ambiguity of the moral case caused by sin then why not apply the same moral logic to abortion. The "liberals" may rejoice in that result, but yet they may at the same time wish the bishops had been more forthright in their condemnation of nuclear war.

41. John Howard Yoder, *The Original Revolution* (Scottdale, Pennsylvania: Herald Press, 1971), 58.

42. Yoder, 60–61.

43. The account of war I developed above is parasitic on Christian presuppositions insofar as a unity of human history is presupposed from which war could be described. But, in fact, there is no such unity in history other than that provided by the church. Otherwise war is relative to each people's history. We thus often seek to deny to the other side the right to describe their violence as war. For example barbarians cannot be warriors since they do not fight in a civilized manner; a bombing in London by the IRA is terrorism, not war. From this perspective war can be seen as a progressive conversation between diverse peoples about the meaning of war itself. World war is a moral achievement as it suggests all sides have the right to describe their violence as war. Insofar as nuclear weapons force all to have a stake in war, they can be seen as a moral advance reflecting our increasing interdependence.

44. For an unrelenting account of war along these lines, see Dale Aukerman, *Darkening Valley* (New York: Seabury Press, 1981). Aukerman observes,

> The dual drives to be rid of God and the countering brother—the opposite of the dual loves to which we are called—coincided completely in the drama of the murder of Jesus. Malice toward the visible brother formed a continuum with the rejection of the unseen God; the judicial murder of the brother was at the same time an attempt to do away with God . . . Still, as Christians we can at times discern in ourselves the dual drives to be rid of God and our enemy. The desire to be rid of God lies behind all of my sinning; the desire to do away with the enemy is the identifiable extreme of what is wrong with me. This means that any

manifestation of drive to be rid of a fellow human being—the
hostility-hatred-murder-continuum—carries with it inseparably
the drive to be rid of God and veers back across the centuries into
that crucifixion of the Christ (45).

45. I am indebted to Robert and Blanche Jensen for helping me put the
matter in this way. For the pacifist is tempted to condemn the state to
the necessity of war but if we do so we but become the other side of the
just war position. Theologically we may not know how God can provide
for the possibility of a nonviolent state, but neither can we act as if such
were not a possibility.

46. Such a position is at least suggested by the bishops in *The Challenge of
Peace* as they say,

> Building peace within and among nations is the work of many
> individuals and institutions; it is the fruit of ideas and decisions
> taken in the political, cultural, economic, social, military, and
> legal sectors of life. We believe that the Church, as a community
> of faith and social institution, has a proper, necessary, and dis-
> tinctive part to play in the pursuit of peace. The distinctive
> contribution of the Church flows from her religious nature and
> ministry. The Church is called to be, in a unique way, the instru-
> ment of God in history. Since peace is one of the signs of that
> kingdom present in the world, the Church fulfills part of her
> essential mission by making the peace of the kingdom more
> visible in our time (21–22).

In a manner similar to some of the criticisms I have made, Joseph
Komonchak suggests that some may "wonder why the bishops do not
make more of the redemptive role of Christ and the church as an
instrument in history of his word and grace. The latter, of course, is not
denied, but it certainly does not occupy a major role. If it had, it might
have been possible to stress more than is now done the 'already' aspect
of the Christian faith." "Kingdom, History, and Church," in *Catholics
and Nuclear War,* 109.

47. I am indebted to David Burrell, James Burtchaell, and John Howard
Yoder for reading and criticizing an earlier version of this chapter.
Carol Descoteaux contributed much to the editing of this manuscript. I
owe a special debt of gratitude to Charles Pinches for his close critique
of the manuscript. I only wish I knew how to respond to the many
questions he raised. Philip Rossi, S.J., and Michael Duffey of Marquette University also helped save me from some obvious errors.